Printed by Printforce, the Netherlands

Perspectives on Teaching and Learning Chinese Literacy in China

MULTILINGUAL EDUCATION

VOLUME 2

Series Editors:

Andy Kirkpatrick
Director, Research Centre into Language Education and Acquisition
in Multilingual Societies
Hong Kong Institute of Education

Bob Adamson
Head, Department of Curriculum and Instruction
Hong Kong Institute of Education

David C.S. Lee
Department of English
Hong Kong Institute of Education

Editorial Board:

Jan Blommaert, University of Tilburg, The Netherlands
Feng Anwei, University of Wales at Bangor, UK
Ofelia Garcia, The Graduate Centre, City University of New York, USA
Saran Kaur Gill, Universiti Kebangsaan Malaysia
Gu Yueguo, The Chinese Academy of Social Sciences
Hartmut Haberland, University of Roskilde, Denmark
Li Chor Shing David, The Hong Kong Institute of Education
Li Wei, Birkbeck College, University of London, UK
Low Ee-Ling, National Institute of Education, Singapore
Tony Liddicoat, University of South Australia
Ricardo Nolasco, University of the Phillipines at Diliman, Manila, The Philippines
Merrill Swain, Ontario Institute of Studies in Education, University of Toronto, Canada
Virginia Yip Choy Yin, Chinese University of Hong Kong

For further volumes:
http://www.springer.com/series/8836

Cynthia B. Leung • Jiening Ruan
Editors

Perspectives on Teaching and Learning Chinese Literacy in China

Springer

Editors
Cynthia B. Leung
College of Education
University of South Florida
 St. Petersburg
St. Petersburg, FL, USA

Jiening Ruan
Jeannine Rainbolt College of Education
University of Oklahoma
Norman, OK, USA

ISSN 2213-3208　　　　　ISSN 2213-3216 (electronic)
ISBN 978-94-007-4821-7　　ISBN 978-94-007-4822-4 (eBook)
DOI 10.1007/978-94-007-4822-4
Springer Dordrecht Heidelberg New York London

Library of Congress Control Number: 2012949324

© Springer Science+Business Media Dordrecht 2012

This work is subject to copyright. All rights are reserved by the Publisher, whether the whole or part of the material is concerned, specifically the rights of translation, reprinting, reuse of illustrations, recitation, broadcasting, reproduction on microfilms or in any other physical way, and transmission or information storage and retrieval, electronic adaptation, computer software, or by similar or dissimilar methodology now known or hereafter developed. Exempted from this legal reservation are brief excerpts in connection with reviews or scholarly analysis or material supplied specifically for the purpose of being entered and executed on a computer system, for exclusive use by the purchaser of the work. Duplication of this publication or parts thereof is permitted only under the provisions of the Copyright Law of the Publisher's location, in its current version, and permission for use must always be obtained from Springer. Permissions for use may be obtained through RightsLink at the Copyright Clearance Center. Violations are liable to prosecution under the respective Copyright Law.

The use of general descriptive names, registered names, trademarks, service marks, etc. in this publication does not imply, even in the absence of a specific statement, that such names are exempt from the relevant protective laws and regulations and therefore free for general use.

While the advice and information in this book are believed to be true and accurate at the date of publication, neither the authors nor the editors nor the publisher can accept any legal responsibility for any errors or omissions that may be made. The publisher makes no warranty, express or implied, with respect to the material contained herein.

Printed on acid-free paper

Springer is part of Springer Science+Business Media (www.springer.com)

Contents

    Introduction... ix
    Cynthia B. Leung and Jiening Ruan

1 **Historical Perspectives on Chinese Written Language
    and Literacy Education in China**........................... 1
    Liqing Tao and Gaoyin Qian

2 **Literacy in Ancient China: A Culturally and Socially
    Situated Role in Historical Times**......................... 19
    Liqing Tao and Gaoyin Qian

3 **Foreign Literature Education in China's Secondary Schools
    from 1919 to 1949**...................................... 35
    Hongtao Liu and Jiening Ruan

4 **Influences of the Cultural Revolution on Chinese Literacy
    Instruction**.. 49
    Cynthia B. Leung and YiPing Wang

5 **Chinese Language Pedagogy and Human Dignity:
    The Special Rank Teacher in the Aftermath
    of the Cultural Revolution**............................... 61
    Po Yuk Ko and Bob Adamson

6 **Early Literacy Education in China: A Historical Overview**...... 81
    Nancy Pine and Zhenyou Yu

7 **Chinese Youth Literature: A Historical Overview**.............. 107
    Minjie Chen

8 **Primary School Chinese Language and Literacy Curriculum
    Reforms in China After 1949**.............................. 129
    Jiening Ruan and Lijun Jin

9	**High School Chinese Language and Literacy Curriculum Reforms**...............................	141
	Jiening Ruan and Guomin Zheng	
10	**Chinese *Lian Huan Hua* and Literacy: Popular Culture Meets Youth Literature**........................	157
	Minjie Chen	
11	**Information and Communication Technologies for Literacy Education in China**.........................	183
	Xun Ge, Jiening Ruan, and Xiaoshuai Lu	
12	**Family Literacy in China**...............................	199
	Cynthia B. Leung and Yongmei Li	
Index...		211

Contributors

Bob Adamson is Professor of Curriculum Studies at the Hong Kong Institute of Education. He publishes in the areas of language education, curriculum studies, and comparative education.

Minjie Chen received her doctoral degree in Library and Information Science from the University of Illinois, Urbana-Champaign. She studies children's literature and library services for youth.

Xun Ge is Professor of Educational Psychology at the University of Oklahoma. Her research interests include designing and integrating learning technologies to support learning and instruction.

Lijun Jin is Professor of Elementary Education at Towson University in Maryland. Her research interests are early literacy and culturally responsive teaching.

Po Yuk Ko is Director of the Centre for Learning Study and Assistant Professor in the Department of Curriculum and Instruction at the Hong Kong Institute of Education. Her research interests include learning study, teacher professional development, and Chinese language education.

Cynthia B. Leung, co-editor of this volume, is Professor of Literacy Education at the University of South Florida St. Petersburg. Her research interests include second language acquisition, early literacy, vocabulary development, and responses to multicultural literature.

Yongmei Li is an Academic Assessment Coordinator and Assistant Professor of Education at Shaw University. Her research interests include English language learners, quantitative research methods, and survey methods.

Hongtao Liu is Professor of Comparative Literature at Beijing Normal University. His research interests are world literature theory, foreign literature in China, and Chinese literature abroad.

Xiaoshuai Lu received her master's degree in Higher Education with an emphasis in Information and Communication Technology from China University of Petroleum-Beijing.

Nancy Pine is director of the Bridging Cultures: U.S./China Program at Mount St. Mary's College, Los Angeles. Her research focuses on young children's literacy learning, the semiotic potential of very young children, and identifying unique teaching methodologies of China and the United States.

Gaoyin Qian is Professor of Literacy Education at Lehman College, the City University of New York. His research interests are epistemological thinking, conceptual change learning from text, and early literacy development among children from immigrant families.

Jiening Ruan, co-editor of this volume, is Associate Professor of Reading/Literacy Education at the University of Oklahoma. Her research interests include beginning literacy development among Chinese monolingual and bilingual children, culturally responsive teaching, and using technology to support teacher reflection.

Liqing Tao is Associate Professor of Literacy Education at the College of Staten Island, the City University of New York. His research interests focuses on literacy acquisition of young children, technology and literacy acquisition, and ancient Chinese literacy practices and theories.

YiPing Wang is an academic librarian at the University of East & West Medicine in California. Her research interests include multicultural issues and the influence of Chinese Culture on learning.

Zhenyou Yu is Associate Professor in the Department of Pre-School Education at China Women's University, Beijing. His research interests are language development and education, early literacy development and instruction, and ESL learning and instruction in China.

Guomin Zheng is Executive Dean of Teachers College and Professor of Chinese Reading Education at Beijing Normal University. His major areas of research include Chinese reading curriculum and pedagogy and the history of Chinese reading education.

Introduction

Cynthia B. Leung and Jiening Ruan

As China plays an increasingly important role on the world stage, people around the world have shown great interest in learning about various aspects of China and Chinese culture. Nothing provides better insight into a society than taking a close look at its education system and its means of socializing its youth, and within the field of education, no discipline is more important to the existence of a culture and society than literacy.

In this first book of our two-volume series on literacy teaching and learning in China, we present to our readers a diverse collection of chapters related to Chinese language and literacy teaching and learning from historical, philosophical, and sociocultural perspectives. The second volume focuses on English literacy and English literacy education in the People's Republic of China.

While this volume traces literacy in China from ancient times to recent curriculum reform efforts to improve Chinese literacy education, it also covers a wide array of topics, including the nature and role of Chinese written language, early literacy development, foreign translated literature, youth literature, popular culture materials for literacy teaching and learning, family literacy, and the integration of information and communication technologies to support Chinese literacy development. Together, the chapters provide a comprehensive, cross-disciplinary look at changes in Chinese literacy practices and literacy instruction over time and the philosophical and sociocultural influences that led to these changes.

Even though the contributors of this volume come from different academic disciplines, one common thread running through all the chapters is a critical understanding that human learning is culture-based and deeply situated in sociocultural contexts consisting of socioculturally specific understandings, practices, and traditions (Bruner 1996) and that literacy reflects the institutional and cultural superstructures and realities of a given society and occurs within the contexts of that society (Gee 2007). Various sociocultural and political factors, nationwide or localized to specific communities or geographic regions, as well as individual factors, constantly interact to shape literacy acquisition and literacy education in China.

It is also crucial to understand that literacy is never neutral. Literacy is political and serves the purposes of those in power. It perpetuates the status quo and facilitates the reproduction of the existing power and social structure (Bernstein 1971). In China, literacy has been used as a cultural tool to indoctrinate the Chinese people and to instill ideologies promoted by the ruling class, be it Confucianism or socialism. One can compare the Chinese written language to the concept of *elaborated codes* that enable upward social mobility, while local dialects are *restricted codes* that hinder one's opportunities to move up the social ladder. Bourdieu's (1986) concept of *cultural capital* is also pertinent to the Chinese context. Literacy in Chinese society is a highly desirable form of capital. In particular, historically, strong competence in and command of the Chinese written language could enable a person from a lower class to gain entry into the class of wealth and power.

Chinese Language: A Complex System

Some basic background knowledge about the Chinese language is important in order for readers to fully understand Chinese literacy and literacy education. Chinese is one of the most complex languages in existence in human history. For Western readers from countries that have an alphabetic orthography (i.e., spelling or writing system), it is crucial to understand that the Chinese writing system is character-based, syllabic, and logographic. The relationship between its spoken language and written language is vastly different from that of an alphabetic language, such as English or Spanish. In written Chinese, visual symbols (characters) represent meaning units rather than individual sounds or phonemes of the oral language. Meanwhile, each character also represents a mono-syllabic sound so it can be read aloud. Readers can refer to Chap. 1 for a more detailed discussion of the nature of the Chinese language and the relationship between spoken and written Chinese.

There are seven major dialects and numerous sub-dialects spoken in different regions of China. The dialects are basically unintelligible to people using other dialects. Historically, multiple attempts were made for the country to have one universal spoken language, but such efforts never materialized until the founding of the People's Republic of China in 1949. The local dialect used in the Beijing area (a.k.a. Mandarin Chinese or *Putonghua*) was set as the standard, official spoken language of the nation, and the Chinese government has been actively promoting it ever since. Mandarin Chinese is a tonal language that contains five tones. One has to be alert to tonal differences because different tones of the same sound can mean drastically different concepts or things. For beginning readers in contemporary China, pinyin, a Romanized script similar to an alphabetic language, was developed by the Chinese government to aid character recognition. However, the role of pinyin is limited and only applies to beginning reading.

Pinyin functions mainly as a crutch for children who are in the process of learning to decode and recognize characters. Once they have mastered a sizable number of characters, pinyin is only used as a tool to self-teach and find the pronunciation and meaning of characters from a dictionary or reference book. It is important to note that outside of schools and official business, dialects and sub-dialects are still widely used by people within their own communities in various geographical regions of China.

Unlike the situation with spoken dialects of Chinese, there is only one universal written language in China that serves as the major carrier of Chinese culture and a tool for communication between and among people who do not understand each other's spoken language. However, the Chinese written language is extremely complex. It is difficult to learn and takes a long time to develop. Therefore, historically, literacy, the ability to read and write, has separated the educated and uneducated, and a majority of the Chinese population was illiterate for thousands of years. There are multiple structures that govern how characters are formed. Most notable, four categories of characters are widely recognized (see Chap.1 for a detailed discussion).

Traditional Chinese characters remained relatively stable over the last few millennia until 1949. In order to increase the country's literacy rate, the Chinese government made multiple efforts to simplify its written script. The first reform was initiated in 1954. The government published a key policy document entitled *A Plan to Simplify Hanzi (a.k.a., Chinese Characters)* [简化汉字方案] to guide the reform effort. Along with the document, a chart containing 7,000 standardized simplified Chinese characters, *Universal Hanzi Chart* [通用汉字表], was developed and promoted for use across the country. The government also banned the use of the traditional form of those prescribed characters (Jia and Zhao 2011). Since then, simplified characters have been taught in schools and adopted for use in all forms of publications in China. In 1978, another reform effort was made to simplify or add more Chinese characters to the list of existing simplified characters. However, due to strong opposition from scholars and the public who feared such an effort would further interfere with the preservation of traditional Chinese language and culture, it was aborted. In 2009, a trial version of *Universal Standardized Hanzi Chart* [通用规范汉字表] was released by the Chinese Ministry of Education and input was sought from the public. This government initiative to further standardize and simplify Chinese characters reignited another round of heated debates between its supporters and opponents across the country (Cao and Xuan 2011). Again, due to strong opposition, the final decision about this initiative has not yet been made. Therefore, in China, literacy and literacy education have always been political and closely tied to social and cultural contexts. It is also important to take note that even though simplified characters are used in China, traditional Chinese characters are still used in Taiwan, Hong Kong, Macao, and other traditional Chinese territories that have different social and political systems.

Future Directions

Although this book addresses a wide variety of topics related to Chinese literacy and literacy education, we have identified several important issues that have been left unaddressed or minimally addressed by the scholarly community studying Chinese literacy and literacy related issues.

First of all, we feel that although abundant literature can be found on the linguistic nature of the Chinese language and how Chinese learners acquire reading and writing skills, scant scholarly discourse can be found on how teacher preparation and teacher quality specifically impact students' literacy development. It is common knowledge in the West that teacher quality is one of the most significant variables in students' literacy learning (Snow et al. 1998). This should come as no surprise due to the high social status teachers have enjoyed historically (except during the Chinese Cultural Revolution) as exemplified in a famous Confucian saying, "A teacher for a day is a father for a lifetime." It is against Chinese cultural tradition to criticize teachers for a students' failure in literacy learning or academic performance in general. Chapter 5 in this book addresses this limitation. However, more research and examination of this topic can help improve literacy education in China.

Secondly, most literature focuses on literacy development and literacy education in urban settings. Limited information can be found regarding literacy development and instructional practices of teachers in rural or economically disadvantaged areas in China. In addition, issues of poverty and social economic status, two influential variables in student learning, are rarely addressed in the literature. With the increasing popularity of information and communication technologies in China, the issue of the digital divide deserves further study.

Thirdly, since China is extremely rich in its spoken language diversity with numerous local dialects spoken around the country, more research on how dialect differences impact students' literacy development is needed. In particular, dialect differences usually relate to differences in discourse styles. It is important to understand how these particular factors transpire in literacy classrooms and connect to student learning.

Last but not least, we have noticed a severe lack of attention to the development of new literacies among the existing literature on Chinese literacy and literacy education. We have encountered numerous scholarly works on various aspects of teaching and learning low-level Chinese reading skills, but limited discussion can be found on cultivating and developing critical thinking, technology literacy, media literacy, and other forms of literacies so essential to a person's success and the country's ability to meet different challenges in the twenty-first century. We would like to call for more work to be done in this area.

So far, inquiries into Chinese literacy have mainly focused on its linguistic and cognitive aspects. It is our intention to push the boundary of the scholarship and discourse to highlight the complex and multidimensional nature of Chinese literacy and literacy education. We hope this book becomes essential reading for scholars, researchers, policy makers, and university students who want to learn more about the historical development and the effects of philosophical, social, cultural, and political factors on Chinese literacy and literacy education. We also hope teachers of Chinese find the chapters in this volume helpful in terms of leading them to a better understanding of the origins of and changes to particular instructional practices. Finally, we hope teachers of English language learners who have Chinese as their home language can gain valuable knowledge about their students' native language and culture and use this knowledge to better support their students' English literacy development.

References

Bernstein, B. (1971). *Class, codes and control* (Vol. 1). London: Paladin.
Bruner, J. (1996). *The culture of education*. Cambridge, MA: Harvard University Press.
Bordieu, P. (1986). The forms of capital. In J. G. Richardson (Ed.), *Handbook for theory and research for the sociology of education* (pp. 241–258). New York: Greenwood Press.
Cao, D., & Xuan, H. (2010). 通用规范汉字表研制中的三对关系 [Three sets of relationships to be addressed in Universal Standardized Hanzi Chart]. *安徽师范大学学报(人文社会科学版)*, *39*(2), 208–214.
Gee, J. (2007). *Social linguistics and literacies: Ideology in discourses* (3rd ed.). London: Taylor & Francis.
Jia, Q., & Zhao, H. (2011). 汉字规范化工作探析 [An exploration of standardizing Chinese characters]. *语文教学通讯·D刊*, *1*, 58–59.
Snow, C. E., Burns, M. S., & Griffin, P. (Eds.). (1998). *Preventing reading difficulties in young children*. Washington DC: National Academy Press.

Chapter 1
Historical Perspectives on Chinese Written Language and Literacy Education in China

Liqing Tao and Gaoyin Qian

1.1 Introduction

Chinese as a written language has a long history. The earliest existing evidence of written records dates back to the Shang Dynasty (about 1700–1050 BC) with archaic Chinese characters carved on tortoise shells or ox scapulae (Bai 1982). These carvings are usually referred to as oracle bone characters and were mainly used in divination for royal families and for state affairs. Since then, Chinese characters as a writing system have undergone several major changes in configuration and styles, but most of them have retained their logographic/ideographic orthography (Qiu 2009; Weiger 1965). Therefore, before we outline characteristics of literacy education in ancient China, we provide a brief description of the Chinese writing system. Instead of providing a technical linguistic description of Chinese writing, we treat Chinese written script as a generally consistent entity, without specific attention to configuration and form changes over time, unless necessary. On such occasions when differences between ancient and modern written Chinese may confuse readers, we use the term "archaic Chinese" to refer to ancient forms of written script and point out the differences. Since the purpose of this chapter is to focus on the historical development of Chinese written language and its acquisition, we believe such a holistic treatment of Chinese written script is justified.

L. Tao (✉)
Literacy Education, College of Staten Island, City University of New York,
New York, NY, USA
e-mail: liqing.tao@csi.cuny.edu

G. Qian
Literacy Education, Lehman College, City University of New York,
New York, NY, USA

1.2 Dialects and Chinese Written Language

Two unique aspects of the Chinese language are important to one's understanding of the history of Chinese literacy education: the relationship between Chinese oral dialects and written script, and the relationship between dialects and a standard universal oral language. Aside from minority languages, seven major dialects are spoken in present-day China by more than a billion Chinese Han Nationality people. These seven dialects are Mandarin, Wu (吴), Min (闽), Yue (Cantonese) (粤), Kejia (Hakka) (客家), Gan (赣), and Xiang (湘) (Chang and Chang 1978; DeFrancis 1989; Duanmu 2007). Sub-dialects of the major dialects further extend language differences between regions. While these dialects share some lexical, phonological, and tonal similarities, they are usually not intelligible to each other in oral communication, except to the trained ear. These dialects share one common bond that makes the Chinese language a unique case in the world: a common written script. It is not a common script for mapping different pronunciations across different dialects. It functions instead as a means of capturing what needs to be conveyed. Therefore, it is not uncommon to witness people who speak different dialects of Chinese resort to writing as a means of communication when their spoken dialects are mutually unintelligible to each other (Chang and Chang 1978). This common written script is character-based, mono-syllabic, and ideographic or logographic.

While we have emphasized the mutual unintelligibility among Chinese dialects, it should be pointed out that it is wrong to conclude the Chinese have never attempted to make oral communication possible among people speaking different dialects. One persistent effort throughout Chinese history has been to promote a universal oral language for all Chinese people to communicate (Duanmu 2007). A common practice has been to adopt the dialect around capital regions as a universal oral language for communication and educational needs. For example, as far back as 551–479 BC, Confucius used Ya Yan (gracious oral language), the common oral language of that time, for reading classics and performing rituals (Confucius, 479 BC/1980; Duanmu 2007). Ya Yan was adopted from the region around the Eastern Zhou's capital near the current city of Luoyang. Later dynasties used other dialects common around their own capitals for universal oral languages. Modern-day China has adopted Beijing Mandarin, a dialect around the Beijing area, as the officially sponsored and promoted universal oral language of communication and education. The dialect is referred to as Putonghua in the People's Republic of China (PRC) and Guoyu in Taiwan. This means of determining a universal language has implications for current Chinese language education since official promotion and use of a universal oral language based on a certain dialect means users of all other dialects must learn to speak the official dialect. In schooling in the PRC, learning Putonghua, therefore, becomes an educational objective (Chinese Ministry of Education 2001), and literacy, thus, has an additional meaning and practice for users of other dialects in China.

We want to add one more point here to caution the reader of an over-simplified view of ancient China's dialect situation. There is some evidence that China's dialects have changed over time, particularly with regard to tones and ending stop consonants, adding to the complexity of China's dialect issue (Ren 2004). However, we need to point out that these changes do not alter the nature of dialect differences as we now know them. Therefore, while we need to be aware of the complexity involved (DeFrancis 1984, 1989), it does not affect the points we want to make in the next chapter.

1.3 Characteristics of Chinese Written Script

1.3.1 Logographic/Ideographic Nature of Written Chinese

Five characteristics of the Chinese written language are most relevant to literacy education. First, Chinese written script is logographic/ideographic with the character as its basic unit. Out of the six categories of character formation principles originally proposed by Shen Xu in the ancient Han Dynasty, four types of characters are widely recognized by contemporary scholars of the modern Chinese writing system (Taylor and Taylor 1995; Wu et al. 1999). These are pictographic characters (象形/xiangxing), simple ideographic characters (指事/zhishi), compound ideographic characters (会意/huiyi), and semantic-phonetic compound characters (形声/xingsheng), among which semantic-phonetic compound characters account for about 90% of modern Chinese characters according to Qiu (2009).

Students are taught that pictographic characters are those that directly show the objects of the labels that describe them, such as the archaic Chinese character 日 (sun); ideographic characters point to concepts the labels describe, such as the characters 上 (up) and 下 (down); compound ideographic characters indicate the meaning of characters that usually combine radicals or stand-alone characters, such as the character 信 (trust) that has a radical "person" and a stand-alone character "say"; and semantic-phonetics point towards the possibility of syllable sounds of characters, such as the character 氛 that has a phonetic indicator/radical 分 (open) and a semantic indicator/radical 气 (gaseous).

Most Chinese characters capture oral language through a single-syllable and somewhat phono-morphemic approach, rather than through phoneme-mapped letters related to pronunciation and letter patterns as in alphabetic languages. In other words, the characters do not directly reflect the regularity in sound patterns, but they are semantically loaded, meaning-based units of written language. To illustrate the logographic/ideographic nature of Chinese characters, we offer some visually similar, but not identical, Chinese characters that do not cue the reader phonetically: 日 (sun, pronounced/ri/), 旦 (morning, pronounced/dan/), 亘 (spatially or temporally continuous, pronounced/gen/). While these examples of characters are not phonetically connected, they provide both visual semantic cues in the form of early ancient writing and etymologic associations among them. In that sense, Chinese characters do not directly signify exact meanings, given the abstract onfiguration of characters, but rather they provide more semantic cues than phonetic matches between visual patterns and sounds. However, phonetic cues in Chinese characters do exist for many semantic-phonetic compound characters in the form of syllabic hints for readers who already have a solid fundamental understanding of Chinese written script. We will elaborate on this a bit further when we discuss the fourth feature of Chinese characters, the use of radicals and phonetics.

1.3.2 Characters as Meaningful Language Units

Second, the basic and meaningful units in Chinese written script are characters, rather than morphemes in an alphabetic language. The characters we cited above offer some examples. Characters are usually used in set expressions in modern Chinese, though they were used more as single expressions of meaning in archaic Chinese. It is worth pointing out that some linguists would argue these characters are morphemes (DeFrancis 1984; Ku Anderson 2000; Shu 2003; Shu et al. 2000), as their counterparts are labeled in an alphabetic language such as English (e.g., *re-* as in regain, *-s* in plans, or *-ed*, in leveled). This argument has its merits in that it offers both a familiar structure and a lens for Western linguists to examine written Chinese and provides a feasible platform on which initial comparative analyses of written Chinese and alphabetic languages can be conducted. However, the limitations are also immediately obvious to any Chinese user. The subordinate nature of bound morphemes in English (for example, *re-*, *un-*) does not capture the associative roles Chinese characters play in forming set expressions. Usually, Chinese word or phrase formation is similar to the way English free morphemes form compound words (such as *classroom*). In addition, grammatical indicativeness, in the form of affixation of some morphemic units in alphabetic languages such as English (e.g., *-ment*, *-ness*), is not directly available in written Chinese characters. More importantly, for beginning learners of Chinese, the morphemic view of characters is not helpful in assisting learners to identify word boundaries in modern Chinese since it assumes both that there is a complete functional unit called words and that morphemes would not contain other smaller semantic indicators. Neither of these morphemic assumptions is always true with Chinese characters. We will further address this in the fourth point below. Even though there is an overlap between the concept of a morpheme in English and that of a character, the latter is easier to grasp in practice, particularly for beginning learners of Chinese. In a sense, characters have a more independent role in written Chinese than this single morphemic argument allows. From a historical perspective, characters have remained the basic functional units of meaning in written script throughout Chinese literacy history into modern day China (Tang 1981; Weiger 1965).

1 Historical Perspectives on Chinese Written Language and Literacy Education...

1.3.3 Syllables as Pronunciation Units

Third, syllables are the most important pronunciation units to understand Chinese. Each character represents one syllable in pronunciation. Modern Chinese can have about 1,600 possible syllables with four distinguishable tones, much less than the syllable number in English. In fact, some estimation puts actual Chinese syllables at 1,300 (Duanmu 2007), much less than the estimated range between several thousand (Taylor 2002) and 20,000 (Li et al. 2002) in English. This would at least be essential to two aspects of character processing: difficulty in homophonic differentiation and insignificance of phoneme recognition.

Let us first address the difficulty created for homophonic differentiation. The 1,300 syllable sounds cover more than 48,000 different characters in Chinese, creating a tremendous amount of homophones, theoretically about 40 homophones on average for each tonal syllable sound (Anderson et al. 2003; Taylor 2002). Such a massive number of homophone characters would be confusing if syllables were used alone. However, different visual configurations and verbal collocational contexts—sequences of words that occur together both at the levels of set expressions and sentences—provide some necessary means for further distinction among homophones. For example, the following pairs of characters would be indistinguishable by sounds alone: 津津, and 斤斤 (all pronounced as jinjin with a first flat tone). Yet, they are recognizably different in visual form and in the following possible collocations: 津津乐道 (dwell on something with a passion), and 斤斤计较 (be picky). For beginning Chinese learners, the match between pronunciation of characters and their visual forms is acquired through both configuration recognition and functional contexts.

The second aspect of character processing relates to syllable recognition. The ability to break syllables down into phonemes is not necessary for syllable recognition. The phonemic ability so indispensable in processing alphabetic languages such as English (Ehri 1991) is not needed at the beginning stages of learning Chinese but will be partially useful in advanced stages of learning Chinese poetry. There is some evidence that points to the non-essentiality of phonemic awareness among proficient users of Chinese (see McDowell & Lorch 2008). What we stress here is phoneme awareness can be bypassed in learning Chinese characters, even though learning standard Mandarin Chinese would definitely benefit from knowledge of its phonemes.

1.3.4 Radicals and Phonetics in Compound Characters

Fourth, we will highlight two features that mark many compound Chinese characters: the use of radicals and the use of phonetics (also called phonetic radicals) in the making of Chinese characters. Radicals are a key component of many compound Chinese characters. Their function is similar to that of English morphemes in that they can be divided into either stand-alone radicals or affixed radicals. Radicals are used as a component to form compound characters. These radicals can usually offer semantic clues to the meanings of the compound characters they form. Even though they cannot offer exact meanings of those characters, radicals can often provide semantic information to the categories of characters. For example, a character that has a 木 radical (wood) such as 树 (tree) would usually indicate the character refers to a substance that has something to do with wood. More examples would include 根 (root), 柳 (willow), and 梨 (pear). Historically, radicals have been recognized as an important component for understanding Chinese characters in their capacity to indicate possible semantic categories of characters (Xu 100/1989).

The use of phonetics is another way a semantic-phonetic compound character can be made, usually in combination with semantic radicals. Phonetic components or phonetic radicals can be stand-alone characters themselves, used with radicals to form compound characters. While phonetic components are only capable of pointing towards broad phonological information in compound characters, they can offer some possibilities of pronunciation. The resultant compound character can either sound the same as the phonetic component, can have the same onsets or rimes, or can have a different tone or sound. For an extreme example, characters having 者 (zhe) as phonetic components can have close to 20 different pronunciations in modern-day Chinese (Qiu 2009), making it a very unreliable pronunciation predictor. The phonetic radical 者 (zhe) can be found in "zhu" (猪, pig), "chu" (储, deposit), and "shu" (暑, summer). While phonetic components are not reliable indicators of pronunciation, they can be a useful assistance to Chinese learners due to the massive number of them in Chinese characters. In fact, about 90% of modern Chinese characters contain phonetic radicals, even though the percentage of phonetic radicals in high frequency characters is lower at about 74% (Qiu 2009). However, to access correct meanings and pronunciations of characters using phonetics would require somewhat advanced and special knowledge of Chinese.

1.3.5 Writing Strokes in Chinese Script

Last but not least, Chinese characters cannot be spelled due to a lack of direct letter representation of sounds. Eight basic writing strokes in Chinese script are essential to the physical formation of Chinese characters. These strokes have distinctive names and can be called out. In an alphabetic language, the spelling of a word is possible through auditory means. This is of course made possible by the limited letters that all have a name, as well as the directionality of arranging letters in a word. Given the limited number of letters available, orally spelling words is both a cognitively manageable means for acquiring the fundamental units of an alphabetically written language and a powerful instructional strategy to facilitate such acquisition. Furthermore, the horizontal writing directionality highlights the importance of the sequence of letter arrangement and mitigates at the same time the spatial configuration of words. Therefore, calling out the letter names of a word in their letter sequence can create the word orally. Yet, Chinese presents a case with reverse characteristics. All strokes within Chinese characters are configured spatially but not directionally or sequentially as letter arrangements are in English words. Having an additional stroke can make a substantive difference to a character. For example, the character 大 (large, pronounced /da/) is semantically and phonologically different from the character 天 (sky, pronounced /tian/) that has an added stroke on top. Spatial configuration is all that matters in forming a Chinese character, and the sequence of strokes within a character is more procedural than substantive. Naming the strokes as one writes, though imposing a façade of temporal sequence, is not very useful in indicating the position of a stroke within a character, nor does it enhance the acquisition of a character. For example, calling out the strokes of a character such as 日 would not be cognitively functional or instructionally facilitative in learning the character since the listener would not know where the strokes should fall within the character, nor could he or she use this auditory input as a mnemonic tool for retaining the character. In fact, it may even confuse learners given the possibility that these similar strokes could form a different character with strokes positioned in a different configuration. In sum, oral spelling is not a very useful means to learn and use Chinese, which is not designed for visually accommodating auditory finesse at the phoneme level.

We need to point out that radicals behave similarly to strokes in the configuration of characters. Radicals within different characters can assume different positions and usually different sizes. Characters, however, remain an identical size in spite of the number of radicals and strokes in the different characters. This unique feature of Chinese characters complicates the task of learning to write or "spell" since both strokes and radicals retain their shapes, but not their size and position, in different characters. While position is key to the formation of Chinese characters, conventions play a large role in the position of strokes and radicals.

1.4 Ancient Chinese Literacy Education: Historical Perspectives

1.4.1 Shang Dynasty

Chinese literacy education, reading and writing instruction, must have begun when a systematic written language was already in consistent use, at least during the oracle bone character time of the Shang Dynasty (about 1700–1050 BC). However, due to a lack of historical documents, we cannot trace literacy education back that far to understand how reading and writing were acquired at that time. From archeological evidence of oracle bones, we know the system of Chinese written language was already well established and would have required prolonged training to acquire. We also know specific cultural conventions that were captured through writing were also dependent on the writing itself to continue and develop, even though the practice was restricted only to ruling institutions (Chen 1985; Qiu 2009). Therefore, literacy acquisition during the Shang Dynasty must have been very specific and limited to only specially selected clerics and diviners, who recorded divinations and important warring events on meticulously prepared bone surfaces (Zhang 2011).

1.4.2 Zhou Dynasty

Brief mention of elementary education institutions in the Zhou Dynasty (about 1050 BC–256 BC) indicates that children went to school to learn reading and writing at around the age of eight, but no mention is made of how exactly reading and writing were taught (Hu 1990; Weiger 1965). A character book entitled 史籀篇 (*Shi Zhou Character Book*) appeared at this time and is generally believed to be the central government's effort to standardize the configuration and shape of character writing. While there is no written record of its use for beginning learners, the book was intended for any character user as a guide for correct characters and is believed to have been used by beginning learners (Ban, 111/1991). During that period, literacy acquisition was included in the education of aristocrats, and formal character text was in existence (Sun 1991). We also know from Confucius' educational practice that education was no longer limited to aristocrats (Bai 1982; Fu 2007). It is worth noting that the second half of the period, consisting of the Spring and Autumn period and the Warring States period, witnessed one of the most acclaimed fertile grounds for cultural and philosophical activities in China's history, producing such intellectual giants as Confucius, Lao Zi, Zhuang Zi, Mencius, Mo Zi, and Xun Zi. Most of these philosophers had their own schools and followers to advocate and practice their thoughts, situating literacy skills as a central means for intellectual exchange and distribution. Corresponding books of various schools were produced and circulated, greatly facilitating the spread of literacy among the general populace and occasioning at the same time the regional adoption of multiple styles of Chinese characters (Qiu 2009).

1.4.3 Qin Dynasty

During the Qin Dynasty (221 BC–206 BC), the first unified nation state in China, written script universalization was first officially enforced in China. The resultant character text 苍颉 (*Cang Jie*) was written in archaic Chinese style (Small Seal style) and provided examples for all users throughout China, including beginners. Up to that time, writing surfaces were mainly bamboo, wood, and, on rare occasions, silk, with brush pens and carving tools as writing implements. Descriptions of literacy education at that time are hard to find, but character enforcement from the central government must have further de-aristocratized and streamlined literacy acquisition in a way that all other script styles previously in use were outlawed. The focus now was on communicative capacity and cultural identity as the most salient functions of literacy (Sun 1991).

1.4.4 Han Dynasty

The Han Dynasty (206 BC–220 AD) that followed saw the publication of the first and most well-known Chinese character dictionary, *Shuowen Jiezi* (Xu 100/1989), which explicitly laid out six principles of making Chinese characters. Paper also came into existence during this dynasty. Some limited descriptions of elementary education indicate the number of characters learned became the focus of literacy education, even though this learning still occurred in the context of learning Confucian texts, which were officially endorsed for the first time in the first half of the dynasty (Bai 1982; Zhang 1992). Character texts written at the time were morally oriented and focused on immediate daily use. There is some evidence that multi-age teaching in large classes was the norm at the elementary level. Using paper, a cheaper means for writing, at the end of the dynasty would have promoted literacy learning and practice. For the first time, characters formally embraced a simplified style called Li or Cleric style and became less picture-like and easier to write, signaling a move towards the modern character style in China (Xu 2009).

1.4.5 Wei-Jin Southern and Northern Dynasties

For the ensuing period of the Wei-Jin Southern and Northern Dynasties (220–589), we have similar sketchy descriptions of literacy education, but three important events clearly influenced literacy education: the emergence of the phonetic analysis of Chinese characters (Liu 2004), widespread use of character styles that were simplified in strokes but abstract in configuration (still in use today), and the popularity of Buddhism throughout the period (Bai 1982; Qian 1996). We would expect these events to contribute to literacy education by including the learning of correct pronunciation of characters in the universal language as a part of literacy acquisition, somewhat simplifying the task of learning characters in simplified character styles, and promoting repeated reading and writing of texts in the Buddhist tradition. Brush pens and paper became standard instruments of learning to read and write characters, and a well-known character text 千字文 (*Qian Zi Wen*) was produced by the end of this period.

1.4.6 Sui and Tang Dynasties

Few descriptions of literacy education during the Sui (581–618) and Tang (818–907) Dynasties exist, but circumstantial evidence abounds. For example, the civil service examination system for selection of officials started during this time and lasted for the next 1,300 some years. Part of the examinations assessed the literacy skills of candidates. In addition, poetic creations that depended on phonetic analysis of rimes and tones reached an unprecedented peak. The block printing technique was developed in this period and made writing more accessible to a larger audience than before. In addition to the types of character texts of previous dynasties, character texts for initial preparation for civil service examinations were introduced during the Sui and Tang Dynasties, thus situating character learning also in the context of moving up in the social ladder through official-scholar preparation (Bai 1982; Lee 2000).

1.4.7 Song Dynasty

The Song Dynasty (960–1279) was the time when elementary education came to the forefront of educational concerns. Various texts of characters and rules for elementary schools were published. From a technical viewpoint, the maturity of the block printing technique was reflected both in the standard printing fonts available and in the highly sophisticated book-binding format of the butterfly style that made information in books more accessible, even though the movable font printing technique invented then was not put into use until the late 19th century in China (Bai 1982; Tsien 1985). From a socio-economic perspective, the development of printing presses across the country greatly reduced book prices and made books more accessible to a large audience (Lee 2000). Clear instructions about learning to read and write were described in rules for elementary students. The literacy qualifications of teachers were clearly stated. Students were divided into different levels, and characters were learned through repeated reading aloud and writing. The emphasis was on learning characters and Confucian texts but not on understanding what was read (Chi 1998). Character texts of the time, however, did take into consideration motivational aspects of young people's learning by making texts more interesting and easier to remember. A character text 三字经 (*San Zi Jing*) produced during the Song Dynasty has been continuously used up to modern times (Zhang 1992). Schools of various types, ranging from government schools to community schools to seasonal schools, were reported.

1.4.8 Yuan and Ming Dynasties

More accounts of literacy education exist for the ensuing Yuan (1206–1368) and Ming (1368–1644) Dynasties than for previous dynasties. Thanks to the mature technique of block printing in the Song Dynasty, books were now printed in large numbers (Bai 1982; Sun 1991). Elementary schools were systematized as part of the educational system in the Yuan Dynasty and were almost everywhere in Ming times. The influence of civil service examinations on elementary school learning, particularly on literacy learning, was more extensive throughout these dynasties. Educators at the time must have noticed the weight of these examinations on young students and began to emphasize teaching to students' interests, but this was a practice followed by individual teachers rather than a formalized teaching procedure. Accompanying pictures for the first time appeared in some texts for learning characters, catering to the needs of young learners (Chi 1998; Zhang 1992).

1.4.9 Qing Dynasty

The Qing Dynasty (1616–1911) saw heightened attention paid to literacy education, both popular literacy and elementary literacy, but instruction continued to follow traditions set during the Song Dynasty (Bai 1982; Rawski 1979). Previous character texts were still very popular. More textbooks of character learning were published with an emphasis on moral and Confucian content, as well as purely on character learning. The influence of civil service examinations was strong, continuously affecting both character learning modes (such as repeated reading and recitations) and the content of texts. Popular literacy was also promoted at the time by Western educated scholars and teachers, particularly among poor communities and religious congregations (Bai 1982; Rawski 1979). For the first time in Chinese educational history, language reform in the direction of alphabetizing Chinese written script was discussed and became a serious scholarly and social endeavor, though it came to little avail as far as the nature of written script was concerned (Bai 1982; Chen 1999; Ichikawa and Komatsu 2008). However, reform efforts that began at that time later were subsumed into modern efforts of indexing pronunciations and simplifying characters (Zhou 2004).

1.5 Literacy Learning and the Nature of Chinese Orthography

Based on the above brief overview of historical evidence of literacy education in ancient China, we next will summarize the main ancient Chinese perspectives on literacy learning in the context of Chinese orthography. We believe literacy learning is ultimately necessitated by the needs and functions of written script in a society and is eventually realized through learners' insights into the nature of the written script. Therefore, we will approach this summary both from the context of the history of literacy learning in China and the uniqueness of Chinese orthography, moving from social concepts to educational concepts and practices.

In ancient China, written language and literacy played an essential role in society from the very beginning. The divination of oracle bones—the presumed power of foretelling the future through characters on the bones—was recorded through literacy. In Confucian times, the centrality of literacy was clearly demonstrated through Confucius' own words and deeds. In later times, whether in the enforcement of character universalization in the Qin Dynasty, the introduction of paper as a writing surface in the Han Dynasty, or the initiation of literacy intense civil service examinations in the Sui and Tang Dynasties, words represented in characters became the carrier of social and cultural conventions. Therefore, literacy at both its basic and advanced levels became an absolute necessity for social and cultural participation, whether to grow into a gentleman (君子, junzi), to become a scholar-official, to simply follow ceremonial rituals, or to be a devotee of the Buddhist religion. This was, and to some extent still is, the context in which literacy acquisition occurred. In traditional Chinese society, teachers and scholars were called "persons who read," highlighting the central role literacy played in defining a respectable person in society. With regards to literacy learning in general, this type of writing-centered milieu provided incentives and motivation for learners. Repeated reading aloud and character writing became methods to develop literacy skills from the beginning.

It is also clear from the brief review of the history of literacy education above that Chinese texts using characters moved from formats that fit all users to formats considered appropriate for beginning and young learners. In about 1,500 years from the remnants of 史籀篇 to 三字经, we notice an educational awakening to both the unique nature of Chinese orthography and the special needs of young children's character learning. Over time, character texts became more rhythmic and limited in the number and complexity of characters. The texts became an initiation into common knowledge of nature and society, interspersed with stories, and were a stepping stone for further advanced learning of Confucian texts. The variety of character texts in the later years of ancient China is testimony itself to the needs and sensitivity towards the initial stages of character learning. Characters could be learned in small steps through accretion, at different rates according to different abilities, and through different texts for different functional purposes. It is also clear that moral messages and Confucian thoughts continued to serve as the contexts in which most of the character texts were written and taught.

When it comes to educational practice, literacy learning and teaching usually involved the following components in ancient China: reading aloud single or contextualized characters, repeated readings of characters, tracing and writing the characters, recitation of texts and poems, and learning the basic character-making principles (Sun 1991; Tao and Zuo 1997). We will briefly discuss each of these teaching methods here.

1.5.1 Reading Aloud to Learn Characters

Reading aloud to learn characters was extremely popular and was recorded at the earliest in the Han Dynasty. It may not surprise anyone that a beginner learns to read through reading out loud, but it was especially relevant to learning Chinese characters because of the existing dialect differences, the non-alphabetic nature of the script, and the homophonic similarity of numerous characters. Reading aloud made it possible for a beginner to acquire character pronunciations in the universal language of the time, to establish immediate connections with the pronunciation of characters to achieve automaticity, and to develop a foundation for further differentiation of characters in contexts. Repeated reading of characters and texts was a practice that enhanced the result of reading aloud but could become very boring and monotonous when the texts used were limited. However, the advantage of repeated reading was also obvious in that it reinforced auditory-visual connections that were needed in reading and identifying characters within a non-alphabetic script. It also made automaticity possible even if it was very shallow at this stage. The resulting oral fluency would be useful to familiarize students auditorily with concepts and characters that were not within their daily vocabulary and concepts, setting the stage for later advanced learning.

1.5.2 *Tracing and Writing Characters*

Tracing and writing characters were always a part of beginning character learning. Not only did tracing start students off right in learning characters (as it was well known in China that one's writing reflected one's personality), but also it helped in learning the strokes, positions of strokes, and radicals within characters, and more importantly in recognizing the visually identifiable features that would be useful in differentiating homophonic characters. To be more specific, Chinese characters have unique spatial configurations that require meticulous attention to the stroke and radical details within identically-sized characters. In order to learn a Chinese character, one must acquire the procedural and visual insight that a stroke or a radical is resizable in a character, but the characters themselves are not resizable. This adds an additional obstacle in learning to "spell" characters. Tracing and writing characters from the beginning of instruction provides a procedural means for the learner to acquire both insight into and practice of correct character writing. Therefore, tracing and later writing characters was a primary task for beginners (Wilkinson 2000).

1.5.3 *Recitation of Character Texts and Poems*

Recitation of character texts and poems was a must, especially after the civil service examinations were introduced, since students who set their eyes on a high social status would need to have the basic skill of knowing traditional classics by heart. As we pointed out in our description of literacy in the Song Dynasty, children were not required to understand the meaning of characters or texts at the beginning stage of learning, but remembering the characters was essential. However, effort is not always sufficient for learning, as some educators realized, so they would introduce texts that catered to the interests of children and set the order of learning classics from easy to advanced texts. From the perspective of learning characters, it should be understood that characters are better remembered in the context of continuous texts. Classic character texts such as 千字文 and 三字经 provide good examples of texts that have been recited for about a thousand years by beginning Chinese learners (Zhang 1992). Modern day Chinese curriculum in Mainland China also has recitation as one of the main instructional practices and learning objectives (Zhou 1999).

1.5.4 Six Principles of Character Writing

After learning a few characters, beginners in ancient times were also introduced to the principles of character writing. While it was usually referred to as the six principles, as described earlier in this chapter, we believe the most relevant principles are the four that help learners see the nature of Chinese characters: pictographic, simple ideographic, compound ideographic, and semantic-phonetic aspects. These principles of character writing provided students with opportunities to be more independent in their literacy learning. However, it was usually understood that the utility of the four principles was not equal for all beginners. The fourth principle seemed to be the most useful, but learners needed substantive knowledge of a large number of characters in order to fully benefit from it.

1.6 Conclusion

We have briefly discussed the characteristics of Chinese written script, sketched an outline of literacy education through Chinese history, and summarized ancient Chinese perspectives on learning to read and write. Chinese literacy acquisition throughout Chinese history centered on the essential role of written language in the society of the time. Individual efforts following Confucian traditions were conceived as necessary and essential to learning Chinese script. Social ambitions for literacy acquisition were fueled by the government-sponsored official-selection mechanism of civil service examinations. Also, the characteristics of Chinese orthography and unique language and dialect issues made some educational practices salient features of ancient Chinese literacy learning.

In conclusion, we would like to offer five implications of our historical survey that are relevant to current literacy educators and policy makers. First, social and cultural functions of literacy are important for the promotion of literacy acquisition. Confucius' thoughts on learning and civil service examinations greatly influenced literacy learning processes and content in Chinese history. Second, technology development fundamentally affected the way literacy spread, but only in the context of social and cultural functions of literacy. Changes from bamboo and wood writing surfaces to paper, and from copying to block printing altered the accessibility of literacy texts. However, we need to keep in mind that paper was not invented initially for writing and the movable font printing technique was not used when it was first invented about 1,000 years ago. Take movable font print as an example. It was not seen as absolutely necessary given the availability of block print at the time (Shen, 1090/1997). In fact, it was not in tune with the writing traditions of ancient China where an individual's writing of characters was regarded as capturing his personality. Movable font print did not do justice to this appreciation of character writing in ancient China where there was no urgency to acquire information.

Third, the orthographic nature of a written script needs to be taken into consideration in literacy instruction and acquisition. For example, learning Chinese characters without engaging in understanding some principles of how the characters are made will be less effective, just as learning English without understanding the alphabetic principle will be equally ineffective. Of course, as we pointed out, not all principles are equally useful for beginners. Fourth, writing at the beginning literacy stages is beneficial. Writing has always been a necessary part of Chinese literacy learning due largely to the spatial positioning of strokes and radicals within Chinese characters, but writing will also enhance the precision of identification of characters and can strengthen our understanding of the nature of the script. The same should be true for other scripts, be they alphabetic or ideographic. Last but not least, the changes in character texts from no attention to reader characteristics to more attention to the special learning needs of children resulted from a realization that we need to understand who we are teaching. This realization is equally important for us literacy educators today. In this multicultural and technologically-advanced age, we need to find ways to make literacy learning relevant and effective from the perspectives of diverse learners.

References

Anderson, R., Li, W., Ku, Y., Shu, H., & Wu, N. (2003). Use of partial information in learning to read Chinese characters. *Journal of Educational Psychology, 95*(1), 52–57.
Bai, S. (Ed.). (1982). *An outline history of China*. Beijing: Foreign Languages Press.
Ban, G. (111/1991). 汉书 [*History of Han*]. Hunan: Yuelu Academy Press.
Chang, R., & Chang, M. (1978). *Speaking of Chinese*. New York: Norton.
Chen, Y. (1985). 简明中国文学史 [*A brief history of Chinese literature*]. Shangxi: People Press.
Chen, P. (1999). *Modern Chinese: History and sociolinguistics*. New York: Cambridge University Press.
Chi, X. (1998). 中国古代小学教育研究 [*A study on China's ancient elementary education*]. Shanghai: Shanghai Education Press.
Chinese Ministry of Education. (2001). *Yuwen curriculum standards for full-day compulsory education – Trial version*. Beijing: Beijing Normal University Press.
Confucius. (479 BC/1980). 论语 [*The Analects with explanatory notes by Yang Bojun*]. Beijing: Chinese Publishing Bureau.

DeFrancis, J. (1984). *The Chinese language: Fact and fantasy*. Honolulu: University of Hawaii Press.
DeFrancis, J. (1989). *Visible speech: The diverse oneness of writing systems*. Honolulu: University of Hawaii Press.
Duanmu, S. (2007). *The phonology of standard Chinese* (2nd ed.). Oxford: Oxford University Press.
Ehri, L. C. (1991). Learning to read and spell words. In L. Rieben & C. A. Perfetti (Eds.), *Learning to read: Basic research and its implications* (pp. 57–73). Hillsdale: Erlbaum.
Fu, S. (2007). 傅斯年战国子家与史记讲义 [*Fu Sinian's lecture collection on schools of the Warring Period and Grand History*]. Tienjing: Tienjing Classics Press.
Hu, Y. (1990). 中国教育史 [*An educational history of China*]. Lanzhou: Lanzhou University Press.
Ichikawa, I., & Komatsu, A. (2008). 百年华语 [*Chinese language over the past hundred years*]. Shanghai: Shanghai Education Press.
Ku, Y., & Anderson, R. C. (2000). *Development of morphological awareness in Chinese and English*. Champaign: Center for the Study of Reading.
Lee, T. H. C. (2000). *Education in traditional China: A history*. Leiden: Brill.
Li, W., Anderson, R. C., Nagy, W., & Zhang, H. (2002). Facets of metalinguistic awareness that contribute to Chinese literacy. In W. Li, J. S. Gaffney, & J. L. Packard (Eds.), *Chinese children's reading acquisition: Theoretical and pedagogical issues*. London: Kluwer.
Liu, Y. (2004). 中国字典史略 [*A brief history of Chinese dictionaries*]. Beijing: Chinese Publishing Bureau.
McDowell, H., & Lorch, M. P. (2008). Phonemic awareness in Chinese L1 readers of English: Not simply an effect of orthography. *TESOL Quarterly, 42*, 495–515.
Qian, M. (1996). 中国文化史导论 [*An introduction to the cultural history of China*]. Beijing: Commerce Press.
Qiu, X. (2009). 文字学概要 [*An introduction to the study of Chinese characters*]. Beijing: Commerce Press.
Rawski, E. S. (1979). *Education and popular literacy in Ch'ing China*. Ann Arbor: The University of Michigan Press.
Ren, J. (2004). 汉语语源学 [*Chinese etymology*]. Chongqing: Chongqing Press.
Shen, K. (1090/1997). 梦溪笔谈 [*Pen talks in the dream brook*]. Yangzhou: Jiansu Guangli Classics Press.
Shu, H. (2003). Chinese writing system and learning to read. *International Journal of Psychology, 38*, 274–285.
Shu, H., Anderson, R. C., & Wu, N. (2000). Phonetic awareness: Knowledge of orthography--phonology relationships in the character acquisition of Chinese children. *Journal of Educational Psychology, 92*, 56–62.
Sun, P. (Ed.). (1991). 中国教育史 [*An educational history of China*]. Shanghai: East China Normal University Press.
Tang, L. (1981). 古文字学导论 [*An introduction to the study of ancient Chinese characters*]. Jinan, Shangdong: Qilu Press.
Tao, L., & Zuo, L. (1997). Oral reading practice in China's elementary schools: A brief discussion of its unique roots in language, culture, and society. *The Reading Teacher, 50*, 654–665.
Taylor, I. (2002). Phonological awareness in Chinese reading. In W. Li, J. S. Gaffney, & J. L. Packard (Eds.), *Chinese children's reading acquisition: Theoretical and pedagogical issues* (pp. 39–58). Boston: Kluwer.
Taylor, I., & Taylor, M. M. (1995). *Writing and literacy in Chinese, Korean, and Japanese*. Philadelphia: John Benjamins.
Tsien, T. H. (1985). Paper and printing. In series J. Needham (Ed.), *Science and civilisation in China, (Vol. 5, Pt. 1)*. Cambridge: Cambridge University Press.
Weiger, L. (1965). *Chinese characters: Their origin, etymology, history, classification and signification: A thorough study from Chinese documents*. Dover: Courier Dover Publications.

Wilkinson, E. (2000). *Chinese history: A manual*. Cambridge, MA: Harvard University Press.
Wu, X., Li, W., & Anderson, R. (1999). Reading instruction in China. *Journal of Curriculum Studies, 31*(5), 571–586.
Xu, S. (100/1989). 说文解字 [*A dictionary to elucidate Chinese characters*]. Beijing: Chinese Publishing Bureau.
Xu, J. (2009). 简明中国文字学 [*A short history of Chinese characters*]. Beijing: Chinese Publishing Bureau.
Zhang, Z. (1992). 传统语文教育教材论——暨蒙学书目和书影 [*On traditional Chinese education and texts with a bibliography of character texts and book reprints*]. Shanghai: Shanghai Education Press.
Zhang, L. (2011). 甲骨文史话 [*A brief history of oracle-bone inscriptions in China*]. Beijing: Social Sciences Academic Press.
Zhou, Q. (1999). 语文教学设计论 [*On Chinese curriculum and instruction*]. Nanning: Guangxi Education Press.
Zhou, Y. (2004). 周有光语言学论文集 [*A collection of linguistic essays by Youguang Zhou*]. Beijing: Commerce Press.

Chapter 2
Literacy in Ancient China: A Culturally and Socially Situated Role in Historical Times

Liqing Tao and Gaoyin Qian

2.1 Introduction

The focus of the present chapter is on the cultural and social effects of Chinese written script in ancient China. Specifically, we highlight the cultural, political, and social interactions that occurred in ancient times because of or related to the unique characteristics of Chinese written language. In Chap. 1, we briefly reviewed some relevant characteristics of Chinese writing. In the present chapter, we focus on aspects of life in Chinese society that were affected by the nature of the written script.

We have adopted a sociocultural literacy and historical perspective for the present chapter (Gee 2007; Resnick and Resnick 1977). This perspective posits that literacy resonates with and is in response to the institutional, cultural, and social superstructures of a given society. We apply this perspective to our analysis of the roles of Chinese written language in China's history, particularly the role of linguistic features that facilitated social and cultural functions of character writing.

2.2 Characteristics of Chinese Characters

While we refer the reader to Chap. 1 of this book for an overview of the unique characteristics of Chinese written script, we would like to highlight here that Chinese written language is single-syllabic, character-based, multi-homophonic, and ideographic. Unlike alphabetic languages, Chinese written language does not rely on

---

L. Tao (✉)
Literacy Education, College of Staten Island, City University of New York, New York, NY, USA
e-mail: liqing.tao@csi.cuny.edu

G. Qian
Literacy Education, Lehman College, City University of New York, New York, NY, USA

phonemes to configure words. But its structural components (strokes), morphemic components (radicals), and syllabic units (characters) constitute the basis of Chinese script. These features have significance for learning to read and write in Chinese, but they also have ramifications for Chinese society. All written languages record and sustain human civilizations. Chinese written language is no exception. It crystallized Chinese civilizations, captured history, and offered an effective means for sustained social and cultural activities. Moreover, the nature of Chinese written language provided a context in which social and cultural phenomena peculiar to Chinese society took shape.

2.3 Cultural, Social, and Political Roles of Chinese Written Language

In this section, we discuss the sociocultural and political implications of Chinese written language in ancient China. While we divide the following into two subsections for the convenience of presentation, they should be viewed as fundamentally interrelated in that they show a complex picture of ancient Chinese culture, society, and people as contextualized in Chinese language.

2.3.1 Chinese Written Language: A Means of Cultural and National Identity

Written language, as a means of extending the capacity of oral language spatially and temporally, provides a necessary foundation for any civilization that sustains and evolves through a process of continuously building on its heritage and maintaining and improving its social, cultural, and political infrastructures and superstructures. In other words, written language constitutes the very means by which civilization has been carried on and evolves (Havelock 1976; Ong 2002; Goody 1987). Without a written language, any large-scale coordination of core social activities would not be possible, and any civilization would not see its traditions being handed down over a sustained period of time. Given the diverse populations and dialect situation across such an expansive territory as China, Chinese written language has served cultural, political, and social purposes of maintaining national identity, communicating, and governing various regions where people speak extremely different dialects. Transcending these dialect differences, Chinese written language has served as the only official written script for China. It even extended beyond China's historical borders and served as a written script for some of its Asian neighbors, such as Japan and Korea, who have had very different oral languages. Chinese was sometimes nicknamed the "Latin of the Far East" but was much more sustainable than Latin in the Middle Ages in Europe (Fischer 2003).

While the power of Chinese civilization was undeniably the main force fostering the formation and popularity of Chinese written language, the logographic/ideographic characteristics of the written script also contributed to the lasting and dominant use of Chinese script in China and some neighboring countries (Chu 1973).

2.3.2 Capacity of Chinese Script to Accommodate Different Dialects and Oral Languages

A brief overview of the history of Chinese written script shows that from oracle bone characters to the Qin Zhuan [篆], Han Li [吏], Cao [草], Kai [楷], and Xing [行] styles, different character styles appeared at different times, eventually settling on the Cao, Kai, and Xing styles in the Wei-Jin Southern and Northern Dynasties (220–589) and formal Kai style in the Tang Dynasty (618–907). Since then, the only salient style modification to Chinese written script was the introduction of the print font style, the Song or Fan-Song fonts in the Song Dynasty (960–1279) and Yuan dynasty (1206–1368) that catered to the needs of block printing (Zhu 2005). Modern Chinese script still uses these styles that retain the logographic/ideographic nature of writing in their squared characters (Chu 1973; Xu 2009). In other words, Chinese written script has continuously been used by people speaking different dialects over more than 3,000 years without metamorphosing into a script that could capture in its visual form the phonological aspects of oral language in the same way its alphabetic counterparts did.

It would be inconceivable that no one was aware of the cumbersome nature of using the ideographic/logographic script to represent the thoughts and concepts coded in different dialect sounds. Indeed, there were several major scholarly and governmental efforts in ancient China to impose some uniformity onto the means of written communication. The character book 史籀篇 during the Zhou Dynasty was one of the earliest efforts known to make characters uniform (Hu 2005). Later, the Qin Dynasty's (221–206 BC) edict to use only the Zhuan style launched the most comprehensive campaign to streamline character use for the sake of consolidating dynastic rule (Sun 1991). Dictionaries were also made starting around 100 AD to strengthen "correct" character writing and weed out other forms (Liu 2004). Efforts were also made to promote a universal oral language to facilitate oral communication, particularly on formal diplomatic or scholarly occasions (Wilkinson 2000). During Confucius' time Ya Yan was made the literary language (Confucius, 479 BC/1980). In later times dynastic rulers promoted their own universal oral language, usually dialects spoken around their dynastic capitals (Duanmu 2000). All these efforts point towards an awareness that China would need consistency in a writing system and intelligibility in speaking to support its civilization and society. Yet, these efforts never touched on the nature of logographic/ideographic script itself, the non-alphabetic nature of the writing system. In fact, until later in ancient China, Chinese written script never went in the direction of regularly matching its visual representations to its sounds, as alphabetic languages do.

One may wonder whether the Chinese in ancient times were informed of advantages of capturing spoken sounds through limited visual figures, such as letters to form words. In fact, ever since Buddhism was introduced into China during the later years of the Han Dynasty around the third century AD, the Chinese were aware of the existence of such written languages through Sanskrit. Shortly afterwards, serious study of the phonology of Chinese script began and resulted in a Chinese character sound-indexing system called *fanqie* (反切), a technique using two Chinese characters to indicate the sound of a target character (Zhou 2004). This method effectively analyzed a target character into its onset and rime, with the first character indicating the onset and the second indicating the rime and tone. This type of insight into character pronunciations might have led to an alphabetized script. But it never happened in China due to reasons we will discuss in the following sections.

2.3.3 *Chinese Characters as Representations of Cultural Identity*

One of the main reasons Chinese written language retained its logographic/ideographic nature may lie in the Chinese people themselves, particularly Chinese scholars who felt the squared characters reflected their cultural identification. Chinese writing held a cultural status that compared to nothing else at the time. Over a long period in ancient China, Chinese written language, among other cultural creations, was a proud artifact to be imitated and learned (Chu 1973). From the Tang Dynasty onwards, China enjoyed a highly advanced society, both economically and culturally the envy of its neighbors. Neighbors of China, such as Japan, Korea, and Vietnam, all adopted Chinese written language as their national written language for a lengthy period of time (Chu 1973). In a fundamental sense, the written script so adopted showed its capacity for accommodating various oral languages and dialects, as well as its prestige in being the carrier of a rich heritage. Identification with this script was a source of great pride for scholars. This could be best shown through Chinese calligraphy, an essential artistic skill for traditional Chinese scholars (Lee 2000; Wang 1988).

2.3.3.1 Chinese Calligraphy as an Art Form

Character writing as an art matured around the same time as the phonological analysis of Chinese characters was developed and paper of various types was made available for painting and writing (Lu 2009; Pan 1983). Poetry began to benefit from the clear delineation of rhyming and tonal patterns, an intended result of phonological analysis (Hu 2005). It was in the Wei-Jin Southern and Northern Dynasties and the Tang Dynasty that calligraphy in several of the most common styles became the norm for scholars. Masters of calligraphy emerged who were emulated and followed over the next 1,300 years to the present time (Pan 1983; Wilkinson 2000). Dynasties after the Tang Dynasty each produced some historically famed calligraphers, but none seemed to command more prestige than the calligraphers of the earlier times. A calligrapher in ancient China enjoyed high artist status, and still does in modern China and several Southeast Asian countries. In fact, calligraphic writing in ancient China was an art that shared the same origin as painting and used similar tools (Schirokauer 1989). This was unique in that the spatial configurations of Chinese characters paralleled those of Chinese painting since both emphasized using lines to create spatial configurations.

The nature of Chinese written script allowed this special attribute of character calligraphy. It took years of consistent calligraphic practice to skillfully and appropriately use a Chinese brush pen, adequately mix and apply ink on absorbent papers, and express oneself through lines formed through this unique process. The importance of character writing also was reflected in civil service examinations in which participant scholar candidates were subjected to rigorous scrutiny of their calligraphic character writing (Wang 1988). Therefore, calligraphy in a sense was not merely associated with painting but was also officially endorsed as an attribute needed for a government scholar-official. In addition, calligraphic skill captured one's personality and expressed one's character (Schirokauer 1989). That might be the reason the government official selection system included calligraphy as an important qualification.

But perhaps more importantly, it became a common practice in ancient Chinese culture to judge the merit and character of individuals by their handwriting. Wang Xizhi (303–361) in the Eastern Jin Dynasty serves as an excellent example of the Chinese cultural admiration for calligraphy. Even in modern China, his essay 兰亭集序 (A preface to the collection of poems composed in Lan Ting), written some 1,600 years ago, is well known mainly because of its beautiful Xing style calligraphy and his Taoist personality. A reverse example is the hated Prime Minister Cai Jing of the Northern Song Dynasty (960–1279), who, because of his notoriety as a traitor, was later removed posthumously from history books as one of the four noted calligraphers in the Song times (Pan 1983). Culturally, the calligraphic characters became a scholar's identity in ancient China, and consequently, a representation of Chinese cultural identity. To substantiate these anecdotal examples, we can see this emphasis on Chinese character writing in the government's use of stone carvings for important laws, the emperors' writings, calligraphic examples, poems on scenic spots, and in the ubiquitous practice of almost all Chinese families of placing poetic couplets on their door frames for Chinese New Year.

Such cultural associations with Chinese written script were both facilitative and prohibitive forces for written language practices and innovations. When the movable printing technique was first invented in China around the eleventh century (Shen 1090/1997), it was never put to serious use until late in the nineteenth century, partly because of its inability to convey the calligraphic power in writing Chinese characters, which was literally preserved in block printing (Tsien 1985). This fascination with character writing was one reason the innovative movable printing technique was overlooked. For an alphabetic language, such innovations would certainly be viewed more from a cost-effective economic perspective (Eisenstein 1980) than from an aesthetic perspective as in ancient China.

On a positive note, emphasis on character writing had its reward. In ancient Chinese education, writing, particularly brush pen writing, was a required practice

(Lee 2000). In addition to the functional importance of writing for communication among speakers of various dialects, high esteem commanded by the handwriting itself undoubtedly facilitated the educational practice of emphasizing writing from the very beginning of literacy learning. This educational practice, in turn, was beneficial to learners in their language acquisition and proficiency. Character recognition was seldom divorced from character writing in ancient Chinese education (Chi 1998).

2.3.3.2 Effects of Ideographic Feature of Characters on Daily Life

Aside from character writing as an art, the ideographic feature of Chinese characters has had a profound effect on the daily life of Chinese people and on Chinese culture as a whole. The practice of using implicit morphemic radicals or characters to indicate or hint at an unspoken character has permeated almost all walks of life in China and Chinese communities. We will use some examples from the classic Chinese novel 三国演义 (*The Strives of Three Kingdoms*) to illustrate how the ideographic nature of characters was deftly explored by scholars in their interactions (Luo 1400/1992). In one instance, General Cao Cao 曹操 inspected a newly built garden and left a character 活 (live) on its entrance gate. No scholars accompanying him could figure out what it meant except for one. That one scholar told them that the general complained the gate was too broad since the character broad 阔 is a compound character, with the character 活 inside the character 门. A similar instance was described when the general left three characters 一合酥 on a case of sweet soft cake in a single column, a usual way of writing Chinese until fairly recently (Xu 2009). No other scholars knew why he described the cake on its case except for the same scholar who took a bite out of the cake and invited others to join him, explaining that the general wanted them to have a piece of it. Since the second Chinese character 合 could actually be divided into three different characters as 人一口, the whole sentence could then be read from top to bottom as 一人一口酥, which literally meant that everyone takes a bite of the cake. Both examples utilized the radicals either in combining or segmenting indicative characters to arrive at their intended meaning.

Such examples are not limited to the scholarly community. A common practice of a similar kind is the character riddles that can be played on various occasions, particularly during the Spring Lantern Festival in the middle of the first month of every Chinese New Year. We will use two examples to show the popularity of using ideographic character features (Luo 2002). The first example is a riddle phrase 身残心不残 (literally meaning "truncated body with a non-truncated heart"). The answer is the character 息 (rest), which is formed by two radicals, 自 and 心. The radical 自 looks like the character 身 (body) except it is missing the lower half, while the radical 心 is complete. Thus, deciphering the character riddle requires insight into both the ideographical and pictorial elements of Chinese characters.

Another example uses a similar strategy of character segmentation, but it focuses more on ideographic than pictorial understanding. The riddle is the phrase

两人同去一人归 (literally meaning "two persons went and only one returned"). The answer to the riddle is the character 丙 (third). The character 两 has two person radicals inside it while 丙 has only one person radical. Therefore, moving from the character 两 to the character 丙 is to change from having two person radicals to having only one person radical. Almost all literate Chinese participate in and enjoy these riddle games during the popular Spring Lantern Festival.

Other commonly observed applications of ideographic features of Chinese characters, such as introducing a homophonic family name, occur in social interactions. An example would be a situation where people are first introduced to each other. There are two family names pronounced "zhang" (章 and 张). Mr. 章 may introduce himself by saying, "I am 章, 立早 (pronounced "li zao") 章." Mr. 章 describes his family name as 立早 zhang, separating the character 章 into its two radicals 立 and 早, rather than 弓长 (pronounced "gong chang") zhang, which would be a homophone for his surname, a common Chinese surname 张. Using radicals orally to distinguish among most common homophones, particularly in homophonic surnames, is a widely observed practice in Chinese culture, deeply rooted in the ideographic feature of characters.

In sum, we suggest that if there is something unique that helped consolidate the Chinese people as a culture and a nation, it must be Chinese written script that overcame dialect barriers (Wang 2004), crystallized elements of China's history (Yin and Wang 2008), and demonstrated unparalleled calligraphic capacity (Pan 1983) because of its logographic/ideographic visual representational nature.

2.3.4 Chinese Written Language: A Means of Institutional Maintenance

While Chinese characters provided a unique foundation for communicating and uniting people with diverse regional and dialect differences, its social and cultural function of identity creation also lent itself conveniently to rulers who wanted to maintain the status quo through formal written representations of themselves and their reign. Rulers and scholars of ancient China, over its long and continuous history, paid meticulous attention to its written records. A brief survey of Chinese history would reveal numerous histories written and recorded over the past 2,500 years (Wilkinson 2000). In the following section, we briefly delineate how history writing in ancient China bestowed prestige on the role of written language. We also discuss the pivotal function of Chinese characters in politics and culture as captured in verbal taboo practices.

2.3.4.1 Role of Written Script in History Writing

Ever since written language came into being in ancient China, it was used on important occasions, such as royal rituals and for recording royal chronicles and lineages. Consequently, ancient Chinese histories recorded rulers, court events, wars, and important lessons associated with dynastic processes and changes (Ng and Wang 2005). For example, 尚书 (*Book of History*), one of the earliest extant histories consisting of a cumulative collection of various court documents, rituals, and other state business starting with the Shang Dynasty (about 1,600 BC) and focusing on the Western Zhou Dynasty (1,100 to 771 BC), was exclusively court-centered (Jian 1983). Almost all known historians in ancient China were court appointed, with their main responsibilities being to record in archives the whereabouts, daily activities, and events of the royal families and to summarize from archival records for dynastic histories (Ng and Wang 2005).

Great ancient historians, such as Sima Qian (author of 史记, *History*), Ban Gu (author of 汉书, *History of Han*), and Sima Guan (author of 资治通鉴, *Comprehensive Mirror for Aid in Government*) were masters at using written language to capture history with unequivocal stances (China's Social Science Academy 1983). Even those great historians had to work within the constraints of serving royal purposes while still adhering to their highly sensitive consciousness of reflecting historical reality. Therefore, there were always tensions in Chinese histories between legitimizing the ruling class and faithfully capturing historical reality. True historians should have been able to represent history in unambiguous words that would impact social development. This can be seen vividly in Mencius's comment on the political effect of Confucius' 春秋, a book of history of State Lu: "When Confucius finished the writing of *The Spring and Autumn Annals*, the rebellious ministers and undisciplined subjects were in a panic" (Mencius, 372-289 BC/1990, p. 125). Confucius had used wording that explicitly expressed his moral stance towards historical events during that warring period, thus highlighting the important nature of historical writing.

To have control over this type of potentially damaging written record of themselves and their reign, rulers in ancient China usually discouraged and even banned private history writing and to a great extent had achieved a monopoly on official history. Abuse of histories occurred often in ancient China (Yu 1993). Yet, private histories kept showing up in such forms as 笔记 (notes and essays), particularly when block printing spread literacy widely and enabled the market to entertain various forms of literary output (Liu 1988). This was an important source for future generations to triangulate historical data. On the other hand, while official histories were meticulously selective when written about the current ruler, many histories commissioned by rulers were more realistic about previous dynasties. Despite this, histories in ancient China tended to be controlled and manipulated by the ruling classes.

Such a tendency was also obvious in the ways rulers treated other writings, including philosophical works and poetry. In order to consolidate his rule, Qin Shihuang (259–210 BC) ordered hundreds of Confucian scholars in the capital to be buried alive and Confucian writings burned, due to their daring opposition to his governing policy and the potentially disruptive effects of the writings on his power and rule (Jian 1983). Later emperors used scholars in the court and academies to compile strictly selected collections of past works, both with the intention of purposively preserving the past, but more importantly with a focus on impressing later generations with their own righteousness and legitimacy. The largest collection ever in China's history of various works of Chinese philosophy, history, literature, sciences, and other areas was 四库全书 in the eighteenth century. This was the most comprehensive collection of Chinese works even though the selection criteria still reflected the Qing rulers' will to weed out rebellious and taboo words (Zhang 2004). Opposite views and their representative writings were often destroyed together with the authors and promoters of such thinking. Each new succeeding dynasty would deliberately eliminate or distort some historical records of the past and would re-write the history of the past dynasty to legitimize their ruling of the country (Yang 1961). History writing or re-writing was regarded as a legitimate way of consolidating one's rule in ancient China.

2.3.4.2 Homophone Taboos

All of the situations we have discussed so far could have happened in other countries and with other languages. In fact, Socrates would be a good example in Western history of a philosopher being persecuted due to his threatening "heresy." However, there was another situation that was only possible with Chinese characters: persecution through homonyms, particularly homophone taboos. These played upon the homophonic overlapping of numerous characters that could be extremely different orthographically and morphemically. Due to the tremendous number of homophones in the Chinese language, as well as the spatial configurations of characters, this type of cultural and political taboo could only occur in the Chinese context. Ancient China witnessed numerous occasions when such taboos were exercised, many times resulting in political persecution (Shanghai Bookstore Press 2007; Zhang 2004). We will discuss this phenomenon in terms of two types of taboos: individual prohibition as part of the cultural heritage and political persecution of officials.

Cultural taboos with regard to homophones and character configurations were popular throughout China's history, due to the importance attributed to written language, the overwhelming number of morphemically different but homophonic characters, and the ability of some characters to be further divisible into smaller components. These cultural taboos shared the same Confucian origin—to maintain existing social hierarchy, social stability, and harmony. To Confucius, it was necessary to have name taboos for elders and superiors (Zhang 2004). Such a practice was intended to maintain the status quo of a society so it would remain peaceful and harmonious. An ideal society would keep its social order through the efforts and understanding of each member sticking to his/her own position and fulfilling his/her own duties (Qian 2005). Any deviations beyond one's corresponding duties and positions, whether filial or societal, would disrupt the status quo. Therefore, "rectification of names" was an essential principle for Confucius to restore the ideal social order (Confucius, 479 BC/1980). Consequently, as a crucial procedural means, name taboos would establish a mentality of respect for elders and superiors, in addition to sustaining order within the immediate family, community, or society.

Chinese characters nurtured a fertile ground for the existence of such taboos. These taboos included, for example, avoidance of using the names of one's elders or superiors, avoidance of homophonic characters used in one's elders' or superiors' names, and avoidance of using any characters or words that pointed to or hinted at negative attributes of one's elders or superiors (Wang 1997). Some well-known examples have already become part of Chinese language usage. In the Tang Dynasty, Emperor Li Shimin (李世民), with given names shi (世) and min (民), created verbal taboos that changed forever the use of these two characters in very specific ways. Shi (世) was replaced from the then high-frequency phrase referring to "generations" (about 30 some years) by the character dai (代), and the character hu (户) was substituted for the character min (民) in the title of the Ministry of Revenue (户部). This title remained in use in ensuing dynasties. Such examples are plentiful in China's history and show how rulers capitalized on the abundance of homophones for the sake of maintaining political stability through name taboos (see Wang 1997; Zhang 2004).

The above social etiquette taboos were realized through the homophonic nature of Chinese characters. The following examples demonstrate the extensive impact such sensitivity to homophones has had on Chinese culture and the everyday life of Chinese people. While not as abrupt and disruptive as the taboos about one's elders and superiors, these taboos could have a profound influence on social and cultural communications. For example, in the southern part of China where many people depended on rivers for their livelihood in ancient time, they were always afraid of being late or afraid their ships would be too slow. Since the Chinese word "chopsticks" 箸 was pronounced "zhu," the same pronunciation as "stop" 驻, ship crews changed the character 箸 to 筷, the same pronunciation as 快 "quick," hinting at the good speed they hoped for their ships. Subsequently, the old taboo pronunciation for chopsticks used by ship crews receded into oblivion and the substitute term has been embraced by the general population of China ever since (Zhang 2004). Another similar case of a popular daily taboo relates to the word clocks (钟, pronounced "zhong"). Giving a gift of clocks to friends or relatives is taboo, due to the similar pronunciation of clocks and the character 终, meaning "the end of one's life." There are numerous instances of these popular taboos made possible by multiple homophonic characters in Chinese. This sensitivity to homophones is necessary cultural knowledge.

In addition, political utilization of the homophonic taboos was a convenient means of getting rid of one's political opponents. As the absolute power symbol of the country, an emperor or a dynasty could justify political purges in the name of Confucian tradition. So numerous were the instances of political persecution that later generations created a term for these political cruelties: 文字狱 (verbal persecution). We will cite two examples to make our point here. The first case occurred at the beginning of the Ming Dynasty (1368–1644) when the first Ming emperor exercised extreme control and employed unimaginable measures to consolidate his rule, frequently subjecting official scholars to a cruel death on very shaky accusations (Fairbanks and Goldman 1998). According to the Ming practice, all local government units would send verbal tributes to the emperor on ceremonial occasions. Official scholars would try their best to use the most respectful words in their tributes. One official scholar from Beiping (nowadays Beijing) used the following phrase to praise the emperor: "垂子孙而作则" (set examples for the sons and grandsons). The character 则 (pronounced /ze/, example) was similar in sound to the character 贼 (pronounced /zei/, thief) and was interpreted by the emperor as a negative comment about him. Consequently, the scholar was executed (Zhang 2004).

A similar execution happened to a Hangzhou official scholar who wrote "光天之下, 天生圣人, 为世作则" (a saint is born into this bright world who sets examples for all). The character 光 (bright) also carried the meaning "bald." The characters 圣 (pronounced /sheng/, saint) and 则 were, respectively, interpreted as 僧 (pronounced /seng/, monk) and 贼 (thief). In the context of the whole phrase, the emperor interpreted it as insinuating that in his past he was a head-shaved monk and that he was being accused of being a thief (Zhang 2004). In the case of this emperor, since his native dialect pronunciation of these characters was almost identical, the homophonic taboo offered him a good opportunity to show off his despotic authority at the time when he was stabilizing his government (Jian 1983).

The second case was equally brutal, absurd, and predicated upon the ideographic configuration of Chinese characters. It is representative of the harsh punishments that ran rampant in the Qing Dynasty (1616–1911) and often ended in cutting short the lives of those who were punished (Shanghai Bookstore Press 2007). During the short reign of Yong Zheng (雍正), verbal persecutions were notoriously severe (Wang 2007). A representative case happened when a scholar official who was dispatched to Jiangxi to oversee the triannual civil service examinations adopted a phrase from the classic *Book of Poetry* "维民所止" (the land is for people to dwell and live on) as the essay title for the civil service examination candidates' policy essay. However, two of the characters (维, 止) from this phrase happened to be part of the royal title of the emperor Yong Zheng (雍正). The two characters were, respectively, two and one top-positioned strokes short of the emperor's title. Evil-minded opponents seized the opportunity to create a forced and false interpretation of the intent of such an essay title, saying the title contained the top-removed (or beheaded) characters used in the emperor's title. Consequently, the scholar official was executed and his extended families exiled on the charge that he was implying the symbolic act of beheading the emperor in the essay title. Such a far-fetched interpretation culminated in the cruel execution of the scholar official and explicitly illustrates how Chinese characters are capable of insinuated interpretations due to their configuration of strokes.

Verbal persecution originated from the Confucian tradition of verbal taboos and was conveniently wrought through the unique characteristics of Chinese characters, including both their homophonic similarities and configurative proximities. Abundant examples were reported in various books. Wang's (1997) collection of about a thousand verbal taboo instances in past history represents a recent effort to document the widespread effects of the practice, particularly its political usage. Verbal persecutions lent a convenient hand to the government's institutional maintenance, ridding itself of political opponents, sending a warning message to other potential opponents, and justifying its own ruling status. The extent and scale of such convenient political persecutions would not be possible without the homophonic and stroke-based characteristics of Chinese written script. While we are not claiming that such political persecutions could not happen in the context of alphabetic languages, we are making the argument that convenient political persecutions through verbal means at the character level was certainly a unique Chinese practice.

2.4 Conclusions

Before we proceed to the conclusions and implications, we need to point out that Chinese script, itself, could not exert such a great influence on the cultural, social, and institutional structures of a country. We believe that the cultural and social purposes served by written language in ancient China were the direct result of social and cultural trends that worked their way into the fabric of the society and were abetted by the unique features of the written language. Without the social and cultural foundations, it would not be possible to make social and cultural use of the features of the written language. However, the written language not only satisfied the cultural and social needs of ancient China, but it actually was able to consolidate and carry on social, cultural, and political traditions, as well as practices.

As we have discussed in the above sections, Chinese written language was used to exert a significant influence on the Chinese people—creating a sense of cultural and national identity and maintaining social order and stability. It was not surprising that whoever came into power in ancient China was eventually enculturated into Chinese culture through the written language (Qian 2005). It was equally amazing to see the same written language being used by people speaking extremely different dialects, making it possible for these people to share the same sense of identity and belonging. The characteristics of Chinese written language allowed the cultural and national identity to overlook regional dialect differences such that functional communication, as well as cultural heritage, was shared and passed on among these people. Furthermore, the rulers were highly conscious of the power of the written language and saw to it that its power was maximized to consolidate their rules. Vestiges of such practices are still visible in cultural and social practices and provide evidence of the role of Chinese written language in ancient times.

2.5 Implications

We believe there are several different ways to examine the implications of the nature of Chinese script for modern Chinese policy makers, Western readers, and educational professionals. First, it behooves policy makers to take into consideration the uniqueness of Chinese written language in understanding the nature of Chinese culture and society. For example, understanding the multi-dialect situation of modern China through the perspective of the unique role of written language in ancient China provides a better view of modern efforts at literacy promotion, Romanization of Chinese characters, popularization of a universal language, and the role of dialects in communication and popular media.

Second, Western readers can benefit from knowledge of the verbal taboo practice in ancient China when examining some modern day practices of character use in Chinese culture. Even though the practice is no longer officially sponsored and exercised, it should be understood that verbal taboos of various types permeate Chinese culture and societies even today. Accommodating or appreciating these cultural specificities can allow outsiders to interact better with the culture and the people.

Third, education professionals can benefit from understanding the social and cultural roles Chinese written language played in sustaining the culture and society in ancient China. This would serve as more than a necessary piece of background knowledge in educational practice. The capacity of the written language to accommodate cultural and institutional needs through its unique features can be a powerful tool for literacy education. The verbal taboos we discussed above shed some light on the social nature of language acquisition that could be capitalized on in literacy education. The study of homophones, for example, could be an instrumental approach to heighten students' appreciation of Chinese written language, creating verbal contexts in which students could practice their knowledge of the language in authentic situations.

Fourth, understanding the roles written language used to play in ancient China can offer some insight into identity issues Chinese students in a foreign country might experience. For example, when the written language is still serving as a link to one's cultural and national identities, losing touch with the language can be a devastating blow to one's sense of identity. It is beneficial for educators to be keenly aware of the possibility of lost identity and to try to provide language and linguistic supports that can function to transition immigrant students into the roles they will assume in the new culture.

Fifth, the power of written language in ancient China can provide some food for thought for literacy educators both in modern China and in foreign countries. Literacy is not merely a functional tool for communication but also an aesthetic means to experience the beauty and necessity of writing, consequently establishing an atmosphere of respect for the written language, as well as a desire to put forth effort to engage in character writing. Such respect and emphasized practice of basic written script can certainly be a force in enhancing literacy acquisition. This can go hand in hand with the current practice of engaging beginning readers in beginning writing processes in order to facilitate their literacy acquisition.

Last but not least, we offer some advice to readers who tend to take for granted the abstract nature of alphabetic languages in accentuating the role of phonetics. The Chinese written language, though phonologically-prone in the final analysis (Chen 1999), is complex in that meanings are accessed both through sounds and visual configurations. That phenomenon should at least alert us to the possible hypothesis that different aspects of a written language interact with the oral and dialect capacity of users and learners in realizing its functional purpose of communication. Therefore, it is not the nature of a written language that decides its communication and acquisition efficiency, but the utilization of the characteristics of a written language that makes it efficient in communication and acquisition. In the case of Chinese written language, understanding the role of character configuration, including both phonetic and semantic structural components, will be beneficial for learners and users.

In short, the present chapter has offered some historical cases for a better understanding of the nature of Chinese written language in the context of Chinese culture and society. We also believe we have provided some comparative perspectives for Western readers, particularly for those who interact with Chinese culture and for educators who are involved with Chinese immigrant students in their classrooms.

References

Chi, X. (1998). 中国古代小学教育研究 [*A study on China's ancient elementary education*]. Shanghai: Shanghai Education Press.
Chen, P. (1999). *Modern Chinese: History and sociolinguistics*. New York: Cambridge University Press.
China Social Sciences Academy. (1983). 中国文学史 [*A history of Chinese literature*]. Beijing: People's Press.
Chu, Y. (1973). The Chinese language. In J. Meskill (Ed.), *An introduction to Chinese civilization* (pp. 587–615). New York: Columbia University Press.
Confucius. (479 BC/1980). 论语 [*The Analects with explanatory notes by Yang Bojun*]. Beijing: Chinese Publishing Bureau.
Duanmu, S. (2000). *The phonology of standard Chinese*. New York: Oxford University Press.
Eisenstein, E. (1980). *The printing press as an agent of change: Communications and cultural transformations in early modern Europe* (Vol. 2). Cambridge: Cambridge University Press.
Fischer, S. R. (2003). *A history of writing*. London: Reaktion Books.
Fairbank, J. K., & Goldman, M. (1998). *China: A new history*. Cambridge, MA: Harvard University Press.
Gee, J. (2007). *Social linguistics and literacies: Ideology in discourses* (3rd ed.). London: Taylor & Francis.
Goody, J. (1987). *The interface between the written and the oral*. Cambridge: Cambridge University Press.
Havelock, E. (1976). *Origins of Western literacy* (Monograph Series, No. 14). Toronto: Ontario Institute for Studies in Education.
Hu, Q. (2005). 中国小学史 [*A history of Chinese elementary education*]. Shanghai: Shanghai People's Press.
Jian, B. (1983). 中国史纲要 [*China: A brief history*]. Beijing: People's Press.
Lee, T. H. C. (2000). *Education in traditional China: A history*. Leiden: Brill.
Liu, Y. (1988). 中国文化史 [*A history of Chinese culture*]. Shanghai: China's Encyclopedia Press.
Liu, Y. (2004). 中国字典史略 [*A brief history of Chinese dictionaries*]. Beijing: Chinese Publishing Bureau.
Lu, S. (2009). 文字学四种 [*Four essays on Chinese written language*]. Shanghai: Shanghai Classics Press.
Luo, G. (1400/1992). 三国演义 [*The strives of three kingdoms*]. Nanking: Jiangsu Classics Press.
Luo, P. (2002). 千古佳迷 [*A collection of time-honored riddles*]. Hefei: Anhui Arts Press.
Mencius. (372-289 BC/1990). 孟子今译 [Mencius' quotations with modern interpretation and commentary by Liu Fangyuan]. In T. Xia, M. Tang, & F. Liu (Eds.), *Modern interpretations of the classic four books*. Nangchang, Jiangxi: Jiangxi People's Press.
Ng, O., & Wang, E. (2005). *Mirroring the past: The writing and use of history in Imperial China*. Honolulu: University of Hawai'i Press.
Ong, W. (2002). *Orality and literacy*. New York: Routledge.

Pan, B. (1983). 中国书法简论 [*A brief discussion on Chinese calligraphy*]. Shanghai: Shanghai People's Arts Press.

Qian, M. (2005). 国史新论 [*Recent interpretations of Chinese history*]. Beijing: San Lian Press.

Resnick, D. P., & Resnick, L. B. (1977). The nature of literacy: An historical exploration. *Harvard Educational Review, 47*, 370–385.

Schirokauer, C. (1989). *A brief history of Chinese and Japanese civilizations*. Stamford: Thomson Learning.

Shanghai Bookstore Press. (2007). 清代文字狱档 [*Archives for verbal persecutions in the Qing Dynasty*]. Shanghai: Shanghai Bookstore Press.

Shen, K. (1090/1997). 梦溪笔谈 [*Pen talks in the dream brook*]. Yangzhou: Jiansu Guangli Classics Press.

Sun, P. (Ed.). (1991). 中国教育史 [*An educational history of China*]. Shanghai: East China Normal University Press.

Tsien, S. (1985). Paper and printing. In series J. Needham (Ed.), *Science and civilisation in China* (Vol. 5, Pt. 1). Cambridge: Cambridge University Press.

Wang, D. (1988). 科举史话 [*Introduction to a history of the civil service examination system*]. Beijing: Chinese Publishing Bureau.

Wang, Y. (1997). 历代避讳字汇典 [*A dictionary of taboo characters in Chinese history*]. Zhengzhou: Zhongzhou Classics Press.

Wang, X. (2004). 中国古代传播史 [*A history of ancient China's communications*]. Taiyuan: Shanxi People's Press.

Wang, Y. (2007). 中国文字狱 [*Chinese verbal persecution*]. Guangzhou: Huacheng Press.

Wilkinson, E. (2000). *Chinese history: A manual*. Cambridge, MA: Harvard University Press.

Xu, J. (2009). 简明中国文字学 [*A short history of Chinese characters*]. Beijing: Chinese Publishing Bureau.

Yang, L. (1961). The organization of Chinese official historiography: Principles and methods of standard histories from the T'ang through the Ming dynasty. In W. G. Beasley & E. G. Pulleyblank (Eds.), *Historians of China and Japan*. London: Oxford University Press.

Yin, J., & Wang, R. (2008). 现代汉语文字学 [*Contemporary Chinese characters*]. Shanghai: Fudan University Press.

Yu, Z. (1993). 中国伪书大观 [*A comprehensive survey of forged books in Chinese history*]. Nanchang: Jiangxi Education Press.

Zhang, F. (2004). 古闻今说 [*Modern musings on ancient stories*]. Beijing: Capital Normal University Press.

Zhou, Z. (2004). 周祖谟文字音韵训诂讲义 [*Zhou Zumo's lectures on Chinese characters, phonology, and semantics*]. Tianjin: Tianjin Classics Press.

Zhu, B. (2005). 图示汉字书体演变史 [*A history of Chinese character style changes illustrated through photo samples*]. Jinan: Qi-Lu Press.

Chapter 3
Foreign Literature Education in China's Secondary Schools from 1919 to 1949

Hongtao Liu and Jiening Ruan

3.1 Introduction

In higher education in China, foreign language teaching is a distinct discipline from Chinese language and literature teaching. Each discipline has its own department and its own curriculum and teaching materials. At the college level foreign literature is taught in departments of foreign languages. In secondary education, however, foreign literature translated into Chinese is an important source of teaching material for the teaching of Chinese Yuwen (language and literacy) (Liu 2001). Because of the various factors involved in studying foreign literature—such as the spirit of the times, the translator, and the nature and status of the translated work—translated foreign literature plays an irreplaceable role in contemporary secondary school Chinese teaching.

Since the spread of secondary education has been more extensive than higher education in China, teaching foreign literature at the secondary level opens the readership of foreign literature to a larger audience, for one must be educated in order to appreciate and understand foreign literature. Under the systematic and compulsory education system of China, translated foreign literature has the potential to greatly impact Chinese learners.

Foreign literature played a significant role in the New Culture Movement that started in 1915 and the subsequent May Fourth Movement in 1919. The New Culture Movement, also called the Chinese Renaissance Movement, was led by a group of influential Chinese intellectuals who returned to China after receiving education in Western countries, carrying with them ideals such as democracy,

---

H. Liu (✉)
Comparative Literature, Beijing Normal University, Beijing, China
e-mail: htliu@bnu.edu.cn

J. Ruan
Reading/Literacy Education, The University of Oklahoma, Norman, OK, USA

freedom, science, and modernization of the country. They rejected traditional Chinese feudal culture and its ideologies. They also considered Archaic Chinese or Classical Chinese (文言文) the carrier of the old culture and, therefore, thought it should be abandoned. They advocated for the creation of a new culture that would embody modern, progressive ideals. To achieve this goal, they considered it essential to start a New Literature Movement to produce new literature that championed new ideas, using a new language medium called Vernacular Chinese (白话文) (Liu 2001). Cultural and literary giants, such as Xun Lu (鲁迅), Shi Hu (胡适), Zuoren Zhou (周作人), and Dun Mao (茅盾), are some of the most well-known representatives of the movement. They have left indelible marks on Chinese literary history and remain influential in contemporary Chinese culture and literature.

During the nearly 30 years from 1920 to 1949, foreign literature education was a significant part of literature teaching and learning in secondary and higher education in China. After the founding of the People's Republic of China in 1949, secondary school Chinese teaching followed a different pattern. This chapter aims to present a focused discussion of the history and impact of translated foreign literature on secondary school Chinese curriculum between 1915 and 1949, which is also referred to as the Modern Period in China.

3.2 Nature of Translated Foreign Literature in Chinese Textbooks

Vernacular texts that upheld the spirit of the New Culture Movement were to a large extent used in Chinese literary education, and translations of foreign literature in the vernacular were a critical part of literary education at the time. Translated foreign literature made its first appearance in Chinese textbooks in 1920 with the publication of China's first vernacular textbook for secondary school students, *Model Works of Vernacular*. The four volumes of this work were compiled by Beiping Hong and Zhongying He and published by Commercial Press. Among the foreign literary works translated into Chinese for this textbook series were the novel *The Last Class* by the French writer Alphonse Daudet, translated by Shi Hu; the poem "Song of the Shirt" by English poet Thomas Hood, translated by Bannong Liu; and the two short stories, "Navigation" by the French writer Ivan Sergeevich Turgenev and "Three Questions" by the Russian writer Leo Tolstoy, both translated by Jizhi Geng. In the 30 years thereafter, foreign literature became an important part of high school Chinese textbooks (Liu 2001).

In secondary school Chinese, literary education was composed of two parts: (a) instruction on the history of literature and (b) cultivation of literary appreciation, ability, and creativity. In *Regulations of the Implementation of Secondary School Principles* promulgated by the Education Ministry of the Republic in 1912, the third item dealt with the aim of Chinese teaching that included the cultivation of interest in literature. Although little mention was made specifically of the status of foreign literature, the report included titles of foreign literature as examples of texts that met the selection standards. For example, "The Speech of Brutus" (extracted from William Shakespeare's play *Julius Caesar*) was listed, among others, as an example of "practical writings." In *Secondary School Curriculum Standards* of 1932, emphasis was placed on the instruction of representative works of all times, the literary schools they belonged to, and their evolution.

For texts that would be read more intensively, "instructions should be made on their status in history, their literary values, and the authors' historical background and their personal styles." In *Secondary School Chinese Course Standards* promulgated in 1936 by the government, a position was made known regarding text selections to be included in textbooks. It proposed that textbook developers select representative works of the main writers of different times, conforming to the sequential development of literature from ancient times to modern times, so students could attain a systematic concept of the origins and evolution of literature.

Literary education is an important feature that distinguishes modern Chinese teaching from traditional Chinese teaching. Traditional Chinese teaching did not include literary education while modern Chinese teaching did. The academic world seemed far more enthusiastic and active than the government about this issue. For example, Benwen Sun (1919) in *Chinese Teaching in Secondary Schools*, proposed: "The teaching of literature should focus on developing students' capabilities in understanding realistic and idealistic common essays and literary works and in presenting one's ideas. It should also help cultivate student understanding and ethics" (p. 3). Lianggong Sun (1923) considered literary teaching a crucial issue in the decisive battle between new literature and old literature. In *The Position of Literature and Art in Secondary Education and the Dalton System*, Sun (1922) made a strong and powerful defense for literary education in secondary school Chinese teaching, pointing out that the lack of emphasis on real or aesthetic literature and excessive emphasis on practical writings in the traditional teaching of Chinese was problematic. He strongly advocated literary education, arguing that it would help students realize educational goals, foster their aesthetic understanding, and improve their language ability.

In secondary school Chinese education, translated foreign literature was considered an integral part of Chinese new literature. For example, in *Zhu's Middle School Chinese* (World Book Company 1933) the eras of the works selected and the number of works from each era were as follows: Zhou and Qin (周秦, 7 pieces); Han and Wei (汉魏, 11 pieces); Jin, Six Dynasties, Tang, and Song (晋六朝唐宋, 32 pieces); Yuan, Min, and Qing (元明清, 90 pieces); and modern (including both Chinese works and translations in Chinese, 196 pieces). Among the Chinese works were 24 translated foreign literary works spread across six volumes, with an average of four translated works in each volume.

Mu Qian (1920) described the evolution of literary styles in his *Discussion on Secondary School Chinese Teaching*. Looking at Chinese literature from a historical perspective, he divided the development of literary styles into four periods: argumentation, embellishment, high style, and Europeanization (著述文、藻饰文、格调文、欧化文). According to Qian, the Europeanized style referred to new literature and translations of foreign literature. *Suzhou Secondary School Curriculum Outline*, a Chinese curriculum published in 1930, includes a section that describes the history of Chinese literature. The last part, "modern times," addresses two items: (a) the rise of the recent new literature and its future and (b) the modern literary translation. The above documents show that translated foreign literature was considered transnational literature and a part of Chinese literature during that period.

There were also some scholars who tried to find support for the close relationship between foreign literature and modern Chinese literature from the perspective of the development of modern vernacular Chinese. In "Introduction to Western Literature," an article collected in the eighteenth volume of *Kaiming Secondary School Lecture Notes*, the author pointed out that foreign literature has had a significant influence on the formation of vernacular Chinese (Liu 2001).

While Classical Chinese is essentially the pure native language, modern Vernacular Chinese has a substantial absorption of foreign vocabulary, syntax, and imagery and can be considered a greatly Westernized language. Therefore, there is no clear boundary or substantial difference between learning Vernacular Chinese taught in schools and learning foreign literature translated into the Vernacular. Since modern times, scholars have never theoretically defined the nature of foreign literature in secondary school Chinese teaching and learning, either because they have accepted the identity of the nature of the two or because they have ignored the differences between them.

3.3 Uses of Translated Foreign Literature in Chinese Instruction

To identify uses of translated foreign literature in secondary Chinese instruction during the period of 1920–1949, we reviewed textbooks of that time period and found four main uses of translated literature in literary instruction. The first use was as an example of a style of literature. Secondary school Chinese teaching adopted teaching units, with the division of units usually based on different styles of texts, such as lyrics, narratives, scenery descriptions, expositions, argumentations, business writings, etc. Foreign literature texts were distributed among different units according to their styles.

The second use was to bring awareness to important issues. Many textbooks built units around different types of issues, which reflected the concern of the New Culture Movement for life issues while at the same time meeting the authorities' requirements for ideological and moral education. For example, in the first volume of *Zhu's Middle School Chinese* (World Book Company 1933), a novel by Italian writer Edmondo De Amicis was classified as narrations on "parental admonishments," and "First Snow" by American poet James Russell Lowell (1819–1891) was grouped into descriptions of "snow sceneries". In the second volume, the poem "The Flower School" by Rabindranath Tagore appeared in the section on "narrations of the life and stories of the flowers." The limitation of this type of text arrangement is obvious since the identification of so-called "issues" is too subjective, without established, accepted standards. In fact, the vast majority of textbooks adopted a combination of the two methods when dividing literary works into units, that is, issue-oriented with texts of the same style in one unit. Also, for women's issues Shi Hu's *The Life of Li Chao* and Henrik Ibsen's *Nala* were put together in the same unit.

The third use of foreign literature in secondary school Chinese was as a tool for students to develop knowledge of the world, as well as knowledge of Chinese language and literacy. Ziqing Zhu (1925) proposed that high school Chinese education should focus on world literary trends and academic thinking in ancient China, deeming these two areas subjects for a higher phase in the cultivation of students' Chinese capabilities. Zhu was not alone in this view. In *Junior High School Chinese Textbook Series* compiled by Lianggong Sun (1923), the first and second volumes focused on narratives, grouped according to the clarity and ease of comprehension and the length of texts. The third and fourth volumes were mainly argumentations, grouped according to the different issues discussed in the texts, while the fifth and sixth volumes were composed completely of translations of foreign fiction masterpieces, arranged according to different nationalities and eras of the authors. Although Lianggong Sun did not give an overall explanation for his arrangement of texts in his textbook series, it is obvious that the difficulty of the articles and the introduction of new thoughts and ideas were behind his decision to put foreign literary works in the fifth and sixth volumes.

The fourth use of translated foreign literature was as material for the teaching of writing. In *High School Chinese Course Standards*, published in both 1932 and 1936, there appeared a type of writing practice that involved translating short articles from a foreign language into Classical Chinese or Vernacular Chinese.

Modern scholars had different views on the use of foreign literature in secondary school Chinese and discussed its significance and limitations. Zhong Yin, in his *Criticism upon and Suggestions to the Present Secondary School Chinese* (1920), expressed his opposition to the inclusion of ancient Chinese literature in secondary school Chinese textbooks, calling on teachers of Chinese to stop being conservative and courageously save themselves from the famine of knowledge by absorbing new knowledge from outside, including knowledge of foreign literature.

In the "Preface by the Compiler" of *Selected Model Chinese Works* compiled by Houwen Ma (1935), at the very beginning of the article, Ma affirmed the significance and positive impact of learning foreign literature:

> The excellent translated foreign literary works, though coming from foreign lands, are also enlightening about China's conditions; or, just as the saying goes, by other's faults, wise men correct their own; by making the textbook inclusive, the outlook of the students will be broadened, their interest in literature deepened. (p. 5)

But he also realized the possible situation of foreign literary works failing to be in line with Chinese perspectives due to cultural differences and cautioned against including foreign literary works that showed extreme views or lapsed into too much romance. He stressed that much thought was needed in the process of text selection and that it was not advisable to include foreign works blindly.

Zhongying He (1920) opposed most of the Chinese classical novels selected for secondary school Chinese textbooks. As for foreign literature, he advocated treating different kinds of foreign literary works differently. For example, according to He, Western dramas should not be selected as texts, on the grounds that the content of translated Western dramas was not closely aligned with the Chinese people's lives and ideologies. Therefore, they were improper for use as textbook texts. But translated novels like Alexandre Dumas's *The Count of Monte Cristo* could be selected as texts because the translation was simple, clear, and accurate. He thought the translator had gone through great pains to polish his language, instead of mechanically translating the foreign language into Vernacular Chinese.

3.4 Popular Authors and Translators of Foreign Literature

To determine the distribution of foreign literary works in secondary school Chinese textbooks of China's modern period (1920–1949), we analyzed the content of 24 popular junior high school Chinese textbooks (see Appendix A) and 7 high school Chinese textbooks (see Appendix B) used for the teaching of Chinese in secondary schools during that time period. There appears to be no authoritative models for inclusion of literary works in secondary school Chinese textbooks since we found great differences in the selection of literature in different textbooks. The compilers of each textbook appeared to select literature for inclusion according to their own personal views and interests. Some of the textbooks included very few foreign literary works, sometimes one or two translated works. The textbook with the most works of foreign literature was *Junior High School Chinese Textbook Series* (six volumes) published by Shanghai Minzhi Bookstore Publishing in 1922. The fifth and sixth volumes of this textbook series were exclusively dedicated to works of foreign literature. Some textbooks had a moderate proportion of translated foreign literature, four in each volume.

In view of the findings listed above, there seems to be little significance in gathering statistics on the proportion of works of foreign literature in these textbooks nor in analyzing the genres of foreign literature in secondary textbooks because the predominant form of foreign literary works in the textbooks was short stories. Occasionally included were pieces of prose, drama, expository texts, and/or speeches. Therefore, we found it more meaningful to focus on the authors and translators of literary works in secondary Chinese textbooks. Table 3.1 presents the top 15 authors whose works were selected for inclusion in the junior high Chinese textbooks, followed by the titles and frequency of their works occurring in the textbooks. Numbers in parentheses show the number of appearances of the same work across the textbooks we analyzed. Also included in the table is information on the translators of the selected works.

Among the top 15 authors, most were European and Russian. Examination of the translators also reveals interesting information. Table 3.2 shows the translators who were most popular with textbook compilers.

We gathered statistics from the seven most widely used textbook series. Altogether, 31 different foreign literary works occurred in these textbooks. A sample of

3 Foreign Literature Education in China's Secondary Schools from 1919 to 1949

Table 3.1 Top 15 authors, literary works, frequency of selection, and translators (Junior high textbooks)

Author	Literary work	Frequency and number of appearances	Translator(s)
1. Edmondo De Amicis (Italian, 1846–1908)	"The Little Patriot of Padua" (9), "The Little Florentine Writer" (6), "A Noble Action" (3), "The School" (3), "The Little Vidette of Lombardy" (3), "My Brother's School-Mistress" (2), "Admonishment about Primary School" (2), "The Infant Asylum" (2), "The Street" (1), "A Well-Awarded Medal" (1), "The Sardinian Drummer-Boy" (1), "The First Day of School" (1), "The Sick Master" (1), and "Papa's Nurse" (1)	14 works 32 appearances	Mianzun Xia
2. Alphonse Daudet (French, 1840–1897)	"The Last Class" (11), "The Siege of Berlin" (9), "The Boy Traitor" (4), "Seguins' Goat" (2), and "The Ferry" (1)	5 works 27 appearances	Shi Hu Zhongsu Huang
3. Guy de Maupassant (French, 1850–1893)	"Two Friends" (7), "A Parricide" (3), "Minuet" (1), "The Blind Man" (1), "In the Wood" (1), "The Prisoners" (1), and "The Necklace" (1)	8 works 16 appearances	Shi Hu
4. Eroshenko Vasil (Russian, 1889–1952)	"Spring and Its Power" (2), "The Small Cage" (2), "A Fragment of My School Life" (2), "The Universal Language and Its Literature" (2), "The Sadness of the Fish" (2), "Beside the Pool" (2), "Father Time" (1), "Excessive Grace" (1), "Tragedy of a Chicken" (1), and "Mission of the Intellectuals" (1)	10 works 15 appearances	Shi Hu Xun Lu
5. Leo Tolstoy (Russian, 1828–1910)	"A Spark Neglected Burns the House" (2), "Innocence" (2), "Three Questions" (2), "A Prisoner in the Caucasus" (1), "A Grain as Big as a Hen's Egg" (1), and "The Prayer" (1)	6 works 9 appearances	Yancun Deng Fuyuan Sun
6. Anton Chekhov (Russian, 1860–1904)	"A Work of Art" (2), "A Letter to Golky" (1), "A Gentleman Friend" (1), "In a Strange Land" (1), and "The Lottery Ticket"(1)	5 works 6 appearances	Shi Hu Tongzhao Wang
7. Ivan Sergeevich Turgenev (Russian, 1818–1883)	"Navigation"(2), "The Sparrow"(1), The Living Mummy (1), and The Old Lady (1)	4 works 7 appearances	Jizhi Geng
8. Tsurumi Yosuke (Japan, 1885–1973)	"Diligent Studying in Vain" (3), "Methods of Reading" (2), "On the Disposition of Business" (1)	3 works 6 appearances	Xun Lu

(continued)

Table 3.1 (continued)

Author	Literary work	Frequency and number of appearances	Translator(s)
9. Olive Schreiner (South Africa, 1859–1920)	"The Dawn of Civilization" (2), "Three Dreams in a Desert" (2) and "The Artist's Secret" (2).	3 works 6 appearances	Zuoren Zhou Yuzhi Hu
10. Maxim Gorky (Russian, 1868–1936)	"The Waves Striving for Freedom" (3), "The Life of a Useless Man" (1), and "Enemies" (1)	3 works 5 appearances	Yanbing Sheng Qiufang Dong
11. Henryk Sienkiewicz (Polish, 1846–1919)	"The Lighthouse Keeper" (1), "Yanko the Musician"(1), "Wish You Good Luck"(1), and "Across the Prairies" (1)	4 works 4 appearances	Zuoren Zhou
12. William Shakespeare (England, 1564–1616)	"The Merchant of Venice" (2), and "The Speech of Brutus" (3)	2 works 5 appearances	Shu Lin
13. Emile Zola (France, 1840–1902)	"A Cat's Heaven" (2) and "Unemployment" (2)	2 works 4 appearances	Fu Liu
14. Hans Christian Andersen (Denmark 1805–1875)	"The Little Match Girl" (6)	1 work 6 appearances	Zuoren Zhou
15. A. Agdronjan (Armenia, dates unknown)	"A Drop of Milk" (5)	1 work 5 appearances	Zuoren Zhou

authors with more than two occurrences of works across the textbooks, whether with one title or several titles, is listed below with the genre and names of their works.

- Argumentation: "Observation on Changes" (3) and "Evolution and Ethics Preface VII" (2) by British philosopher Aldous Huxley, translated by Fu Yan
- Travel notes: "Jottings on West Lake" (2), "Suzhou" (1), and "The Stage" (1) by Japanese writer Ryūnosuke Akutagawa, translated by Mianzun Xia
- Short story: "The Necklace" (2) by Guy de Maupassant, translated by Hui Chang, and "Moonlight" (1), translated by Zuoren Zhou
- Drama: Tales adapted from Shakespeare's dramas *Timon of Athens* (2) and *The Merchant of Venice* (1) by Charles and Mary Lamb, translated by Shu Lin
- Travel diary: "Westminster Abbey" (3) by Washington Irving, translated by Shu Lin
- Short story: "The Happy Prince" (3) by Oscar Wilde, translated by Zuoren Zhou

Because compilers of junior high school textbooks and high school textbooks are usually different people, it was common to see a text appearing both in junior high and high school textbooks, such as the short story "A Drop of Milk" by Agdronjan, translated by Zuoren Zhou.

A close examination of the translators shows that most translators of the selected foreign literature were major names in the New Literature Movement who also

Table 3.2 Translators of foreign literature (Junior high textbooks)

Translator	Frequency	Origin of translated works
Zuoren Zhou	32 translations 52 appearances	Russia, Japan, Eastern and Western Europe, the Nordic nations, Africa
Shi Hu	11 translations 41 appearances	France (most works by de Maupassant)
Mianzun Xia	14 translations 36 appearances	Italy (most works by Amicis)
Xun Lu	15 translations 22 appearances	Russia, Japan (most works by Eroshenko and Tsurumi Yosuke)

strongly fueled the spread of the New Culture Movement. Not only were they highly accomplished writers, but they were also men who enlightened the Chinese population with progressive ideas and inspired millions of Chinese people in the fight for a better and more just Chinese society.

3.5 Educational Ideas and Teaching Methods

Foreign literature in secondary school Chinese shouldered the two missions of ideological and moral teaching and literary education. Ideological and moral teaching encompassed three areas: patriotism education, enlightenment education, and education of outlook on life.

Patriotism is a common theme of foreign literary works selected for textbooks. All the most frequently selected foreign works, such as "The Siege of Berlin," "The Last Class," "The Little Patriot of Padua," "The Boy Traitor," "The Little Vidette of Lombardy," and "Two Friends," show the spirit of patriotism in ordinary people of various nationalities.

Guy de Maupassant's "Two Friends" tells the story of how ordinary men do not forget their share of responsibility in protecting their country. At the most difficult moment of the siege of Paris by Prussian aggressors, two fishermen went fishing out of town, feeling unbearable distress, but were caught by Prussian soldiers. They thought they had never felt cordial feelings towards their own country. However, when the Prussians tried to force them to tell the password into their town, threatening them with death, both fishermen chose death.

The protagonist in Edmondo De Amicis' "The Little Patriot of Padua" is an 11-year-old Italian boy, who, under unbearable abuse in his circus life, fled to the Italian consulate for protection. On the ship back to his motherland, the boy, who was ragged and looked sick but was travelling by tourist class, caught everyone's attention. After getting to know his story, the ladies and gentlemen all opened their wallets for him. The boy was happy for the unexpected money. However, when three drunken men indulged in insults against his motherland, Italy, the boy did not hesitate to thrust the money in their faces because he did not want money from those who spoke ill of his country.

Enlightening works with themes such as revolting against tyranny, striving for national freedom from foreign oppressors, exploring ways for developing a nation, and probing rosy perspectives on human life occupy a large proportion of the selected foreign literary works. Works by Russians, Eastern Europeans, and South Africans mostly have such themes, including Maxim Gorky's "The Waves Striving for Freedom," "The Life of a Useless Man," and "Enemies," and Olive Schreiner's "The Dawn of Civilization" and "Three Dreams in a Desert." In particular, "The Waves Striving for Freedom" is a truly magnificent prose poem, an ode to the ocean. The rocks on the coast symbolize the power of constraint and oppression while the mountainous and overwhelming waves through perseverance finally beat them.

In foreign literary works appearing in textbooks, another theme often found is life issues, especially those related to the school life of teenagers. In De Amicis's "A Noble Action," a child from a poor family, when having a conflict with his classmate, poured ink on the teacher. When the teacher asked about the disturbance, another student initially assumed the blame. At last the conflict between the teacher and the students was resolved through forgiveness. "The School" was about encouraging people to go to school, and "My Brother's School-Mistress" sang praises of a kind-hearted female teacher. In "A Well Awarded Medal," a student was awarded a medal by the inspector. Although his grades and conduct were well worthy of this prize, the inspector particularly mentioned that the main reason for awarding him the medal was his optimistic temperament, courage, and constant filial piety. The student's father, who was a blacksmith, was also invited to the school. With everyone's congratulations, he felt regret about his maltreatment of the child and felt a new sense of love and pride for his son. We can see that De Amicis thinks highly of the spirit of caring, love, and compassion. "Diligent Study in Vain" by Japanese writer Tsurumi Yosuke gives a list of various examples to demonstrate the harmful effects of being a bookworm, and "Methods of Reading" introduces one by one some good reading methods in a friendly chatting manner.

Although there are a number of foreign literary works in secondary school Chinese textbooks, their ideological content basically falls into the three categories discussed above.

As a part of literary education, the teaching of translated foreign literature had a very different approach from later nationally accepted teaching methods for literature. Some modern scholars have explored this matter and have provided valuable information. In *A Study on the Courses of Secondary School Chinese* (the eighth book of the National Zhong Shan University Education Institute Series), Zhen Ruan (1934) listed "modern world literature" among the general elective courses of the third grade of high school, the class hours being 2 h per week for 1 year, and the total credits being four. He proposed four specific goals of teaching world literature: to help students get a general idea about masterpieces of modern world literature and develop a general appreciation of the works; to help students attain a general understanding of the thought and art of modern world literature and its influence on modern Chinese literary creation, while preparing them to study and criticize modern literature; to expand students' literary horizons, helping them to compare ancient and modern

Chinese literature; and to instruct students on different schools of modern world literature, so they can form specific concepts in their minds about different literary schools and confirm the knowledge they acquired from a general introduction of literature.

Ruan (1934) did not ask teachers to make detailed analyses of literary works in class, but suggested they only needed to assign students the amount and methods of reading without designating specific books to read. Students could do the reading after class according to their own interests in order to cultivate their interest in literature. The main basis for evaluation would be reading notes or reports written by the students. He specified reports should focus on the main idea, overall structure of the work, exemplary paragraphs, language of the translator, and student's thoughts provoked by reading the book.

In *The Position of Literature and Art in Secondary Education and the Dalton System*, Lianggong Sun (1922) gave an overall view of teaching methods for translated foreign literature. In common with Zhen Ruan (1934), he also stressed students' extra-curricular reading, but at the same time he designed more specific types of homework to ensure reading quality. One such homework assignment was the *book-oriented homework method*, which involved writing reading notes or keeping a reading diary after reading each book. The contents of the writing would include a summary, analysis of characters (the characters' ages, personality traits, personal beliefs, and their relationships with each other), theme analysis, and reflections on the book. Another assignment was the *writer-oriented homework method*. For this assignment, students wrote a comment or several comments about the same writer, or they wrote a general comment on works by different writers who had similar characteristics. The content of the writing included the author's life, his doctrines, artistic opinions and schools, the influence of the times and environment on the author, some examples and comparisons of different writers or different works by the same writer, and some other types of reflections or comments. The third method was the *nation-oriented homework method*. Students were to write about the nations the writers belonged to and, through comments on writers of different nations, discuss artistic ideas of different nations. The last approach was the *issue-oriented method*, which involved asking ideological or artistic questions about different works and commenting on every issue present in the work or making a general comment on all of the issues.

Foreign literature in modern Chinese textbooks was a part of literary education, but at the same time it had its distinct qualities because of the additions and cuts by translators in the process of translation and other arbitrary changes made to the text content. When selecting translations of foreign literary works for Chinese textbooks, the focus was most frequently on translations by master translators and the smoothness and beauty of the language, instead of the fidelity of the translations. Huaishen Hu (1936) in *Problems in Secondary Chinese Teaching* held that translation problems should be discussed carefully in foreign literary teaching. He gave several examples of awkward situations faced by teachers of translated foreign literary works when Chinese expressions did not convey the exact meaning as in its original language. One example was the last sentence in Daudet's "The Last Class," which Shi Hu translated as: "(The teacher) wrote vigorously on the blackboard three words: '法兰西万岁' (Chinese for "long live France")." In French, of course, it is three words, but in Chinese it is five characters.

3.6 Conclusion

Championed by a group of highly influential Chinese scholars, translated literature became an inseparable part of the New Culture Movement in China and contributed to the spread of the movement in the Modern Period in China (1919–1949) and beyond. In addition to serving as material for literary education and Chinese language education in secondary schools, translated literature provided an opportunity for Chinese secondary students to reflect on the conditions of the country, as well as social and life issues they faced at the time. It also expanded the world view of the students and facilitated the dissemination of Western ideals, such as democracy, freedom, and science.

Secondary literary education has undergone a huge transformation since the early part of the twentieth century and is at the present time in a critical stage of development. Learning from history is undoubtedly significant in our search for a better education for our students. This study suggests translated literature once was a powerful conduit of ideas and greatly contributed to the social and cultural changes in modern China. Translated literature deserves more attention and recognition from Chinese secondary educators and should continue to remain a critical part of secondary education in China.

Appendix A: The 24 Junior High School Chinese Textbooks Reviewed

1. *Junior High School Chinese Textbook Series*, compiled by Lianggong Sun and Jiu Zhong, Shanghai Minzhi Bookstore Publishing, 1922 edition.
2. *Modern Junior High School Textbook—Chinese*, six volumes, compiled by Shi Zhuang, the Commercial Press, 1924 edition.
3. *Chinese Textbook under the New Teaching System*, six volumes, the Commercial Press, 1924 February edition.
4. *Junior High School Chinese Readings*, 11 volumes, compiled by Beijing Kongde School, 1926 edition.
5. *Junior High School Chinese Textbook*, three volumes, compiled by Yixing Shen, Zhonghua Book Company, 1927 edition.
6. *New Age Chinese Textbook*, six volumes, compiled by Huaishen Hu, the Commercial Press, 1928 edition.
7. *Junior High School Chinese Textbook*, six volumes, compiled by Yifu Zhou, the Commercial Press, 1932 edition.

8. *Junior High School Chinese Selected Reading*, six volumes, compiled by Genze Luo and Yuangong Gao, Lida Book Company, 1933 edition.
9. *Junior High School Standard Chinese*, six volumes, revised by Jiangsu Provincial Education Department, Shanghai Middle School Students Book Company, 1934 edition.
10. *Zhu's Junior High School Chinese*, compiled by Jianmang Zhu, World Book Company, 1934 edition.
11. *Junior High School Contemporary Chinese*, compiled by Jiangxi Provincial Education Department, Shanghai Middle School Students Book Company, 1934 edition.
12. *Creative Chinese Textbook*, six volumes, compiled by Weinan Xu, World Book Company, 1932 edition.
13. *Experimental Junior High School Chinese Textbook*, six volumes, compiled by Rongling Shen, etc., Zhonghua Book Company, 1934 edition.
14. *Junior High School Chinese Textbook*, six volumes, compiled by Nuchao Sun, Zhonghua Book Company, 1934 edition.
15. *Chinese*, six volumes, compiled by Chucang Ye, Zhengzhong Book Company, 1935 edition.
16. *Junior High School Chinese Textbook*, six volumes, compiled by Songyou Yan, Shanghai Dahua Book Company, 1935 edition.
17. *Chinese Textbook*, six volumes, compiled by Zhen Wang and Shuda Wang, Chinese Books Press of the High School Affiliated to Beijing Normal University, 1937 edition.
18. *Junior High School Chinese*, six volumes, compiled by Chucang Ye, Zhengzhong Book Company, 1934 edition.
19. *New Junior High School Chinese*, six volumes, compiled by Jianmang Zhu, World Book Company, 1937 edition.
20. *Junior High School Chinese Textbook*, six volumes, compiled by Wenhan Song, Wenshu Zhu, Zhonghua Book Company, 1936 edition.
21. *New Junior High School Chinese*, six volumes, compiled by Wenhan Song, Shanghai Zhonghua Book Company, 1937 edition.
22. *Junior High School Chinese*, six volumes, Department of Education Editing Group, 1942.
23. *Chinese*, compiled by Fuyun Fang, etc., State-Designated Seven-Joint Suppliers of Primary and Secondary School Textbooks, 1947 edition.
24. *Chinese*, six volumes, State Editing House, Zhonghua Book Company, 1948 edition.

Appendix B: The Seven High School Chinese Textbooks Reviewed

1. *High School Chinese*, three books, six volumes, compiled by Jianmang Zhu, World Book Company, 1930 edition.

2. *High School Chinese*, six volumes, compiled and edited by Meigong Xu, etc., Jiangsu Province Liyangcheng Secondary School Chinese Branch Conference, 1932 edition.
3. *Du & Han High School Chinese*, six volumes, compiled by Tianmi Du, Chuyuan Han, World Book Company, 1935 edition.
4. *Contemporary High School Chinese*, six volumes, compiled by Jiangsu Province Education Department, notations provided by Wujing Xue, etc., Shanghai Middle School Students Book Company, 1935 edition.
5. *High School Chinese*, six volumes, compiled by Chucang Ye, Zhengzhong Book Company, 1937 edition.
6. *High School Chinese*, six volumes, compiled by Education Department Editing Group, Xinmin Press Co. Ltd, 1940 edition.
7. *New High School Chinese*, six volumes, compiled by Wenhan Song and Zhiwen Zhang, Zhonghua Book Company, 1947 edition.

References

He, Z. (1920). 白话文教授问题 [On the teaching of Vernacular Chinese]. 教育杂志, *12*(2), 9.
Hu, H. (1936). 中学国文教学问题 [*On secondary school Chinese teaching*]. Shanghai: The Commercial Press.
Liu, H. (2001). 中学语文中的外国文学问题 [On foreign literature teaching in secondary school Chinese]. 北京师范大学学报, *1*, 135–141.
Ma, H. (1935). 标准国文选 [*Selected model Chinese works*]. Shanghai: Guangda Publishing House.
Qian, M. (1920). 中等学校国文教授之讨论 [Discussion on secondary school Chinese teaching]. 教育杂志, *12*(6), 1–2.
Ruan, Z. (1934). 中学国文教学目的之研究 [On the goals of secondary school Chinese teaching]. 中华教育界, *22*(5), 21–30.
Sun, B. (1919). 中学校之国文教授 [Chinese teaching in secondary schools]. 教育杂志, *11*(7), 3.
Sun, L. (1922). 文艺在中等教育中的位置与道尔顿制 [The position of literature and art in secondary education and the Dalton system]. 教育杂志, *14*(12), 1–14.
Sun, L. (Ed.). (1923). 初级中学国语文读本 [*Junior high school Chinese textbook*]. Shanghai: Shanghai Minzhi Bookstore Publishing.
World Book Company. (1933). 朱氏初中国文 [*Zhu's middle school Chinese*]. Shanghai: World Book Company.
Zhong, Y. (1920). 对于现在中学国文教授的批评及建议 [Criticism upon and suggestions to the present secondary school Chinese instruction]. 教育杂志, *12*(6), 20.
Zhu, Z. (1925). 中等学校国文教学的几个问题 [Some questions about secondary school Chinese teaching]. 教育杂志, *17*(7), 7.

Chapter 4
Influences of the Cultural Revolution on Chinese Literacy Instruction

Cynthia B. Leung and YiPing Wang

4.1 Introduction

At the first session of the Chinese People's Political Consultative Conference (CPPCC) in Beijing in 1949 that proclaimed the founding of the People's Republic of China (PRC), combating illiteracy was recognized as one of the goals of the Chinese Communist Party (CCP) and was included in the Common Program of the CPPCC (Houn 1973). Thus, from the beginning of the New China, literacy was an important concern of the CCP in order to achieve their twin objectives of transforming the state into a socialist and an industrial society. It is difficult to spread a new social philosophy or ideology without the written word, but it is even more difficult to create an industrial society without a certain degree of literacy in the population. With a literacy rate of only about 20% in 1949, the CPC had a major task set out for itself (Houn 1973).

Wang (2003) identified three phases of educational reform from 1949 to 1976. The first phase involved copying Russian educational models. During the second phase from 1958 to 1965, Mao Zedong (also known as Mao Tse-tung), the Chairman of the Communist Party of China Central Committee (CPCCC), abandoned the Soviet model and encouraged the establishment of an educational system that would be characteristically Chinese. The third phase occurred at the time of the Great Proletarian Cultural Revolution from 1966 to 1976 when "a whole generation experienced a disrupted education" (Meng and Gregory 2002).

This chapter focuses on Chinese literacy education during this third phase. We explore changes to literacy instruction and the functions of literacy during the years

---

C.B. Leung (✉)
Literacy Education, University of South Florida St. Petersburg, St. Petersburg, FL, USA
e-mail: cleung@mail.usf.edu

Y. Wang
UEWM Library, University of East & West Medicine, Sunnyvale, CA, USA

of the Cultural Revolution and describe reading materials used for Chinese literacy instruction at that time, including political propaganda materials and textbooks. We highlight several forms of literacy that became important both in the spread of Maoist ideology and literacy across China during the Cultural Revolution: "Two Newspapers and One Magazine" and Big Character Posters (*Dazibao*). It is important to note that many of the literacy and general educational practices common during the Cultural Revolution did not originate during that 10 year period. Therefore, whenever possible, we also try to place these practices in a historical context for our readers.

4.2 Beginnings of the Cultural Revolution

In May 1966 the Politburo issued a document, the "May 16th Circular," in response to an academic debate about a historical play that led to "sarcastic writings" Mao thought were criticizing him in the media (Hsü 1990, p. 698). The circular announced a "great Cultural Revolution...led personally by Comrade Mao Tse-tung."

> Our country is now in an upsurge of the great proletarian Cultural Revolution which is pounding at all the decadent ideological and cultural positions still held by the bourgeoisie and the remnants of feudalism. Instead of encouraging the entire party boldly to arouse the broad masses of workers, peasants, and soldiers, and the fighters for proletarian culture so that they can continue to charge ahead, the outline [published about the play]...obscures the sharp class struggle that is taking place on the cultural and ideological front. (Mao 1966b)

The May 16th Circular also reported that the Central Committee would dissolve the Group of Five, created in January 1965 when Mao first approached the Politburo about a cultural revolution, and would establish a new group to replace it (Hsü 1990). Thus, under Mao's leadership, the Central Cultural Revolution Group (CCRG) was set up before the end of May. This group included Mao's secretary Chen Boda, Mao's wife Jiang Qing, Premier Zhou Enlai, and five others. This "Left Alliance" led the early stages of the Cultural Revolution (Lin 2009).

The Cultural Revolution was officially launched in August 1966 with the convening of the 11th Plenum of the 8th Chinese Communist Party Central Committee in Beijing (Lin 2009). On August 8, the CCPCC adopted its *Decision of the Chinese Communist Party Central Committee Concerning the Great Cultural Revolution* (also known as the Sixteen Points) that laid out the aims of the "current great proletarian cultural revolution...a great revolution that touches people to their very souls, representing a more intensive and extensive new stage of the development of socialist revolution in our country" (CCPCC 1996b, p. 263). This revolution would center on class struggle and educating the masses. "Reforming the old educational system and the old policy and method of teaching is an extremely vital task of the great proletarian cultural revolution" (p. 272). Education, literature, and the arts would be reformed "to facilitate the consolidation and development of the socialist system" (p. 264).

The CCPCC reaffirmed Mao's thesis that the first stage of a cultural revolution involves work in the "ideological sphere." The "Four Olds"—old ideas, old culture, old customs, and old habits—were still being used by the "exploiting classes to corrupt the mind of man and conquer his heart." Consequently, "the proletariat must squarely face all challenges of the bourgeoisie in the ideological sphere, and use its own new ideas, new culture, new customs and new habits to transform the spiritual aspect of the whole of society" (CCPCCb 1996a, p. 264). Schools were "dominated by bourgeois intellectuals," so "it [was] necessary to completely change the situation" (p. 272). Education must serve "proletarian politics" and academic education must be "integrated with productive labor" (p. 273).

The *Decision* of the 11th Plenum directly affected Chinese language and literacy education since it specified that "teaching material must be thoroughly reformed" (p. 273). The CCPCC called for complex reading material to be replaced by simplified readings related to proletarian politics, and students and teachers should participate in the "cultural revolutionary struggle for criticizing the bourgeoisie" (p. 273). Ancient Chinese texts, including the Confucian classics that had been used for centuries as instructional material, became targets for destruction because they belonged to the Four Olds. Teachers of Chinese classics were targeted for re-education.

In the summer of 1966 at the beginning of the Cultural Revolution, Mao encouraged the young generation to be Red Guards for his revolution. Red Guards quickly formed among high school and college students. They wrote Big Character Posters to expose and criticize crimes and excesses of those thought to be bourgeois anti-revolutionaries, including teachers who taught them old ways of thinking. Many schools and universities closed so students could dedicate themselves to revolutionary struggle. Some Red Guards went to people's homes and ransacked private property, burning or destroying Western objects and anything related to traditional Chinese culture, including ancient Chinese texts and works by Confucius (Hsü 1990). People sometimes were injured during raids on homes or struggle sessions, or committed suicide as a result of public humiliation. Different groups of Red Guards formed and sometimes had conflicts with each other (Lin 2009). Two years into the Cultural Revolution in July 1968, with violence escalating in major cities, Mao met with leaders of the five major revolutionary groups in Beijing to officially end the Red Guard Movement and to inform them order would be restored (Cleverley 1991; Hsü 1990; Langley 2008).

4.3 Political Content of Chinese Language and Literacy Instruction

From the beginning of the PRC, proletarian ideology was integrated into materials to teach Chinese. During the Great Leap Forward beginning in 1958 when the nation experimented in communal living, textbooks included more political content than previously because the party used political exhortation to motivate workers to increase agricultural and industrial output (Cleverley 1991). However, during the Cultural Revolution "political content entered schooling as never before" and was included in lessons in all subjects (Cleverley, p. 186). The *Decision* of the 11th Plenum (CCPCC 1966b) specified, "In carrying out the cultural revolutionary mass movement, it is essential to combine the dissemination of the proletarian world outlook, Marxism-Leninism and the thought of Mao Tse-tung with the criticism of the bourgeois and feudal ideologies" (p. 273). These political ideologies became the content of materials to teach Chinese. The 11th Plenum also emphasized in its *Communique of the Eleventh Plenary Session* (CCPCC 1966a) that "the intensive study of Comrade Mao Tse-tung's works by the whole Party and the whole nation is an important event of historic significance" (p. 285).

4.3.1 Two Newspapers and One Magazine

On June 1, 1966, *People's Daily* published an editorial "Destroy All Evils" to gain the support of the nation in carrying out a proletarian Cultural Revolution (China Media Project 2007/2012). The media played a vital role in informing the public of the latest Communist Party policies. During the Cultural Revolution Mao Zedong Thought was adopted for education of the masses, and re-education of the bourgeois, through three influential media publications referred to as Two Newspapers and One Magazine: the editorials and lead articles in *People's Daily*, *People's Liberation Army Daily* (*PLA Daily*), and *Red Flag* magazine (*Hong Qi Magazine*). *People's Daily* was, and still is, the official newspaper of the Central Committee of the Chinese Communist Party, and *PLA Daily* was the official newspaper of the Central Military Commission. *Hongqi Magazine* (*Red Flag*) published theoretical pieces on Communist party ideology and began publication during the Great Leap Forward in 1958 (CMP, para. 7–9).

Chen Boda, Mao's secretary, set up these media as a "propaganda machine" to deliver Mao's ideological messages to the Chinese people. The three publications published the same editorials, which were "regarded as the loftiest guides for Communist Party behavior and the unification of public opinion" (CMP 2007/2012, para. 1). Two Newspapers and One Magazine was the mouth piece of the Communist Party through which Mao's latest speeches and ideas and the latest political trends were published in editorials, feature articles, and columns. Quotes from Mao's *Little Red Book* and political slogans also were published in Two Newspapers and One Magazine (CMP, para. 4). Almost everyone was expected to learn and understand the most current political situation through various reading groups in cities, rural areas, and schools across the nation. Mao's instructions were studied in school as language and political education.

The editorial "Destroy All Evils" had an immediate effect on Chinese literacy instruction in schools. From the beginning of June, formal teaching was disrupted at some schools. Students studied *People's Daily* editorials and daily columns of Mao's quotations, such as "Chairman Mao is the red sun in our hearts!" Articles from

Two Newspapers and One Magazine became one type of reading material used to teach Chinese Yuwen (language and literacy) during the Cultural Revolution.

4.3.2 Big Character Posters

The writing of Big Character Posters was another literacy practice promoted during the Cultural Revolution that also was used in Chinese Yuwen education at that time. The posters were large wall-mounted displays with large hand-written characters. Chinese calligraphy was written with brushes on large sheets of paper that were later mounted in public places and on classroom walls. Big Character Posters originated in Imperial times but were more common in China after the 1911 revolution when the literacy rate increased (Library of Congress 2012). During the Great Leap Forward when Mao initiated a reform of the education system, Big Character Posters attacking the old style of education appeared on the walls of college and university buildings. Mao praised these posters and saw them as an effective propaganda tool (Cleverley 1991).

In the early days of the Cultural Revolution, Nie Yuanzi and some of her colleagues at Beijing University introduced Big Character Posters as a way to expose and criticize the crimes and excesses of those thought to be bourgeois anti-revolutionaries (Cleverley 1991). On May 25, 1966, they posted Big Character Posters in the dining room of Beijing University to expose crimes of the administration. Students at Shanghai University posted similar Big Character Posters on their campus (Cleverley 1991). Those who were attacked could respond with other Big Character Posters. Mao approved the content of Nie's poster, calling it "China's first Marxist-Leninist big character poster," and it was published with a commentator's article in *People's Daily* on June 1 (Cleverley 1991; Mao 1966a, para. 1).

Also in late May 1966, Red Guards appeared in Beijing, first at the middle school affiliated with Qinghua University (Lin 2009). Students from the middle school wrote two Big Character Posters on May 25 and June 2 and signed them Red Guards (Chesneaux 1979). Over the summer there was much revolutionary fervor throughout the country and many schools and universities closed (Cleverley 1991). Mao was known for his calligraphy and on August 5 created his own Big Character Poster, "Bombard the Headquarters" (Lin 2009; Mao 1966a). The CCP Central Committee considered Big Character Posters an effective way to support the revolution. The *Decision* of the 11th Plenum of the CCPCC adopted on August 8 noted the use of Big Character Posters by "young revolutionaries" and supported the use of these posters for "exposing and criticizing in a big way, firmly launching an attack against those open and covert bourgeoisie representatives" (CCPCC 1966b, p. 264). Big Character Posters were referred to several times in the document to emphasize that

> Full use must be made of such means as big-character posters and large-scale debates so that views and opinions may be aired and the masses helped to elucidate the correct viewpoints, criticize the erroneous opinions, and uncover all demons and monsters. Only in this way will it be possible to make the broad masses heighten their consciousness in the midst of struggle, increase their capacity for work, and distinguish between the right and wrong and the enemies and ourselves. (p. 267)

Big Character Posters became part of the Chinese Yuwen curriculum in schools in the summer of 1966 after the CCPCC circulated the Sixteen Points of the 11th Plenum (He 2002), along with newspaper editorials and Chairman Mao's instructions. "China was full of posters, like a huge bulletin board: school walls, shop windows, buses, staircases, public restrooms and any other blank spaces were filled with revolutionary slogans and announcements of chastisement meetings" (He, p. 309). Students in elementary and secondary schools read from Big Character Posters mounted on school walls and produced their own posters. Creating Big Character Posters gave students opportunities to practice Chinese calligraphy.

4.3.3 Mao's Little Red Book

Some regions in the PRC used *Quotations from Chairman Mao Tse-Tung*, also known as *The Little Red Book*, and articles from Two Newspapers and One Magazine as the primary Chinese Yuwen reading material or as transitional material until new textbooks could be published. *The Little Red Book* was compiled in an office of the *People's Liberation Army Daily* for use first with the army (Han 2012). It went through several versions beginning in January 1964, including a version in 1966 for the new revolution.

The Little Red Book was widely circulated throughout the country in the early days of the Cultural Revolution. *Peking Review* published an article on August 12, 1966 on the mass publication of Mao's works:

> The Central Committee of the Chinese Communist Party has decided to speed up the large-scale publication of Chairman Mao Tse-tung's works in order to meet the urgent needs of the broad masses of the people in studying Mao Tse-tung's thought. It has called on the broad masses of cadres and workers and staff members of publication, printing and distribution departments throughout the country to mobilize immediately, make all-out efforts and take the publication and distribution of Chairman Mao's works as their foremost task. Following the speed-up in the mass printing of Chairman Mao's works this year and next, these works, for which there has been a pressing demand by the broad masses, will gradually come to be in plentiful supply throughout the country. (para. 2)

The CCPCC planned for 35 million sets of the *Selected Works of Mao Zedong* to be printed and distributed in 1966 and 1967 (Peking Review 1966, para. 3). The Ministry of Culture held a national conference in Beijing to "urge printing, publishing and distribution organizations throughout the country to take immediate revolutionary measures" to increase the publication of Mao's works for the masses (para. 5). Under the leadership of Communist Party leaders at various levels, publishers were asked to "mobilize all printing houses, where conditions permit, to undertake the glorious political task of printing Chairman Mao's works" (para. 6). While the original intent was to increase publication of the *Selected Works*, the party's goal shifted to publishing *Quotations of Chairman Mao*, and 720 million copies were published by the end of 1966 (Han 2012).

School children were each given a pocket-sized copy of *The Little Red Book* and told to cherish it. They chanted passages from it over and over again in unison and recited quotations. The repetition acted as a form of indoctrination. However, through memorization and repeated reading, the students learned to read Chinese characters. This was also one practice used to teach peasants and factory workers to read. Recitation and repeated reading were techniques used from ancient times to teach the reading of Chinese logographic characters (see Chap. 1 of this book).

4.3.4 Chinese Literacy Textbooks

Established in December 1950 under the leadership of the Chinese Ministry of Education, the People's Education Press (PEP) was responsible for curriculum research and compiling and publishing teaching materials for the PRC (PEP 2007). The role of the PEP was to interpret and implement state policy through developing syllabi and textbooks for different subjects, including Chinese Yuwen (Language and Literacy). The PEP acted as a bridge between state policy and implementation of curriculum in the schools (Adamson 2004). From 1966 to 1972, however, the PEP was forced to close, along with other educational organizations (PEP 2007), and staff were sent to work on farms or in shops in rural towns (Adamson 2004). Curriculum development work of the early 1960s was completely disrupted.

In 1967 the CCPCC called for old textbooks to be destroyed and new ones to be developed by local teams of textbook writing groups (Adamson 2004; Shen and Sun 2010). Some editorial teams said they consulted with students, revolutionary groups, workers, peasants, and soldiers, but it may not have been a "genuine consultation process" (Adamson 2004, p. 112). Large cities had their own People's Press that published textbooks. Chinese Yuwen textbooks varied in different provinces, cities, and counties since textbook editorial teams made their own selections of material for inclusion in their textbooks. However, reading material and exercises in all textbooks had to conform to the central government's ideology.

Agencies of education management issued guidelines for literacy education, including selection criteria for textbook content (Shen and Sun 2010; Nie 2009a, b). The guidelines for literacy education in Shanghai stated textbook content had to "actively promote Mao Zedong Thought, relentlessly criticize the capitalist class, and strenuously fight for the elimination of the people-exploit-people system on earth" (Nie 2009a, p. 21). Selection criteria should be "politics first, artistic merit second" (p. 21). The majority of published textbooks across the PRC contained articles by political leaders and material about the Cultural Revolution. Writings by Marx, Engles, and Lenin, originally published in German and Russian, were translated into Chinese. The only texts translated from French were *The Internationale* by Eugène Edine Pottier, which was the anthem of the International Workman's Association, and poetry of the Paris Commune (Hong 2012).

Nie (2009a, b) and Shen and Sun (2010) analyzed the content of some Chinese Yuwen textbooks published between 1968 and 1972. In the preliminary Chinese

Yuwen textbook published in 1968 for 7th graders at Shanghai Middle School, 9 of the 22 lessons were Mao's poems, essays, speeches, and quotations (Shen and Sun 2010). About half of the 1972 textbook edition for Shanghai Middle School was writings by Mao and other Communist leaders. This edition also included scenes from Model Plays that focused on modern revolutionary themes, family histories, and a few classical essays and poems (Nie 2009a, p. 21).

The 11th grade Chinese literacy textbook used in Guangzhou contained critiques on ideology and culture written by Marx, Engles, Lenin, and Mao; theoretical pieces on strengthening proletarian control of the country; articles on class struggle and criticism; short stories on uniting the Chinese people against their enemies; and revolutionary stories (Nie 2009b, p. 23). Volume 1 of the 1969 edition of the preliminary middle school textbook published by Zhejiang People's Press had similar content, plus study guides and drills based on Mao's writings. Essays from *People's Daily*, *Zhejiang Daily*, and *Wenhui Daily* also appeared in this edition (Shen and Sun 2010). Volume 2 of the 1971 preliminary Chinese Yuwen textbook for middle schools in Anhui Province adopted essays from *People's Daily* & *PLA Daily* (Shen & Sun).

Revolutionary plays had been initiated as an educational source during the Socialist Education Movement that Mao had instituted in 1962. Under the auspices of Jiang Qing, Mao's wife who became a member of the Central Cultural Revolution Group, "new forms of revolutionary art" appeared in 1964, including the ballet *The Red Detachment of Women* and the play *The Raid on the White Tiger Regiment* (Hsü 1990, p. 696). The Central Cultural Revolution Group engineered the writing and performance of Model Plays promoting class struggle. Segments of these plays were included in some local textbooks.

4.3.5 Revolutionary Diaries

In addition to practicing writing through creating Big Character Posters, students developed writing skills by keeping personal self-reflection diaries. This instructional activity became a common practice in some schools when the school day became more regular with the use of the new Chinese Yuwen textbooks. As students reflected on their thoughts and actions, they remembered Mao's instructions and tied their reflections to quotations from his works. Selections from a 3rd grader's Anti-Selfishness Diary show how in the process of connecting her thoughts to the teachings of Mao, the student learned to critically reflect in writing on her actions.

> May 13, 1970 – Today our class held a "Combating Selfishness" meeting. The teacher said that the Young Pioneers should take the lead in articulating their thoughts. I was initially reluctant to say anything, but upon remembering Chairman Mao's admonition to "combat selfishness and condemn revisionism," I immediately made a statement.
>
> May 21, 1970 – Earlier today while I was playing at a classmate's house, I happily answered the call of another classmate to go and sweep the floor. However, when my pants were dirtied in the process of cleaning, I wanted to quit. At that moment, the sound of

Chairman Mao's words enabled me to overcome my selfishness, and I continued my cleaning task. Afterwards we went home, singing a revolutionary song along the way. I had a stomach ache after returning home, but I believe that my ideology became redder despite the physical discomfort. (Shen and Sun 2010, p. 10)

4.4 Connecting Mental and Manual Labor in the Countryside and Cities

The *Decision* of the CCPCC at the 11th Plenum in 1966 at the beginning of the Cultural Revolution articulated the position of the Chinese Communist Party that schooling should serve the needs of proletarian politics and should integrate book learning with productive labor.

In schools of all types, it is imperative to carry out the policy, advanced by Comrade Mao Tse-tung, of making education serve proletarian politics and having education integrated with productive labor, so that those who get an education may develop morally, intellectually and physically and become socialist-minded, cultured laborers. (CCPCC 1996b, p. 273)

After the initial stage of the Cultural Revolution when schooling was disrupted, productive labor on farms and in factories became a critical part of education. By sharing hardships with peasants, factory workers, and other manual workers, students would learn to relate theory to practice, and class barriers could be broken (Cleverley 1991). During the Great Leap Forward, work study programs had been initiated in primary, junior middle, and senior middle (high) schools, and "productive work was taken more seriously in schools than at any time since 1949" (p. 144). The CCP extended this earlier experience with work study programs to the whole of China in the late 1960s.

In December 1968, the CCP announced the Down to the Countryside Movement and ordered some of the Red Guards and other older urban students "sent up the mountains and down to the countryside" to learn from peasants (Lin 2009). During the height of the Red Guard Movement, students and recent graduates had traveled throughout China interacting with local populations, but the new movement would relocate youth to rural areas to learn about manual labor.

In 1962, Mao had instituted another movement, the Socialist Education Movement, to stress class struggle. The movement included sending party officials and intellectuals to the countryside to learn from peasants (Hsü 1990) and drafting teachers and senior students for investigative teams to go to rural areas and check for corruption and feudal practices (Cleverley 1991). Those referred to as educated peasants were secondary school and university graduates who were sent to the countryside to learn from peasants and work the land during the Social Education Movement, but they had remained in rural areas after the movement ended (Hsia 1972). During the Cultural Revolution's Down to the Countryside Movement, educated peasants were recruited as teachers if they had completed a minimum of 2 years in production work and had politically acceptable class affiliations (Hsia 1972).

There was little opportunity for youth sent to the mountains and countryside during the Cultural Revolution to learn academic subjects. They learned to cultivate food crops, raise livestock, and participate in other types of manual labor carried out by local peasants. Mao also sent intellectuals to the countryside to be re-educated by poor and lower-middle peasants who not only taught them how to work but how to study articles and political writings for "ideological rectification," such as the Three Great Treatises: "In memory of Norman Bethune," "Serve the People," and "How the Foolish Old Man Removed the Mountain" (Chen 1970, p. 198). Dr. Norman Bethune was a Canadian physician who is said to have saved the lives of thousands of soldiers in the People's Liberation Army during the Japanese invasion (Cleverley 1991).

At primary and lower and upper middle schools in urban areas, students attended schools half day to study and the other half day to work in order to learn from the real world of production. It was rather common that in the morning they studied Chairman Mao's instructions, read newspaper editorials, kept revolutionary diaries, and participated regularly at self-criticism meetings. Shortened lesson times caused students to have limited education and limited time to learn and understand.

After the re-opening of schools in Beijing in 1968, *China Pictorial* reported on the progress made in the revolution in education "to transform the old educational system and the old principles and methods of teaching" (China Pictorial, para. 1). Peking No. 23 Middle School was used as an example of a school embracing class struggle as its main educational goal.

> The revolutionary teachers and students of No. 23 Middle School concluded that…students must be infinitely loyal to Chairman Mao and to Mao Tse-tung's thought. They must set up a proletarian world outlook, share the feelings of the workers and peasants and establish a firm proletarian stand. To achieve this aim the school took as its main course the class struggle. They made arrangements with factories and people's communes to allow students to come to learn industrial work and farming. Teaching methods and subject matter were transformed accordingly. Some courses were dropped, some combined, and others concerning knowledge of industrial and agricultural production were added….Chairman Mao's works are the basic teaching material for courses in politics and Chinese. (China Pictorial 1968, p. 22)

In many cities, teachers revolutionized their teaching methods by inviting former poor peasants, soldiers, and workers to deliver lectures and provide guidance on revolution. These guests told stories about the horrible treatment they had received from landlords and capitalists in the old society, and they told students they should appreciate and love the New China (He 2002). Factory training schools were set up for workers with junior middle school education and 5 years of work experience. Textbooks were especially prepared for these schools and included Mao Zedong Thought. Students participated in manual labor and military training (Cleverley 1991).

During the Cultural Revolution barriers holding back children from worker and poor and lower-middle peasant families from attending school were broken and more children were able to attend school (Fraser and Hawkins 1972). New educational policies favored decentralization and local control of schools. Primary schools in rural areas were often managed by production brigades and middle schools by communes, giving peasants more voice in the selection of teachers and curriculum material and in adapting the curriculum to meet local needs (Meisner 1977).

Age limits for school attendance, tuition fees, and entrance exams were abolished making it easier for children of the Red Class to receive formal education. Alternative formats of schooling introduced during the Great Leap Forward, such as part-time schools, half-study and half-work or half-farming schools, and winter schools for adult peasants, "were revised and [became] an established feature of rural life" (Meisner, p. 349).

4.5 Summary

Educational standards across China varied enormously before the Cultural Revolution, and gaps existed between educational opportunities for urban and rural youth (Cleverley 1991). Educational policies instituted during the Cultural Revolution strived to improve educational opportunities for the children of workers and peasants. The mass movement of educated youth to the countryside raised the literacy levels of rural areas when these youth were integrated into the local populace. The writing of Big Character Posters for political campaigns provided opportunities for peasants and urban workers to learn character writing and practice calligraphy (Ebrey 2012).

While widespread literacy was not yet achieved by the end of the Cultural Revolution, changes to educational practices were far-reaching. Larger numbers of students in rural areas were able to receive basic education. However, students who had attended traditional schools in urban settings found their education disrupted and levels of instruction less advanced, especially in the areas of science and technology. Curriculum materials for Chinese Yuwen instruction were politically charged, and literacy acquisition involved learning political propaganda. The Cultural Revolution was a unique period of Chinese History with unique literacy practices. Numerous lessons can be learned from this chaotic period in China so that it will not be repeated again.

References

Adamson, B. (2004). *China's English: A history of English in Chinese education*. Hong Kong: Hong Kong University Press.
Chen, T. H. (1970). Education in communist China. In F. N. Trager & W. Henderson (Eds.), *Communist China, 1949–1969: A twenty-year appraisal* (pp. 175–198). New York: New York University Press.
Chesneaux, J. (1979). *China: The People's Republic since 1949*. New York: Harvester Press.
China Media Project. (2007/2012). *CMP, China Media Project: A project of the Journalism and Media Studies Centre at the University of Hong Kong*. Retrieved from http://cmp.hku.hk/2007/03/20/211/
China Pictorial. (1968). Spring thunder in the proletarian educational revolution: In Peking No. 23 Middle School. *China Pictorial* 1968(2), 22. Retrieved from *Morning Sun: A film and website about Cultural Revolution* at http://www.morningsun.org/living/education/cp_educational_revolution.html

Chinese Communist Party Central Committee. (1966a). Communique of the Eleventh Plenary Session of the Eighth Central Committee of the Communist Party of China (Adopted on August 12, 1966). From the Survey of the China Mainland Press, August 17, 1966 (No. 3762). In A. D. Barnett (1967). *China after Mao* (pp. 277–287). Princeton: Princeton University Press.

Chinese Communist Party Central Committee. (1966b). Decision of the Chinese Communist Party Central Committee concerning the Great Cultural Revolution (Adopted on August 8, 1966) From the Survey of the China Mainland Press, August 16, 1966 (No. 376.). In A. D. Barnett (1967). *China after Mao* (pp. 263–276). Princeton: Princeton University Press.

Cleverley, J. (1991). *The schooling of China: Tradition and modernity in Chinese education*. North Sydney: Allen & Unwin.

Ebrey, P. B. (2012). *Calligraphy in modern China: A visual sourcebook of Chinese civilization*. Retrieved from http://depts.washington.edu/chinaciv/callig/7calmodn.htm

Fraser, S. E., & Hawkin, J. N. (1972). Chinese education: Revolution & development. *The Phi Delta Kappen, 53*, 487–500.

Han, O. L. (2012). *Sources and early printing history of Chairman Mao's Quotations*. Bibliographic Society of America website. Retrieved from http://www.bibsocamer.org/bibsite/han/index.html

He, M. F. (2002). A narrative inquiry of cross-cultural lives: Lives in China. *Journal of Curriculum Studies, 34*, 301–321. doi:10.1080/00220270110108196.

Hong, H. (2012). *A critical survey of translation and reception of the 20th century French literature in China*. Retrieved from http://brown.edu/Programs/Nanjing/content/documents/20thCenturyFrenchLiteratureinChinaHuangHong.pdf

Houn, F. W. (1973). *A short history of Chinese communism*. Englewood Cliffs: Prentice-Hall.

Hsia, A. (1972). *The Chinese Cultural Revolution*. New York: Seabury Press.

Hsü, I. C. Y. (1990). *The rise of modern China* (4th ed.). New York: Oxford University Press.

Langley, A. (2008). *The Cultural Revolution: Years of chaos in China*. Minneapolis: Compass Point Book.

Library of Congress. (2012). *Glossary – China*. Retrieved from http://lcweb2.loc.gov/frd/cs/china/cn_glos.html

Lin, A. H. Y. (2009). *Twentieth-century China: Modernization and transformation*. Lecture 6: From the "Struggle between two lines" to the "Cultural Revolution": China's efforts and setbacks in its quest for modernization in the 1960s and 1970s. Retrieved from http://www.edb.gov.hk/FileManager/EN/Content_3266/modernisation_&_transformation_of_china_lecture09_6.pdf

Mao, Z. (1966a). *Bombard the headquarters – My first big character poster* (August 5, 1966). From *Peking Review, 22* (November 7, 1967). Mao Zedong Internet Archive. Retrieved from http://www.marxists.org/reference/archive/mao/selected-works/volume-9/mswv9_63.htm

Mao, Z. (1966b, May 16). *Communist Party of China on the Great Proletarian Cultural Revolution*. Mao Zedong Internet Archive. Retrieved from http://www.marxists.org/subject/china/documents/cpc/cc_gpcr.htm

Meisner, M. (1977). *Mao's China: A history of the People's Republic*. New York: Free Press.

Meng, X., & Gregory, R. G. (2002). The impact of interrupted education on subsequent educational attainment: A cost of the Chinese Cultural Revolution. *Economic Development and Cultural Change, 50*, 935–959.

Nie, X. (2009a, July 13). 大跃进及文革时期语文教科书乱象 [The chaos of language textbooks during the Great Leap Forward and the Cultural Revolution]. 瞭望, 20–21.

Nie, X. (2009b, July 13). 追问人性内涵的39年 [The thirty years of humanity inquiry]. 瞭望, 22–24.

Peking Review. (1966, August 12). C.P.C. Central Committee decides on large-scale publication of chairman Mao's works. *Peking Review, 9*(33), 13–15.

People's Education Press. (2007). People's education press website. Retrieved at http://www.pep.com.cn/EnglishVersion_1/

Shen, L., & Sun, Y. (2010). Dissecting the Chinese language literacy education and political discourse during the Cultural Revolution. *American Review of China Studies, 11*(2), 1–16.

Wang, X. (2003). *Education in China since 1976*. Jefferson: McFarland.

Chapter 5
Chinese Language Pedagogy and Human Dignity: The Special Rank Teacher in the Aftermath of the Cultural Revolution

Po Yuk Ko and Bob Adamson

5.1 Introduction

The lifetime Special Rank Teacher (SRT) award was established in 1978 by the People's Republic of China with the aim of honoring outstanding teachers in various subjects and at different levels. Over 10,000 teachers have been granted this title since its inception (Cai et al. 1999). The shelves of most education bookshops in the PRC contain numerous biographies, studies of teaching ideology, and exemplar lessons of the SRTs (e.g. Huang and Ni 1991; Liu and Zhang 1996; Wang 1992; Zhang 2001; Zhejiang Special Rank Teacher Association 2002). The SRT reflects contemporary political attitudes of the state towards teachers, as well as the pedagogical excellence awardees are deemed to possess.

The traditional status of Chinese teachers was ambiguous. Culturally, they received great respect, but most teachers in ancient China did not enjoy high social or economic status (Ho 1961; Shi and Englert 2008). While enjoying veneration from the public, teachers were expected to embody knowledge, wisdom, and virtue and to be able to serve as role models for their students. In Chinese educational philosophy, education is not confined to knowledge acquisition. Confucianism places a strong emphasis on moral cultivation, with the ultimate aim of education to develop students as cultivated persons. Confucianism advocates it is the teacher's responsibility to foster moral and ethical development. In *The Analects*, Confucius says, "The Master

---

P.Y. Ko (✉)
Department of Curriculum and Instruction, Hong Kong Institute of Education,
Tai Po, Hong Kong

Centre for Learning Study, Hong Kong Institute of Education,
Tai Po, Hong Kong
e-mail: pyko@ied.edu.hk

B. Adamson
Department of International Education and Lifelong Learning,
Hong Kong Institute of Education, Tai Po, Hong Kong

instructs under four heads: culture, moral conduct, doing one's best and being trustworthy in what one says" (Cited in Lau 1979, p. 89).

In recent times, teachers were strongly affected by political turmoil. During the civil war of 1945–1949 between the Guomindang (Nationalist Party) and the Chinese Communist Party (CCP), remolding teachers to the Communist ideology of teaching began in the area ruled by the CCP. They were involved in educational experimentation that emphasized egalitarianism and pragmatism (Chen 1987). In the early years after the CCP took power, teachers suffered little ideological suppression, as it was essential for the CCP to attract young people to the profession in order to dilute the lingering influence of Confucianism and the Guomindang. However, the policy of remolding teachers was extended when the CCP adopted class struggle theory that differentiated people into class categories. Teachers, together with many other intellectuals, were classified in an undesirable category, bourgeois scholars, as many of them were said to come from families involved in exploitation activities and had received "feudalistic" education (Lin 1991).

Teachers were targets of criticism and subjected to suspicion and ill-treatment during political movements such as the Anti-Rightist Campaign in 1957, the Cultural Revolution from 1966 to 1976, and the Criticize Lin Biao, Criticize Confucius Campaign launched in 1973 within the Cultural Revolution period. They were urged to remold themselves by learning from the workers, peasants, and soldiers in order to adopt the "revolutionary" line of the party. During the Cultural Revolution, many teachers were locked in "cowsheds," temporary jails set up in schools or office buildings to detain the so called "anti-revolutionists," and suffered from serious harassment (Wang 1999; White 1981). Official statements record that over 140,000 cadres and teachers under the Ministry of Education and over 53,000 scientists and technicians were falsely charged and persecuted during the Cultural Revolution (Cleverley 1985). Some teachers who could not stand the torture and humiliation, especially from students they had taught, committed suicide. The events of the Cultural Revolution provided the immediate background to the institution of the SRT award in 1978.

Although the SRTs are mainly frontline primary and secondary school teachers (only a small number are education researchers and tertiary teachers), their roles and status are more complicated than those of ordinary frontline teachers. Many of them have developed distinctive theories or models of teaching that have been formally published in journals or books. Moreover, some of them are associated with an eponymous pedagogical method and with a group of practicing teachers identifying themselves as their disciples or followers. Although many of them were deprived of the opportunity of higher education and formal teacher training due to political instability in the PRC, they seem to have developed rich scholarship, good writing ability, and expertise in teaching (Ko and Marton 2004). Apart from taking up frontline teaching work, they are often invited to give speeches on their pedagogic beliefs, to conduct demonstration lessons that are open to the public, and to serve as consultants for textbook editing, research fellows of teaching research projects, mentors to new teachers, and adjudicators in teaching competitions. Some have been invited to become members of important committees that screen official syllabi and teaching materials. Politically, many are members of the CCP and have been representatives of the People's Congress at the provincial or state level. In sum, they took up the roles of teacher leaders, pedagogical innovators, political representatives, role models in the teaching profession, and at the same time practicing teachers in schools. It seems these frontline teachers were highly valued by the state.

The bestowing of the SRT award essentially suggests the awardees are considered the embodiment of all-round "excellence," in terms of political, as well as moral and professional criteria. This notion differs in many respects from the conception of teaching excellence elsewhere. As revealed by some award systems for teachers in other contexts, such as the Master Teacher Plan or certification for accomplished teachers by the National Board of Certified Teachers (NBCT) in the United States and awards for university teachers in Australia, teaching excellence is often conceptualized as competency or knowledge (see for example Dunkin and Precians 1992; Georgia Professional Standards Commission 2012; Moore 1984). Some studies highlight the personal qualities of teachers as key factors contributing to teaching excellence (e.g. Turk 1992). However, the political background of an expert teacher is seldom stated as a prior condition in the criteria of teaching awards in the West. Indeed, as White (1991) points out, mandated teaching awards that use political criteria to identify outstanding teachers are often shunned by educators as professionally divisive political interference. Moreover, lifetime awards for teachers are also regarded as controversial in some Western systems, such as the Master Teacher Plan in the United States, because there is a worry the awardees might stop performing at the requisite level after holding the rank for a period of time (Moore 1984). Furthermore, Western studies on expertise argue that while experts are able to excel in their particular areas, they might not be able to shine in other areas (e.g. Berliner 2002; Dreyfus and Dreyfus 1986).

It appears, therefore, the SRT award has particular characteristics. What then are the features of their pedagogical models? What beliefs and actions helped them to get through the turbulent period of social change? To answer these questions, this chapter adopts an historical approach. We first explore the major developments in Chinese language teaching in Imperial, Republican, and Communist eras before analyzing the nature of the SRT award in its historical context. Finally, we examine the biographies of 14 SRTs to ascertain their contributions to Chinese language education.

The selection of case study teachers for the biographical study started with a literature search. From a review of collected biographies of famous SRTs (e.g. Huang and Ni 1991; Liu and Zhang 1996; Wang 1992), we chose 14 SRTs whose full life histories and pedagogy were recorded in the literature. This approach creates a small difficulty in interpretation of results in that, although the fame of these 14 SRTs made data more accessible, they are "la crème de la crème" and, therefore, any claims of generalizability across all SRTs need to be tempered with caution. We then carried out in-depth interviews with seven of the SRTs to triangulate and enrich the data.

5.2 Pedagogical Developments in Chinese Language Teaching

Before the fall of the traditional education system in the late Qing period, Chinese language learning was regarded as a handmaiden of classical studies and was linked closely with the preservation of cultural heritage (Chen 1987, p. 2). It was also a tool to achieve public office under the Imperial civil service examinations. In the late Qing period, the political, social, and cultural systems were critically reviewed due to enormous social upheavals. The role of Chinese language education underwent significant changes. In 1903, a new educational system, the Guimou Educational system, was established, representing a victory for modernizers, such as Zhang Zhidong (Hsü 1983). Chinese literature (*Zhongguo wenxue* 中国文学), which referred to the study of Chinese literature and language, was established as an independent subject for the first time (Chen 1987) and was separated from study of the Chinese classics (*du jing* 读经). Two years later in 1905, the civil service examination was abolished and the linkage between Chinese language as a subject and public or political appointments was broken.

Since then, there have been ongoing debates concerning various issues in Chinese language education. One of the debates, concerning the orientation of Chinese as a subject, *wen* (文) versus *dao* (道), began around the May Fourth period (1919). The word *wen* has two meanings, language and literature, while *dao* means cultural and ideological aspects. Scholars such as Lin Shu (林纾) holding a more traditional view have argued that since Imperial times, language study could not be separated from moral and cultural education. To support their argument, they often quoted a popular saying: "Literature is meant to convey the *dao*" (文以载道). There was another group of educators, represented by Ye Shengtao (叶圣陶) and Zhu Ziqing (朱自清), who believed the primary goal of Chinese as a subject should be to help students develop language ability, with moral or ideological education secondary to this goal. The debate resulted in a large number of articles discussing the issue published in journals and newspapers at that time (see e.g. Gu and Li 1991).

Another controversy was the status of *baihua* (白话) (the vernacular) and *wenyan* (文言) (the classical language) in Chinese language curriculum. Throughout history, wenyan was used in classical literature and official documents and hence regarded as a prestigious form of language, while baihua, the vernacular, was used in spoken language and considered an inferior form of language. During the May Fourth Movement, Hu Shi (胡适), a key reformist, argued aggressively that wenyan was a "dead language" because it deviated from the spoken form of language and was difficult for laymen to understand, whereas baihua was a better language for communication, and hence facilitated the modernization program of the country. This viewpoint was supported by many reformist intellectuals of the time and became widely accepted after the May Fourth Movement (Chow 1980). Thereafter, baihua gained its official status in the literary world, as well as in the education field.

However, the debate on wenyan and baihua was not settled. Many school teachers did not welcome the change since the teaching of baihua texts was a new challenge for them. In the past, "translating" wenyan sentence-by-sentence was basically the method used in Chinese language instruction, and teaching Chinese was often referred to as "explaining the book" (*jiang shu* 讲书). As baihua is similar to the spoken form of Chinese, students no longer needed teachers' translations to understand the baihau texts (Zhang 1991). Teachers found they had lost their main duty as translators in the teaching process and were eager to find new methods to deal with the teaching of baihua texts. This subsequently gave rise to much discussion about appropriate methods to teach Chinese and the role of teachers as revealed in articles in educational journals at that time (Chen 1987). There was some interest in foreign ideas, such as the child-centered theory promoted by John Dewey during his visit to China from 1919 to 1921 (Yu 1991). However, the reforms were small scale. The "explaining method" (串讲法) and "lecturing method" (讲解法) were still the prevailing instructional methods among most Chinese language teachers.

Chinese Language was a central school subject in the curriculum of the new People's Republic of China. It was allocated 7 lessons a week at the junior secondary level and 6 at the senior level—more than that of all other subjects according to *The Teaching Programme for Secondary Schools* in 1953 (Zhang 1991). The subject tended to be especially sensitive to political influence, as evidently it was one of the two subjects (the other being History) in which teaching materials used in the Republican era were revised substantially under the new regime (Löfstedt 1980). The most significant change in the content of Chinese Language textbooks was the substitution of many of the classical (*wenyan*) texts in the syllabus with vernacular (*baihua*) texts written by reformists from the May Fourth Movement and Communist leaders (Zhang 1991).

The pedagogical approach promoted by the state at that time was a Soviet model, the Five-Step Model (五环节教学) developed by Kairov (1893–1978), the head of the Ministry of Education of the Soviet Union, in his book *Pedagogy*. The Five-Step Model included organizing and planning, revising and checking, teaching a new topic, reinforcement, and arranging assignments. Although the model suggested a rigid procedure for teaching, many Chinese Language teachers still followed it because, first, it was an officially promoted method and second, teachers did not have many other alternative models to follow (Chen 1987; Yan 1984).

There were two other large-scale, state-sponsored reforms that involved most of the subject teachers in this period, namely the Red-Scarf Teaching Approach (红领巾教学) and the Splitting the Chinese Language Curriculum into Literature and Language Strands (汉语文学分科教学) reform. The Red-Scarf Teaching Approach was inspired by a Soviet professor during his time at a teacher training institute in Beijing in the early 1950s. He criticized the predominance of teacher talk, the emphasis on ideological aspects of the text, and the insufficient attention to the language and literature aspects in lessons he observed (Chen 1987). His ideas were widely disseminated by an influential journal, *People's Education* (Ye 1984). However, the approach was not officially promoted after China broke away from the Soviet Union in the early 1960s. Moreover, the method itself was criticized as having some shortcomings. Researchers commented the approach led to an overuse of questioning in lessons, which they believed was not conducive to students' learning (Chen 1987).

The Splitting the Chinese Language Curriculum into Literature and Language Strands reform took place from 1955 to 1957. The syllabus at that time comprised individual model essays that were texts selected from different sources, including literary works of modern Chinese writers or translated articles of foreign writers. The advocates of the "split" approach, who were mainly experienced teachers, key educators, and linguists, criticized the existing syllabus for being non-systematic and without a clear focus. They believed reorganizing it into two strands, so the language strand focused on linguistic knowledge and the literature strand focused on classical and modern literature, could improve the organization of the subject. More importantly, they advocated Chinese Language teaching should be changed from a text-based to a more skill/knowledge-oriented approach (Chen 1987). This idea gained the support of the Ministry of Education, which produced new syllabi. However, the split approach also attracted a lot of criticism. The classical texts in the literature strand were criticized for being too difficult, and the grammar study in the language strand was said to be too dull and boring. Some opponents of the new initiative believed language teaching should take a holistic rather than a piecemeal approach (Chen 1987).

Around this time, state policy mandated efficiency and high quantity as targets of every production sector, so teachers were urged to develop methods that could attain a greater quantified learning outcome. In many schools, quantitative learning targets (such as the amount of words students should acquire) were set. Some schools set up check counters at the entrance to make sure students could pass the tests on memorization of words before they went back to school (Chen 1987).

The Cultural Revolution had a great influence on education and teachers' lives. During the campaign, schooling at all levels stopped for about 3 years. After classes resumed in 1969, education was highly politicized, with Chinese Language being no exception. The textbooks produced during this period mainly contained articles written by key political leaders or newspaper editorials that were full of political slogans. The "three-oriented approach" (textbook-oriented, teacher-oriented, and classroom-oriented) was criticized severely. An "Open Door approach" that promoted learning taking place outside the classroom was encouraged (Zhang 1991). In Chinese Language lessons, students were allowed to leave the classroom and do so-called social research—observe things on the streets and write compositions or report on the issues. However, since composition skills were not taught, students found it difficult to write reports. Their strategy to cope was to copy phrases and slogans from newspaper editorials, instead of writing original reports. As a result, the content of their compositions was simply an imitation of the official propaganda (Chen 1987). In some schools, workers, peasants, and soldiers were invited to teach lessons. This was called the "Going out and Coming in" policy. The focus of these lessons was political propaganda rather than language teaching (Chen 1987). During this period, Chinese Language was renamed "political-language lessons" (政文课) (Zhang 1991, p. 380).

In the immediate aftermath of the Cultural Revolution era, pedagogical debates on Chinese Language teaching resurfaced. The first discussion was sparked by Lü Shuxiang's article in *People's Daily* in 1978 that criticized the conventional teaching method used by many Chinese Language teachers at that time as being "small in quantity, slow, poor quality, and wasting time" (少、慢、差、费) (Lü 1987, p. 3). Another influential educator, Ye Shengtao, challenged the centrality of prescribed texts in the Chinese Language curriculum. He advocated a skills-based approach to Chinese Language teaching where "language is an instrument" and teaching materials (i.e. prescribed texts) should be used as tools to cultivate students' independent learning ability rather than as content to be remembered (Chen 1987, pp. 314–316). A third educator, Zhang Zhigong, urged the conducting of scientific research on Chinese language teaching to improve the teaching of the subject. The above three language educators' views were influential in the field since they were praised as the "three veterans" (三老) in Chinese Language education (Chen 1987).

Teacher initiated pedagogic innovations flourished in this period. About 38 school-based or teacher-initiated pedagogic innovations in Chinese Language teaching developed from the late 1970s to early 1990s (Dai 1997).

5.3 The SRT Award

When Deng Xiaoping launched the economic modernization drive in 1978, he recognized the crucial role of education in facilitating this policy. He also acknowledged that the teaching profession faced the problem of low morale in the wake of the Cultural Revolution.

> The Gang of Four led young people to bad ways. This was one of their sins. Now we have to change the situation. We hope schools could develop a good environment for young people....We have to investigate how to raise teachers' quality. In the past several years, teachers dare not to teach, but we cannot blame them. Now we hope that they not only dare to teach, but also can teach well. (China Education Yearbook 1984, p. 49)

In 1978, speaking at the National Conference on Education, Deng announced the establishment of the Special Rank Teacher (*teji jiaoshi* 特级教师) (SRT) award to promote teaching excellence, saying that

> We have to raise the political and social status of teachers. Not only should students respect teachers, the whole society should respect teachers....Proper measures should be taken to encourage people to take up education as a career. Outstanding teachers in particular can be appraised as Special Rank Teachers. (China Education Yearbook 1994, pp. 62–63)

The causes of the crisis in the profession had historical roots that went back many centuries before the Cultural Revolution. The solution, bestowing honorific titles, also had precedents in the 1950s. The purpose of the SRT award was to honor the recipients as outstanding teachers and to promote their pedagogy (model teaching) nationally. The SRT award was one of several teaching awards instituted in the late 1970s and early 1980s. Other honors included Model Class Master (*mofan banzhuren* 模范班主任) and Outstanding Teacher (*youxiu jiaoshi* 优秀教师) (China Education Yearbook 1984). Since its inception, more than 10,000 teachers have been granted the title of

SRT, which is the most distinguished and prestigious award in the field. Although it is not a large proportion compared with the enormous teacher population—approximately 15 million in 2007 (Department of Development and Planning, Chinese Ministry of Education 2007)—it is not an insignificant number.

The establishment of the award was confirmed by an official document, *Tentative Regulations on the Appraisal and Selection of Special Rank Teachers*, promulgated by the Ministry of Education in December 1978. The document delineated the nature and objective of the award, the required qualifications, and the selection methods (China Education Yearbook 1984). This "tentative" regulation was not revised until 1993, when it was replaced by *The Regulations on the Appraisal and Selection of Special Rank Teachers* (China Education Yearbook Editorial 1994). The revised document is less politically-oriented compared with the old version and also suggests some changes in the operation of the appraisal system. However, the main ideas concerning the nature of the award in the old version remain unchanged. Table 5.1 summarizes the details of the 1978 document on the SRT award. The major changes suggested by the 1993 version are in brackets.

The SRT award is competitive, with selection occurring only every few years and with an initially low success rate since the award was aimed at excellent people in the profession as defined by the CCP. The success rate increased later. For instance, in Zhejiang province, a total of 144 SRTs were awarded as the sixth cohort in 1998. The number was nearly half the sum of the previous five cohorts (Zhang 2001). The award not only identified such teachers, but also improved their material conditions. Substantial rewards were given to the awardees. The merit pay of 30 Yuan was equal to about one third of the monthly salary of experienced secondary teachers in the early 1980s (Interview: Yu, 17-6-1999). The allowance was raised to 80 Yuan in 1993 and to 300 Yuan monthly from 2008. The award was established by the state, but it operated at the provincial level. Different quotas of SRTs were given to different provinces, which implies the selection sought to achieve geographical balance. Individual teachers were nominated by schools to the county education bureau that would carry out an inspection of the candidates, including on-spot lesson observations, interviews with the candidates' colleagues and students, and a review of documents, such as lesson plans and articles written by the candidates. Reports would then be submitted to the provincial education bureau that would make the final selection. The above process represents "democratic procedures" and "follow the mass-line" stated in regulations and also suggests a focus on pedagogical merits.

However, it is clear from the regulations that the award was initially linked to politics, with an emphasis on loyalty to the CCP, as SRTs would be given appointments to serve in political consultative organizations at the provincial or state level. Good personal conduct was also considered to be an important criterion. Another noteworthy feature is that SRT is a lifetime award. There is no re-evaluation for the awardees, and the merit pay is received for life. In return, the awardees are expected to make contributions to the teaching profession even after retirement. Professional attributes that are esteemed include good subject matter knowledge and teaching skill, being able to improve students' learning, being innovative in teaching, being

Table 5.1 The Special rank teacher award[a]

Content	Details
Aims	To elevate the social and political status of teachers; to praise outstanding teachers in order to keep them in the profession;
	To encourage teachers to contribute to teaching improvement in order to enhance the quality of teaching
	(The 1993 version specifies that the award was for primary and secondary school teachers only.)
Qualifications	Candidate must support the CCP and Communism; be loyal to the CCP and follow the CCP's instructions on education;
	A clean political record with no major political problem. *(Deleted in the 1993 document)*
	Moral integrity; a good reputation among fellow teachers and in the education profession. *(The 1993 version states an SRT should be 'a teacher of exemplary virtue; a model devoted to nurturing students; an expert in teaching'.)*
	Extensive theoretical knowledge and teaching experience; able to teach effectively and show remarkable results; willing to innovate; diligent; produce acclaimed work, such as teaching materials and methods; willing to help new teachers
	Senior secondary school teachers: university graduates in relevant subject; Junior secondary school teachers: university graduates; Primary school teachers: graduates of normal secondary schools; Kindergarten teachers: graduates of training schools for Kindergarten education. *(Criteria for academic qualifications were deleted in the 1993 document.)*
Role and status of the awardees	SRTs will be appointed as committee members of the National People's Congress or the Chinese People's Political Consultative Conference. *(The 1993 version says that SRTs should concentrate on contributing to their profession.)*
	SRTs can be hired by teacher-training institutes, education research organizations, and educational publishers as special teachers, researchers, or editors. SRTs should do research or act as mentors to new teachers. When retired, these teachers may be employed as honorary principals, education consultants, or other posts arranged by academic organizations
Reward	SRT certificate issued by provincial/municipal revolutionary committee. Lifelong reward of 20 Yuan per month for primary school teachers; 30 Yuan for secondary school teachers *(80 Yuan for both primary and secondary SRTs in the 1993 version.)*
Selection method	Party cadres in schools should undertake democratic procedures and follow the "mass-line." After consultation with the masses, cadres nominate potential candidates to the county education bureau. The education bureau carries out inspections and appraisals, including interviews, school visits, documentary reviews, etc. Reports on the candidates sent to provincial education bureaus for final selection
Success rate	About 0.05% of the total number of teachers will be selected in big cities, such as Beijing, Shanghai and Tianjin; elsewhere the ratio of successful candidates should be lower. Selection will take place every 3–5 years. *(Ratio increased to 0.15% in the 1993 version)*

Ko and Adamson (2011). Used with kind permission from Taylor & Francis

[a]*Summarized from "Tentative Regulations on the Appraisal and Selection of Special Rank Teachers" (China Education Yearbook 1949–81, p. 741) and "The Regulations on the Appraisal and Selection of Special Rank Teachers" (China Education Yearbook 1994, pp. 846–847)*

able to produce demonstrable results, such as the development of practical teaching methods or teaching materials for dissemination, and being able to serve as mentors to new teachers. SRTs are expected to contribute to the development of knowledge on teaching, as well as being demonstrators of good practices.

It seems teaching excellence in Mainland China is officially represented by the SRTs, who are considered to be exponents of good practices and holistic models of good teachers. However, an analysis of the biographies of the selected 14 SRTs reveals they all have also suffered a certain extent of political torture, yet they tend to have maintained their fidelity to the state, as evidenced by the fact that many of them are members of the CCP and have been representatives of the People's Congress at the provincial or state level. There seems to be a discrepancy between a criterion stated in the document with the features of the 14 SRTs. The 1978 document stated a SRT should have a "clear political record" with no major "political problem." However, most of the 14 SRTs have not had a clear political record. On the contrary, many of them were given different political black labels during past political campaigns. As shown in Table 5.2, some, like Zhang Xiaochun, Ouyang Daina, Qian Menglong, and Ning Hongbing, had suffered in the purge during the Anti-Rightist Campaign of 1957. They were accused of being "rightists" and downgraded to lower occupations or transferred to do labor in villages. During the Cultural Revolution, nearly all were accused of crimes. For instance, Ning Hongbing, a SRT from Beijing, was vilified as a "member of the black gang," "counter-revolution academic authority," and "spy." He was first sent to a temporary jail, a "cowshed," and later transferred to the countryside to do laboring work (Ning 1992). Liu Yinghui, a SRT from Liaoning province, was only 30 years old when the Cultural Revolution began. She was classified as a member of the group of "monsters and demons" (*niu gui she shen* 牛鬼蛇神). The Red Guard shaved half of her head bald in a criticism meeting in order to humiliate her (Liu 1992).

Qian offers an explanation as to why teachers such as himself could restore their enthusiasm for teaching right after the Cultural Revolution. Although faithful to the CCP's ideals, he was not an uncritical adherent of Party policies:

> Teachers became enthusiastic because we thought we could radiate our vigor to work for our career again. The bitter memory of the Cultural Revolution disappeared very soon. The feeling was like having a "second liberation"....Sometimes I feel that it's strange that we Chinese are so easy to please. Maybe it's because of receiving the propaganda of the Communist Party for a long time. (Interview: Qian, 6-18-1999)

> I separated the politics from teaching. The political errors were the responsibility of the political leaders, whereas teaching was my responsibility towards society. (Interview: Qian, 4-25-1998)

It seems to imply their genuine belief in the Party and the Communist ideology helped them sustain their fidelity to the Party even though they took a non-conformist stance towards the radical political line during adverse circumstances.

Another internal support to the SRTs was a strong commitment to the integrity and dignity of teachers. Among the 14 SRTs, Ouyang Daina's performance in the Cultural Revolution offers the best demonstration of this commitment. She was detained in a "cowshed" for nearly 2 years and on several occasions she was nearly beaten to death

Table 5.2 Biographical details of the 14 SRTs

Ding Jiecao (1925-)[a]

1949: graduate, Department of Chinese, Dongbei University
1953: began teaching in a secondary school in Shenyang
1955: piloted innovations in Chinese Language
1956: granted the *Outstanding Teacher* award
1956: joined the *Chinese Democracy Promotion Association*
1960: became a textbook editor

Cultural Revolution: labelled *revolutionary authority (fandong quanwei)*, no teaching for several years
1976: resumed teaching in Shenyang
1979: granted the SRT award
1988: retired

Professional commitments: Committee member, Language Pedagogy Research Committee, North-eastern District
Political appointments: Member, PCC, Shenyang

Zhang Xiaochun (1926–1992)[b]

1948: graduate, Department of Education, Yingji University, became secondary school teacher
1950s: created "extended language education approach" (*da yuwen jiaoyu*)
1955: Head, Teaching & Research Unit, Education Department, Hebei Province; joined the CCP

1958: accused of being a "rightist"
1961: transferred to be a lower ranking teacher in a secondary school
1977: promoted as a senior teacher in the school
1979: granted the SRT award
1981: honored as *Model Worker of Hebei Province*

Professional commitments: Committee member of NSCLTR *Political appointments:* Deputy, 6th NPC; Member, PCC, Hebei Province

Zhang Fushen (1926-)[c]

1948: graduate, Beijing Chinese Law Institute
1949: began teaching in a secondary school, Dalian
1958: researcher, Liaoning Teacher Institute
1962: became secondary school teacher
Cultural Revolution: no teaching for 3 years; some in early 1970s

1976: resumed teaching in Dalian; joined the CCP
1979: granted the SRT award
1984: Head, Chinese Department, Tieling Institute of Education
1988: honored as *Model Worker of Liaoning Province*

Professional commitments: Committee member, China Writing Association; Committee member, Liaoning Writing Association
Political appointment: Member of the 4th, 5th, & 6th PCC, Liaoning Province

Yu Yi (1929-)[d]

1951: graduate, Department of Education, Fudan University; teacher in Shanghai
1956: granted the *Outstanding Teacher* award
1965: joined CCP Cultural Revolution: arrested and detained in "cowshed" for 3 months, no teaching for 3 years; resumed teaching in early 1970s

1978: granted the SRT award
1986: named *Outstanding member of the Communist Party in Shanghai*
1989: honored as *Advanced Worker of the Nation*
1990: became principal of Shanghai No.2 Teachers College

Professional commitments: Vice-chairman of the NSCLTR; Member, CESSTM; Drafted the CLOSG 1986, 1993
Political appointments: Deputy, 7th, 8th, & 9th PC, Shanghai

(continued)

Table 5.2 (continued)

Ouyang Daina (1930-)[e]

1941: family moved to Yan'an (parents were CCP cadres)	1961: began teaching in Anshan
1946: joined the CCP	Cultural Revolution: labelled "monster and demon"; detained in "cowshed" for 2 years; resumed teaching in 1970 until retirement
1953: graduate, History Department, People's University, continued study in the History Archives Unit of the University	1979: granted the SRT award
1957: accused of being a "rightist"	1982: began writing experimental textbooks
1958: "demoted" to teacher in secondary school, rural Shanxi	1988: granted *Advanced Teacher of the Nation* award

Professional commitments: Member, CESSTM; Committee member, NSCLTR; Drafted the CLOSG 1986, 1993.

Political appointments: 1981: Deputy, PC, Anshan county; 1983: Deputy, PC, Liaoning Province

Qian Menglong (1931-)[f]

Received formal education to secondary three	1976: allowed to teach Chinese Language
1950: began teaching in a primary school	1979: granted the SRT award
1951: began teaching in secondary school	1981: joined the CCP
1956: granted the *Outstanding Teacher* award	1985: established the Jiading Experimental School as first principal
1957: labelled rightist, transferred to work in the countryside	1988: retired, then part-time textbook editor, Shanghai Normal University Press
1960: resumed teaching	1989: honored as *National Model Worker*
Cultural Revolution: Detained in "cowshed" for 2 years; resumed teaching in early 1970s, taught Art	

Professional commitments: Member, CESSTM; Committee member, NSCLTR; Drafted the CLOSG, 1986, 1993

Political appointments: Deputy, PC, Shanghai

Cai Chengqing (1934-)[g]

1954 graduated, Anqing Teaching College, teacher in secondary school	1980: granted the SRT award
1956: joined the CCP	1984: honored as *Model Worker of Anhui Province*
Cultural Revolution: no teaching for 2 years; 1969: resumed teaching	1989: honored as *Outstanding Teacher of the Nation*

Professional commitments: Committee member, NSCLTR *Political appointments:* Deputy, PC, Anhui Province

Liu Feifei (1934-)[h]

1950: army volunteer in Korea, joined the CCP	1977: experimented on the teaching of composition in school
1961: graduated, Beijing Teachers College; began teaching in Beijing	1979: published teaching materials for teaching of composition
Cultural Revolution: no teaching for 3 years; 1970: teaching in Beijing	1985: granted the SRT award

Professional commitments: Committee member, NSCLTR *Political appointments:* Deputy, PC, Beijing

(continued)

Table 5.2 (continued)

Zhang Fu (1935)[i]	
Received formal education to junior secondary level	For 3 years; resumed teaching in secondary school in Nanchang
1955: teacher in primary school, Jiangxi	1980: moved to another school in Nanchang
1960: joined *Chinese Democracy Promoting Association*	1985: granted the *Outstanding Teacher* award
1964: moved to a new secondary school	1986: honored as *National Model Worker in Education*
Cultural Revolution: transferred to work in the countryside as laborer	1991: granted the SRT award

Professional commitments: Chairman, Chinese Language Association of Nanchang; Associate Director, Education Association of Nanchang
Political appointments: Deputy of the 7th and 8th NPC; Vice Chairman, PCC, Nanchang

Ning Hongbing (1936-)[j]	
1955: graduate, Beijing Teacher Training Institute; taught in a primary school for 3 months and then changed to secondary school in Beijing	1976: moved to Beijing No. 80 Secondary School
1957: accused of being a "rightist"	1982: joined the CCP
1965: graduated, Chinese Department, Beijing Television University	1986: granted the SRT award
Cultural Revolution: detained in cowshed; then labor in the countryside	1988: awarded *Model Worker of Beijing City* and *National Model Worker in Education*
1972: resumed teaching	

Professional commitments: Committee member, NSCLTR; Committee member, Beijing Association of Research in Chinese Language Teaching
Political appointment: Deputy, PC, Beijing

Liu Yinghui (1936-)[k]	
1955: graduated, Shenyang No 1 Teacher College, teacher in a secondary school in a suburban area; joined the CCP	1969: resumed teaching
1958: began teaching in Shenyang Railway Secondary School	1983: promoted to principal
Cultural Revolution: accused of being "*monster and demon*"	1986: granted the SRT award

Professional commitments: Vice Chairman, Chinese Language Teaching and Research Committee, Shenyang
Political appointment: Member, PC, Shenyang

Li Zhongyi (1938-)[l]	
1959: graduated, Lüshun Teachers College	1979: joined the CCP; granted the SRT award
1961: began teaching in Liaoning	1985: honored as *Model Teacher of Liaoning Province*
Cultural Revolution: accused of being member of the "*black gang*," no teaching for 3 years; 1970: resumed teaching	1985: became vice principal in a secondary school in Liaoning
	1989: senior teacher, Dailing Experimental Secondary School

Professional commitments: Committee member, Language Pedagogy Research Committee, North-eastern District
Political appointment: Deputy of the PC of Fuxin city

(continued)

Table 5.2 (continued)

Chen Riliang (1939-)[m]	
1960: graduated, Fujian Normal University; teacher, Fuzhou No. 1 Secondary School	1983: promoted as vice principal, joined the CCP
1960–66: research on the "three-model" approach to teaching reading	1988: granted the SRT award; awarded Golden Key prize in the National Teaching Reform in Primary and Secondary Level
Cultural Revolution: research interrupted; 1970: resumed teaching	
Professional commitments: Member, CESSTM; Committee member, NSCLTR; Drafted the CLOSG, 1993; Associate Editor, *Zhongxuesheng yuwenbao [Language Newsletter for Secondary Students] Political appointment:* Deputy, 6th and 7th NPC	
Wei Shusheng (1950-)[n]	
Received formal education to secondary three in Shenyang	1984: granted the SRT award
Cultural Revolution: joined the Red Guards; 1968: teacher in *minban* primary school; 1971: joined the CCP; 1972: worked in political section, electronic factory, Panjin; 1974: denounced in Criticize Lin Biao and Criticize Confucius Campaign	1986: became principal of Panjin Experimental School
	1988: granted honor of *National Model Worker*
	1991: granted Ten Outstanding Young People award
1978: resumed teaching in Panshan No. 3 Secondary School	1995: became Director of Panjin Education Department
Professional appointments: Member, National Educational Science Planning Unit; Vice Chairman, Academic Committee of the NSCLTR	
Political appointments: Deputy, 13th & 14th NPC	

Key *CESSTM* Committee for Editing and Screening Syllabuses and Teaching Materials (*guojia jiaowei zhongxiaoxue jiaocai shencha weiyuanhui*), *CLOSG* Chinese Language Official Syllabus Guideline (*yuwen jiaoxue dagang*), *CR* Cultural Revolution, *NPC* National People's Congress (*quanguo renmin daibiao dahui*), *NSCLTR* The National Association for Secondary Chinese Language Teaching and Research (*quanguo zhongxue yuwen jiaoxue yantaohui*), *PC* People's Congress (*renmin daibiao dahui*), *PCC* Political Consultative Conference (*zhengzhi xieshang huiyi*)

[a]Ding (1992), in Wang (1992), pp. 291–293 & pp. 305–316
[b]Huang and Ni (1991), pp. 146–162
[c]Zhang (1992), in Wang (1992), pp. 261–266
[d]Yu (1992), in Wang (1992), pp. 1–33; Yu (1996), in Liu and Zhang (1996), pp. 3–28. Interview: 17/6/99
[e]Ouyang (1992), in Wang (1992), pp. 161–182; Ouyang (1996), in Liu and Zhang (1996), pp. 395–442. Interview: 14/6/99
[f]Qian (1996), in Liu and Zhang (1996), pp. 537–606; Qian (1992), in Wang, pp. 111–132; Qian (1985). Interview: 24/4/98, 18/6/99
[g]Cai (1996), in Liu and Zhang (1996), pp. 730–783; Huang and Ni, pp. 135–145
[h]Huang and Ni (1991), pp. 39–49
[i]Liu and Zhang (1996), pp. 257–329. Interview: 20/12/98
[j]Ning (1992), in Wang, pp. 213–223; Ning (1996), in Liu and Zhang (1996), pp. 63–118. Interview: 8/8/97
[k]Liu (1992), in Wang (1992), pp. 348–354
[l]Li (1992), in Wang (1992), pp. 317–319
[m]Huang and Ni, pp. 187–195. Interview: 17/11/96
[n]Wei (1996), in Liu and Zhang (1996), pp. 798–842; Wei (1995). Interview: 12–14/6/99

by the Red Guards because she resisted acceptance of the humiliating acts they asked her to perform. Ouyang recorded how she not only managed to maintain her own dignity, but also preserved the identity of being a teacher.

> Sometimes the students shouted slogans at me but made mistakes in their utterance of some words. Some of their "big posters" contained some wrongly written characters. I told them they had made mistakes and what the correct words were. Usually they would yell at me to shut up. Sometimes they would beat me too. But I found that later they would secretly correct the wrong words in their utterance and on the posters. To them, I was still a language teacher, but I was teaching them in a special "classroom" at a special time. (Interview: Ouyang, 6-14-1999)

5.4 The Pedagogic Contribution of the SRTs

The SRTs demonstrated sensitivity to the national trend of pedagogic development in Chinese Language teaching (CLT) and were motivated to try out pedagogic reform long before they were granted the award. The pedagogic innovations they developed sought to tackle practical problems in CLT and to respond to the trend of development of the subject.

Many of the 14 SRTs had been engaged in initiatives such as the Red-Scarf Teaching Approach and Splitting the Chinese Language Curriculum into Literature and Language Strands, but one of the distinguishing features of the 14 SRTs is that they all developed some kind of pedagogic model of or approach to Chinese Language teaching (Table 5.3). For example, Zhang Xiaochun developed *extended language education* (*da yuwen jiaoyu vs. jiaoyu* 大语文教育) that promoted out-of-class language learning activities (Huang and Ni 1991). Ning developed a *three-permissions* (*sange yunxu* 三个允许) policy in his classes and promoted a relaxed and open atmosphere in classroom learning. Students were permitted to make mistakes in answering questions, to change their views, and to query the teacher at any time (Ning 1996).

The approaches the SRT developed were given particular names, such as the *coaching and directing method* (*dianbo fa* 点拨法) by Cai, the *jump and pick approach* by Zhang Fu, the *three-model reading approach* (*san keshi vs. kexing* 三课式) by Chen, and the *three-level model for training of writing* (*zuowen sanji jiaoxue* 作文三级教学) by Liu Feifei. These approaches were usually expressed in technical terms, such as "levels," with very detailed and specific steps in the instructional methods to deal with some practical problems in Chinese Language teaching. This crystallization of theory into a systematic pedagogic formulation facilitated dissemination to other teachers, thus giving the innovations a greater impact.

For instance, Liu's three levels were *observation*, *analysis*, and *expression*. The model delineated a scheme which consisted of six stages and 44 training foci. She also designed teaching packages consisting of sample lesson plans and teaching materials for other teachers to follow (Huang and Ni 1991). Chen focused on the improvement of teaching reading comprehension. His methods consisted of three specific steps, including previewing, discussion, and revision and summarizing (Huang and Ni 1991).

Table 5.3 The pedagogy of 14 SRTs

Name	Approaches/models of teaching	Publications/research/demonstration lessons
Ding Jiecao (1925-)	*Four-step model* in the teaching of classical literature	Presented demonstration lessons in more than 20 cities; Six volumes of senior secondary Chinese Language textbooks
Zhang Xiaochun (1926–1992)	*Extended language education* approach (*da yuwen jiaoyu*)	Extended language learning teaching materials (*da yuwen jiaocai*); led Extended language education research group
Zhang Fushen (1926-)	*Seven steps in essay writing*	Three books on writing pedagogy; carried out five cycles of experiments on the new approach on writing instruction.
Yu Yi (1929-)	*Affective approach in reading instruction*	Five books and over 160 articles on Chinese Language teaching; conducted over 20 videotaped demonstration lessons.
Ouyang Daina (1930-)	Developed a framework for the systematic training of students' reading and writing ability	Junior Secondary Experimental Textbooks (12 volumes); produced about ten videotaped demonstration lessons
Qian Menglong (1931-)	*Tri-center four-model guided reading* approach (*sanzhu sishi yuwen daodufa*) and *Five-step strategy* (*wubu jiaoxuefa*)	Two books and over 60 articles on Chinese Language teaching; Conducted ten video-taped demonstration lessons.
Cai Chengqing (1934-)	*Coaching and directing method* (*dianbofa*)	Three experiments on the coaching and directing approach
Liu Feifei (1934-)	*Three-level training of writing* (*zuowen sanji jiaoxue*)	Four books on teaching writing; two sets of textbooks & several books on teaching writing; experiments, 1977, 1985–1988,
Zhang Fu (1935-)	*Jump and pick approach* (*tiaozaifa*)	3-year longitudinal study of his students from 1985; two books in 1992 and 1997 to promote the innovation
Ning Hongbing (1936-)	Using cards as aids (*kapian jiaoxuefa*); created *Three permissions* (*sange yunxu*): let students make mistakes, change their views, and query teacher any time	Carried out four cycles of study on the approach during 1978 to 1988; monograph, *Articles of Ning Hongbing* (*Ning Hongbing wenji*); 10 videotaped demonstration lessons
Liu Yinghui (1936-)	*Teach with real affection, learn with real affection* (*jiaoyou zhenqing, xueyou dongqing*)	Conducted over 30 demonstration lessons; published 18 articles in national journals; edited learning materials (16 volumes)
Li Zhongyi (1938-)	Developed reading and writing method, *Organize Chinese Language teaching into thematic*	Conducted class-based research; published about 30 articles in subject-based journals; published a book, *Writing Skills* (1985);

(continued)

Table 5.3 (continued)

Name	Approaches/models of teaching	Publications/research/demonstration lessons
	modules (*yi xunlian xiangmu wei danyuan zhuzhi yuwen jiaoxue*)	produced several demonstration videotapes
Chen Riliang (1939-)	Three-model reading instruction (*sanke xing*):	Over 20 articles; produced demonstration videotapes; editor, Chinese Language newsletter for secondary school students
Wei Shusheng (1950-)	Six-step approach (*liubu jiaoxuefa*) for classroom instruction	Classroom research; ten books & many articles; some 530 seminars & over 20 videotaped demonstration lessons

Ko & Adamson (2011). Used with kind permission from Taylor & Francis

The 14 SRTs were also able to produce demonstrable outcomes of two types. The first type involved their classroom practices. As shown in Table 5.3, many of the teachers produced publications of their lesson transcripts to illustrate their innovations. They also taught open classes and videotaped these for the dissemination of their pedagogy. The second type involved students' learning outcomes. Most of the 14 SRTs carried out small classroom-based experiments to evaluate their innovations. They reported positive results of their trials through students' academic achievements on examinations. For instance, Wei's pedagogy targeted academic low-achievers. He reported the academic results of his first experimental class as follows:

> In 1978, I taught a class (junior secondary one) which had eight academic low-achievers with an average score in Chinese Language below 40....In the promotion examination.... all these eight students achieved the scores eligible for senior secondary school or vocational schools. The weakest student, whose score was only 24 when he entered my class, gained 72.5 marks in his Chinese Language in the examination. He was promoted to senior secondary school. (Wei 1995, p. 112)

Some of the SRTs gained support from the local education bureau or universities to carry out larger scale trials on their pedagogy. They also reported positive results from these trials. For instance, the *three-level model for training of writing* developed by Liu gained support from Peking University in order to carry out large-scale experiments. It was reported there were 80 experimental classes in 19 different provinces using her method, as well as the teaching materials she developed for teaching writing from 1985 to 1988. She reported the experimental class yielded an average score of 5.13 higher than the control group in writing attainment in their promotion examination (Huang and Ni 1991).

In summary, the critical features of the professional lives of the SRTs demonstrated they were scholarly teachers with rich subject matter knowledge. Their pedagogic development was self-initiated, and their reforms matched the national trends in Chinese Language teaching. They articulated their ideas and practices as models of teaching with specific instructional procedures and were able to demonstrate their pedagogy in open lessons. Finally, questions of the quality of their pedagogy were answered by reports of their students making academic gains in formal examinations.

5.5 Conclusion

The establishment, aims, and roles of the SRT award can be understood as having roots in contextual factors. The award was a response to the educational problems in the aftermath of the Cultural Revolution, in particular the shortage of teachers and the low morale within the teaching profession. The award aimed to improve the image of teachers, to retain good teachers, and to enhance the quality of teachers in general, by providing a state honor, merit pay, and a public platform for the recipients to disseminate their pedagogical ideas. At the same time, the award was an act of rehabilitation by the CCP for victims of political campaigns who were able to sustain their loyalty to the government.

The SRTs were regarded as holistic representatives of teaching excellence. Each of them was considered an embodiment of a virtuoso character, good subject matter knowledge, excellent teaching performance, and educational scholarship. This conforms with the Confucian concept of respecting teachers and recognizing them as role models and embodiments of the virtue and wisdom of teaching. The dual emphasis on the professional and the political aspects of the SRTs lives also coincided with the Communist concept of expert—the unification of "redness" and "expertise."

Essentially the SRTs were in conformity with the mainstream of societal values of the time. These teachers had a patriotic belief in the political ideology of the country that was developed in their early days. This contributed to their conformity to the ideology of the state despite the very negative experiences they had suffered during the Cultural Revolution. As a result, they were willing to stand as role models for the state.

The SRTs were reformists in that they were reflective and intrinsically motivated to discover their own ways to improve their teaching. They were innovative and skillful in articulating their pedagogic ideas as practical approaches to teaching. They made use of the reform momentum of the post-Cultural Revolutionary era to progress in their career path and so became leader teachers in the field. The SRT award acknowledged and rewarded the exceptional pedagogical skills of the teachers, as well as their political fidelity to the more moderate ideologies of the CCP.

References

Berliner, D. C. (2002). Learning about and learning from expert teachers. *International Journal of Educational Research, 35*, 463–482.

Cai, C. (1996). 蔡澄清 [Cai Chengqing]. In G. Liu & D. Zhang (Ed.), 中国著名特级教师教学思想录 [*The teaching ideology of famous Special Rank Teachers in China*] (pp. 730–783). Jiangsu: Jiangsu Education Press.

Cai, J. et al. (1999). 特级教师专业发展调查 [The survey on the profession development of special rank teacher]. 特级教师期刊, *6*, 1–8.

Chen, B. (1987). 中国现代语文教育发展史 [*History of Chinese language education in China*]. Yunnan: Yunnan Education Press.

China Education Yearbook Editorial. (1984). 中国教育年鉴 1949–81 [China education yearbook 1949–81]. Beijing: China Encyclopaedia Publication Press.

China Education Yearbook Editorial. (1994). 中国教育年鉴, 1994 [China education yearbook, 1994]. Beijing: People's Education Press.

Chow, T. T. (1980). *The May fourth movement* (5th ed.). Cambridge, MA: Harvard University Press.

Cleverley, J. (1985). *The schooling of China: Tradition and modernity in Chinese education*. Sydney: Allen & Unwin.

Dai, R. (1997). 新时期中小学教学方法的改革与实验 [Reform in teaching methods and practice in the last fifteen years in China]. 课程论坛, 6(2), 86–105.

Department of Development & Planning, Chinese Ministry of Education. (2007). 中国教育统计年鉴, 2007 [Education statistics yearbook of China, 2007]. Beijing: People's Education Press.

Ding, J. (1992). 丁洁操自传 [The autobiography of Ding Jiecao]. In W. Wang (Ed.), 当代中学语文教育专家研究 [A study of contemporary Chinese language educators] (pp. 297–316). Beijing: Scientific Education Press.

Dreyfus, H. L., & Dreyfus, S. E. (1986). *Mind over machine: The power of human intuition and expertise in the era of the computer*. New York: Free Press.

Dunkin, M. J., & Precians, R. P. (1992). Award-winning university teachers' concepts of teaching. *Higher Education, 24*, 483–502.

Georgia Professional Standards Commission. (2012). *National Board Certified Teachers*. Retrieved from http://www.gapsc.com/NationalBoard/home.asp

Gu, H. C., & Li, X. B. (1991). 二十世纪前期中国语文教育论集 [The educational essays of the early twentieth century]. Sichuan: Sichuan Education Press.

Ho, P. (1961). *The ladder of success in Imperial China: Aspects of social mobility, 1368–1911*. New York: Columbia University Press.

Hsü, I. C. Y. (1983). *The rise of modern China* (2nd ed.). New York: Oxford University Press.

Huang, L., & Ni, W. (1991). 先进教育思想高超教学艺术 [Advanced ideas and teaching methodology: A study of the special rank Chinese language teachers]. Guangxi: Guangxi Teachers' College Press.

Ko, P.Y., & Adamson, B. (2011). Pedagogy and human dignity – the Special Rank Teacher in China since 1978. *History of Education, 40*, 279. doi:10.1080/0046760X.2010.529829.

Ko, P. Y., & Marton, F. (2004). Variation and the secret of virtuoso. In A. B. M. Tsui & F. Marton (Eds.), *Classroom discourse and the space of learning* (pp. 43–62). Mahwah: Erlbaum.

Lau, D. C. (1979). *The analects of Confucius*. London: Penguin.

Li, Z. (1992). 李忠义自传 [The autobiography of Li Zhongyi]. In W. Wang (Ed.), 当代中学语文教育专家研究 [A study of contemporary Chinese language educators] (pp. 317–319). Beijing: Scientific Education Press.

Lin, J. (1991). *The Red Guards' path to violence*. New York: Praeger.

Liu, Y. 1992. 刘映辉自传 [The autobiography of Liu Yinghui]. In W. Wang (Ed.), 当代中学语文教育专家研究 [A study of contemporary Chinese language educators] (pp. 348–354). Beijing: Scientific Education Press.

Liu, G., & Zhang, D. (1996). 中国著名特级教师教学思想录 [The teaching ideology of famous special rank teachers in China]. Jiangsu: Jiangsu Education Press.

Löfstedt, J. (1980). *Chinese educational policy: Changes and contradictions*. Stockholm: Almqvist & Wiksell.

Lü, S. (1987). 吕叔湘论语文教育 [Lü, Shuxiang's comments on Chinese language teaching]. Zhengzhou: Henan Education Press.

Moore, R. W. (1984). *Master teachers*. Bloomington: Phi Delta Kappa Educational Foundation.

Ning, H. (1992). 宁鸿彬自传 [The autobiography of Ning Hongbin]. In W. Wang (Ed.), 当代中学语文教育专家研究 [A study of contemporary Chinese language educators] (pp. 213–223). Beijing: Scientific Education Press.

Ning, H. (1996). 宁鸿彬文选 [The selected articles of Ning Hongbin]. Guangxi: Lijiang Publisher.

Ouyang, D. (1992). 欧阳代娜自传 [The autobiography of Ouyang Daina]. In W. Wang (Ed.), 当代中学语文教育专家研究 [A study of contemporary Chinese language educators] (pp. 161–182). Beijing: Scientific Education Press.

Ouyang, D. (1996). 欧阳代娜 [Ouyang Daina]. In G. Liu & D. Zhang (Ed.), 中国著名特级教师教学思想录 [*The teaching ideology of famous Special Rank Teachers in China*] (pp. 395–442). Jiangsu: Jiangsu Education Press.

Qian, M. (1985). 语文导读法探索 [*The exploration on guided-reading approach on Chinese language*]. Yunan: Yunan People's Publisher.

Qian, M. (1992). 钱梦龙自传 [The autobiography of Qian Menglong]. In W. Wang (Ed.), 当代中学语文教育专家研究 [*A study of contemporary Chinese language educators*] (pp. 111–132). Beijing: Scientific Education Press.

Qian, M. (1996). 钱梦龙 [Qian Menglong]. In G. Liu & D. Zhang (Ed.), 中国著名特级教师教学思想录 [*The teaching ideology of famous Special Rank Teachers in China*] (pp. 537–606). Jiangsu: Jiangsu Education Press.

Shi, X., & Englert, P. A. J. (2008). Reform of teacher education in China. *Journal of Education for Teaching, 34*, 347–359.

Turk, M. (1992). *Foundations of excellence*. Paper presented at the Eighteenth Annual Conference of the Higher Education Research Society of Australia, Monash University Gippsland Campus, Churchill, Victoria.

Wang, J. C. F. (1999). *Contemporary Chinese politics*. Upper Saddle River: Prentice Hall.

Wang, W. (Ed.). (1992). 当代中学语文教育专家研究 [*A study of contemporary Chinese language educators*]. Beijing: Scientific Education Press.

Wei, S. (1995). 魏书生文选 [*The articles of Wei Shusheng*], Book I & II. Guangxi: Lijiang Publisher.

Wei, S. (1996). 魏书生 [Wei Shusheng]. In G. Liu & D. Zhang (Ed.), 中国著名特级教师教学思想录 [*The teaching ideology of famous Special Rank Teachers in China*] (pp. 798–842). Jiangsu: Jiangsu Education Press.

White, G. (1981). *Party and professionals: The political role of teachers in contemporary China*. New York: Sharpe.

White, W. F. (1991). Search for the excellent teacher and the emergence of the master teacher. *Journal of Instructional Psychology, 18*(2), 93–102.

Yan, Z. (1984). 三十年与四十年 [Thirty years and four years]. In G. Liu (Ed.), 我和语文教学 [*My relationship with language teaching*] (pp. 433–438). Beijing: People's Education Press.

Ye, C. (1984). 我从事语文教学研究工作的三阶段 [The three stages of my research on Chinese language teaching]. In Liu (Ed.), 我和语文教学 [*My relationship with language teaching*] (pp. 45–57). Beijing: People's Education Press.

Yu, X. (1991). *The encounter between John Dewey and the modern Chinese intellectuals: the case of the 1922 education reform*. USA: Bell & Howell Company.

Yu, Y. (1992). 于漪自传 [The autobiography of Yu Yi]. In W. Wang (Ed.), 当代中学语文教育专家研究 [*A study of contemporary Chinese language educators*] (pp. 1–3). Beijing: Scientific Education Press.

Yu, Y. (1996). 于漪 [Yu Yi]. In G. Liu & D. Zhang (Ed.), 中国著名特级教师教学思想录 [*The teaching ideology of famous Special Rank Teachers in China*] (pp. 3–28). Jiangsu: Jiangsu Education Press.

Zhang, L. (1991). 中国语文教育史纲 [*The history of Chinese language teaching*]. Hunan: Teachers' College Press.

Zhang, F. (1992). 张福深自传 [The autobiography of Zhang Fushen]. In W. Wang (Ed.), 当代中学语文教育专家研究 [*A study of contemporary Chinese language educators*] (pp. 261–290). Beijing: Scientific Education Press.

Zhang, C. (2001). *A collection of articles of the special rank teachers*. Hangzhou: Zhejiang Education Press.

Zhejiang Special Rank Teacher Association. (2002). *Special rank teachers' comments on classroom teaching reform*. Hangzhou: Zhejiang Education Press.

Chapter 6
Early Literacy Education in China: A Historical Overview

Nancy Pine and Zhenyou Yu

6.1 Introduction

Literacy teaching of young children remained essentially the same in China for 2,000 years, from the earliest days of the Chinese empire across tumultuous centuries to the beginning of the twentieth century. Although dynasties varied enormously, most literacy training of young children remained unchanged and was derived from ancient Chinese thinking and traditions, with only a little influence from outside China. A half century of change followed this period beginning in 1903 when the first preschools were founded. Political and cultural upheaval surrounded the 1911 collapse of the last dynasty, and the influential May 4th Movement of 1919 took root. Scholars returning from overseas, enamored of Western concepts, influenced education, and ancient Chinese traditions were pushed aside as irrelevant to modern needs.

In 1949 when the People's Republic of China was founded, another major change affected early literacy education. China turned to her then mentor, the Soviet Union, and shut out all other Western influences. Even after the 1960 split with the USSR that led to withdrawal of all advisors and technical support, Soviet educational policy and practice remained entrenched. Only when economic and political reform came to China 30 years later in the late 1970s, led by Deng Xiaoping (邓小平), did a restorative balance begin, integrating Western pedagogical literacy thinking with traditions deeply rooted in the culture and practices of the Chinese people. In the following sections we trace the themes of early literacy theory and practice as they flow across these time periods, adapting to the political and cultural shifts.

N. Pine (✉)
Education Department, Mount St. Mary's College, Los Angeles, CA, USA
e-mail: npine@msmc.la.edu

Z. Yu
Department of Pre-School Education, China Women's University,
Beijing, China

6.2 Period 1. From Ancient Times to 1900

6.2.1 Background

Starting before Confucius (孔子, 55–479 BCE) and stretching across millennia to the early twentieth century, the purpose of receiving an education, including literacy training, was to master the knowledge and acquire the moral integrity considered necessary to pass the imperial exams and win recognition in society. The exam content during that long period was the Confucian classics, memorized by child and adult alike even though children did not comprehend the meaning.

Suggested ways to educate young children of elite families emerged in texts during the Warring States period (475–221 BCE), but not until the Han dynasty (206 BCE-220) is there evidence of widespread circulation and acceptance of theories concerning instruction of small children (Kinney 1995). Early education focused on developing children's morality, so they could become government officials. The earliest extant writing on the topic, *Muyi Zhuan* (*Biographies of Maternal Paragons*) written by Xiang Liu (刘向, ca. 77–7 BCE), one of several Han thinkers, stresses two theories—making early childhood, including the prenatal stage, the starting point in a person's education and granting women an important role in the moral development of their children. Although throughout these millennia girls were not allowed to be part of the Imperial exam system, many became literate, some to a sophisticated degree, and they were frequently responsible for young children's first literacy learning.

Early education had two strands: literacy instruction and moral development. Although some scholars suggested children should not learn to write until 8 or 9 years of age because of their small hands and tender bones (Liao 2006), families often began a son's formal training at two or three when he could hold a brush, with the mother or nurse teaching him his first characters (Cleverly 1985). Families bent on producing Imperial scholars began preparation prenatally. The back of the pregnant woman's mirror was to be inscribed with "Five Sons Pass the Examinations." To have a chance of bearing a gifted son, she must follow proper ways to sit, avoid certain foods, not talk arrogantly, and listen to poetry and the Confucian classics read aloud (Yu 2003). Records of child prodigies in chronicles of the Han Dynasty show some having mastered difficult texts, such as the Confucian *Analects*, as early as 7 years old.

In 124 BCE, Emperor Wu Di (汉武帝; ruled 141–87 BCE), who had declared Confucianism the official state philosophy, created five institutes aligned with the Five Confucian Classics (五经): *The Book of Changes* (易经), *The Book of History* (书经 or 尚书), *The Book of Rites* (礼记), *The Book of Songs* (诗经), and *The Spring and Summer Annals* (春秋). Later the Four Books (四书) were added: *The Analects of Confucius* (论语, a record of speeches and discussions by Confucius and his disciples), *Mencius* (孟子, a collection of conversations of the scholar Mencius with kings of his time), and two chapters from *The Book of Rites—The Great Learning* (大学) and *The Doctrine of the Mean* (中庸). Together, these works outlined the principles of society and government, as well as codes for personal conduct, and were central not just to Imperial exams up to the twentieth century but for several centuries were the texts used for young children's early literacy education even though the children did not understand them (Zhang 2004).

Children entered a school, usually a *Si Shu*, (私塾) at age eight (seven by Western calculations) where more formal learning began. Privately run, a *Si Shu* took a variety of forms (Han 1997). One type was conducted in a home by a family-hired tutor and was likely to have from one to ten students attending from the immediate and neighboring families. Another type was run by tutors in their own village and might be in their home or a community building, such as a temple.

6.2.2 Pedagogy and Curriculum of Early Literacy

Both preschool and primary school students learned to read and write Chinese characters through memorization. The pattern was so consistent over more than 2,000 years that eighteenth and nineteenth century descriptions of learning appear to hold considerable accuracy for much earlier times (Wu 1995). One author wrote the following description of his schooling, looking back on his small town upbringing and the arrangement of the family school where he and his relatives studied and where the tutor lived.

> To the left of the screen-wall stood a small house with a hall and two large rooms which was built to be the family school....I loved to listen to the older children chanting and reciting the classics. The central wall contained a small shrine for the written image of Confucius. Our tutor [lived in] two rooms. In front of the hall was a small garden....A huge thorny tree, called a Tseng...will always remain in my memory. None of my cousins will forget it either, for it could be seen from our desks in the hall, and our eyes were always fixed on it while we recited the classics to our tutor, especially if the recitations were difficult. It gave shade in the heat of summer, and when the tutor allowed us a little rest we would sit or play under it. (Yee 1940, pp. 22–23)

In a much earlier account Chong Wang (27–97) (王充), a Han scholar, wrote in his autobiography about strenuous instruction and how he had to learn to behave with politeness, honesty, benevolence, obedience, propriety, and reverence. He recounts they were whipped for bad writing and daily he read a "thousand characters from *The Analects* and *Shu Jing* [书经, *The Book of History*]" (quoted in Kinney 1995, p. 37).

Tutors were often those who had studied long years for the Imperial exams but had not scored high enough to receive a government post (Han 1997). They had spent their lives studying the Confucian classics and had no knowledge of how to work as a farmer or help in their family's business. Therefore, they could do nothing for a livelihood except teach children. They had no pedagogical training. Memorization and recitation of the classics was the only method they knew for teaching students to read and write.

Character recognition was stressed first. Comprehension came later. According to Zisheng Pan (潘子声) of the Qing Dynasty in *A Dictionary for Young Children* (养蒙针度), every child begins by recognizing characters, and later learns to read and write (Compilation Commission 1990). Learning focused only on the form and pronunciation of characters. Meaning in context was ignored. It was believed beginning readers should not be allowed to read texts until after they recognized many characters. Nevertheless, in ancient China, in contrast to today, those able to recognize a few Chinese characters were considered literate. Over the millennia, teaching strategies remained quite similar. Memorizing, copying exact character forms, and plenty of punishment were central to becoming literate. Students recited in groups at school. Then after school they had to practice the material individually in order to commit it to memory.

Although the West saw a transformation from oral to silent reading, with reading aloud to oneself considered the mark of a poor reader, no such shift occurred in China. A walk across the schoolyard of modern Chinese elementary schools is accompanied by a chorus of strong voices reading or reciting textbook passages. In outdoor spaces before high school and college classes, students are seen bent to their books as they walk and recite, memorizing texts. The tradition dates back thousands of years and seems to have proven efficient or comfortable for teaching children to read in Chinese. For many, the repeated readings emphasize the beauty and cadence of the language and help uncover textual meaning. A saying known to many today is, "Du shu bai bian, qi yi zi jian" (读书百遍, 其义自见; "If you read or recite a book 100 times, the meaning of the book will come out naturally.") This belief was common centuries ago and continues to be an essential part of China's current pedagogical practices.

Historical descriptions are peppered with stories that laud early memorization abilities at 5 years or so. For instance, when he was seven, the mother of a Ming statesman supervised his memorization of *The Classic of Filial Piety* (孝经) until he could recite it without mistakes. Mothers and tutors had young children recite aloud repetitively and memorize various texts before they taught them to recognize characters. At other times character recognition and oral recitation of memorized texts went hand in hand.

Details of how children should learn to memorize and recite were spelled out by some. When reading, as suggested in Yòu Xùn (幼训; *Early Children Training*) by Xuegu Cui, a Qing dynasty scholar, the reader

> should not increase or omit characters, and should not repeat over and over again. The voice shouldn't be too high or too low, too fast or too slow. The worst is if, while reading, the child gets excited and reads like a croaking frog, or when bored, like buzzing flies. (Compilation Commission 1990, pp. 81–82)

Educators of ancient times combined character-recognition and character-writing with adherence to good behavior and high morals. Xi Zhu (朱熹, 1130–1200), an influential Confucian of the Song Dynasty, proposed in *The Analects of Zhu Zi II* (朱子语类辑略. 卷二), that when children read aloud, they needed to do three things: concentrate the mind, focus the eyesight, and move the tongue and mouth. To write clearly a student must form characters carefully, stroke by stroke, but also with his heart fully engaged.

In later centuries, methods were developed for adults to teach young children to read and understand difficult parts of texts (Liao 2006). Concrete strategies to aid character recognition developed. One educator instructed adults to have children listen carefully to each sentence and pay close attention to the individual characters, so they could read the text in front of their peers without any mistakes. Wooden character blocks were also suggested to help learning. Xuegu Cui explained in detail how to teach children characters using cards or books. In "Instructions for Children" he wrote:

> What about recognizing characters on cards? Generally, at the beginning of learning, one should not hasten to teach children to read books. Instead, make small cards and write a single character on the front of the card. On the back write a different character with the same pronunciation. For example "文" [wén, *article*] and "闻" [wén *hearing*], "张" [zhāng, *opening*] and "章" [zhāng, *chapter*], and teach them one at a time.
>
> What about recognizing characters from books? Choose books they have never read. First teach them the words in the books one by one. Circle them with a red brush, and then write them down on the top of the book with black ink. This is the best way to help children recognize the words. (Compilation Commission 1990, p. 79)

Others suggested textbooks could be used for teaching students to write, as well as to read, and writing characters would help children better recognize the characters (Liao 2006). Although there is some evidence the above strategies were used, most tutors of young children appear to have found straight recitation and copying more expedient (Leung 1994; Yu 2003). All assumed connecting character recognition to text meaning was unnecessary for young children.

As this millennia-long period moved towards a close, Yun Wang (王筠, 1784–1854), a philologist in the Qing Dynasty, pointed out in *The Methods of Teaching Children* (教童子法) that teachers should adhere strictly to a step by step process guided by children's developmental sequence (Zhang 2004). Through what he called "practical teaching," he proposed learning strategies that moved away from memorization of texts or isolated copying of characters. He wrote:

> It is unnecessary to read the books intensively. Instead, the ideographic character form should be taught first. For example, teach them the characters of "日" and "月" [*sun* and *moon*], by pointing at the sun and moon in the sky. To teach children "上" and "下" [*up* and *down*], one can point out the character structures to show them. (Li 1990, p. 33)

He also suggested once children recognized the characters, they could be taught other characters through combining elements of the written forms.

Yi (1994) points out that in all time periods, textbooks are one of the most important factors affecting children. This must have been especially true during the long feudal period when Confucian texts dominated. Child-oriented rhymes began to develop quite early, and at times ethical jingles were created for children to sing and memorize (Zhang 2004). Primer-like books with simple character patterns were developed as early as the Qin (221-207 BCE) and Han dynasties (221 BCE-220 CE), but only a few families had access to them. Nevertheless, although pedagogy remained relatively static across the centuries, texts became increasingly appealing and more comprehensible for children.

6.2.3 Textbooks

The oldest known textbooks used for young learners were *The Three-Character Classic* (三字经), an early primer written in rhymes with simple characters, and *The Names of a Hundred Families* (百家姓) (CNSECE 2003; Liu 1985). Both appeared during the Song dynasty (960–1279). With the help of a tutor, children learned to recognize the Chinese characters in these books, as well as write them. *The Three-Character Classic*, one of the first books children memorized, contains a little over 1,000 Chinese characters and only 514 new ones. Directed at both the child and the tutor, the text includes general pedagogical advice infused with moral declarations and admonishments. The following is an excerpt from the book with translations done by Zhuzhang Guo (2004). The first verse reads:

> 人之初　　性本善　　性相近　　习相远
> [Men at their birth
> Are naturally good.
> Their natures are similar,
> And their habits become widely different.]

It then continues with several hundred more lines of advice such as:

> 养不教　　父之过　　教不严　　师之惰
> [To feed without teaching
> Is the father's fault.
> To teach without severity
> Is the teacher's laziness.]
> 子不学　　非所宜　　幼不学　　老何为
> [If the child does not learn,
> This is not as it should be.
> If he does not learn while young,
> What will he be when old?]
> 首孝弟　　次见闻　　知某数　　识某文
> [Begin with filial piety and fraternal love,
> And then see and hear to learn.
> Learn to count,
> And learn to read.]

The book also includes historical and cultural information and descriptions of the natural world.

稻粱菽　　麦黍稷　　此六谷　　人所食
[Rice, millet, pulse,
Wheat, glutinous millet and common millet,
These six grains,
Are those which men eat.]
马牛羊　　鸡犬豕　　此六畜　　人所饲
[The horse, the ox, the sheep,
The fowl, the dog, the pig.
These six animals,
Are those which men keep.]

The Names of a Hundred Families (百家姓), composed in the early Song dynasty (960–1279 CE), placed all of the surnames of the time in rhyming lines of eight characters (Tom 1989). Although nonsensical, it provided children characters to copy and recite.

In the *Thousand-Character Text* (千字文), which was often the next book to be memorized (Cleverly 1985), verse after verse provides general and historical knowledge, as well as Confucian morality. The following verses from the *Thousand-Character Text*, translated by Guo, show how young children were taught the characters even though they could not comprehend most of the text.

盖此身发　　四大五常　　恭惟鞠养　　岂敢毁伤
[Human bodies are from the four main substances,
Man's minds should cherish the five virtues or principles.
Every person should remember the parents' benevolence of rearing them,
And never harm or hurt their own bodies.]
都邑华夏　　东西二京　　背邙面洛　　浮渭据泾
[Among the cities of ancient China,
There were two capitals: one in the east and the other in the west.
The eastern capital, facing the Luo River, was in front of Mount Mang;
The western capital was situated in a place where the Wei River and the Jing River passed.]
矩步引领　　俯仰廊庙　　束带矜庄　　徘徊瞻眺
[When walking, people should be steady and easy in their manners;
Whether bending bodies or raising heads, people should behave themselves as seriously as in temples.
The dress people wear should look neat and dignified,
When taking walks or climbing high, people should pay attention to their appearances.]

Textbooks written especially for little children, such as *The Book of Stories* (书言故事), were also published in the Song dynasty. By the end of the thirteenth century, these and books such as *The Thousand Family Essay* (千家诗) and *Ethical Teachings* (弟子规) became increasingly more popular among schools. Filled with Confucian moral teachings, they were used for both little children and adults.

Child-oriented texts multiplied from then on and served different functions, but all stressed the combination of knowledge, moral principles, and evoking children's interest. They were sometimes illustrated with fine pictures (Zhang 2004). In one

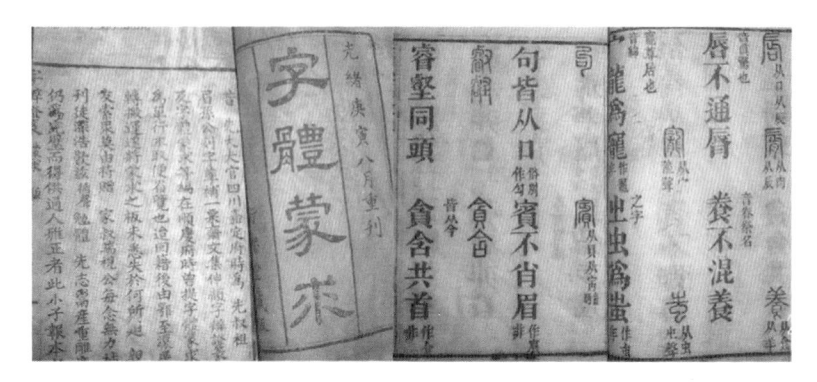

Fig. 5.1 Sample pages from *The ABCs of Chinese Font* (e.g., the *upper right corner* shows the various components that comprise the character 唇) (Photo by Zhenyou Yu)

type, illustrations accompanied a few words or sentences. During the Ming dynasty (1279–1369) illustrated books of all kinds, including those for children, were very popular (Yu 2003). They focused not just on words but on topics of the natural world, such as the four seasons and animals, so children were learning more than just character recognition (Gao 2007). In *A Newly Compiled Illustrated Four-Word Glossary* (新编对相四言), the earliest extant illustrated primer in the world, children "read" pictures about natural phenomena, such as the sun, moon, wind and clouds, animals and plants, and specific parts of the body, such as the eyes and nose. Another of these illustrated texts is *The Three-Character Book about the World* (名物三字书). Later, in the Qing dynasty (1636–1911), *The Initiatory Picture Book* (蒙养图说) and *The Twenty-Four-Picture Book for Filial Piety* (二十四孝图说) were compiled so children could read the pictures accompanying the stories (He 1990; Zhang 2004). In these books morality and nature went hand in hand with learning characters. For instance, in one story an older child gives the larger of two pears to a younger child and keeps the smaller one for himself.

Another type of textbook laid out rules for how to write Chinese characters. Unlike letters in an alphabet, children must learn which of the many strokes in a character is made first, in what direction, and how to balance the character within a square space. These texts were prepared so children, by copying from the book using a brush, could learn the controlled precision needed to write well. In *The ABCs of Chinese Font* (字体蒙求), first published in 1876, for instance, children were instructed about the various components of characters, including their origin and the different steps used to form each character (Fig. 5.1).

In China, traditional textbooks occupy a unique position. Many of those from ancient times remain a part of everyday life today. Published centuries ago, texts such as *The Three-Character Classic* continue to be read (Cleverly 1985). It is as though McGuffey's Readers were still popular in the United States of the twenty-first century.

6.3 Period 2. Early 1900s to the End of the 1940s

6.3.1 Background

Beginning in the twentieth century, early education in China passed through dramatic transformations and reflected the on-going national struggle to integrate and harmonize ancient Chinese wisdom and knowledge with Western ideas and experience (Lu 2001). External events, combined with internal political upheaval, had a profound effect on China. As early as 1840, foreign traders and missionaries began arriving. Through various maneuvers Western countries claimed rights in "unequal treaty" ports. In 1911 the increasingly weak Qing dynasty was overthrown by revolutionaries led by a hero of modern China, Sun Yat-sen (孙中山, 1866–1925), and the Republic of China was born.

The new government leaders introduced Western ideas that wrenched China from a deteriorating dynastic system to a republic and focused on radically changing her direction for the first time in centuries. Intellectual ferment culminated in the May 4th Movement of 1919, an anti-Imperialist, cultural, and political movement resulting from the Chinese government's response to the Treaty of Versailles. The movement led to an upsurge of Chinese nationalism and identified three areas of needed reform: "the emancipation of the individual person as an educational goal, the need for increased study of sciences, and the development of democracy" (Wang 2001, p. 297). It also provided the first major shift away from traditional educational concepts toward critically examining the role of Chinese education and the need for modernization (Wang 2001). The flowering of these new ideas and institutions was juxtaposed, however, against the chaos of Japanese encroachment and invasion from 1935 to 1945, and a year later, civil war between the Nationalists and the Communists that lasted until 1949.

In spite of these unstable and often disastrous times, intellectual ferment continued as China threw off the feudal mantle. More and more Chinese scholars returned from the West (mainly from the United States) and began to promote new education theories and practices. John Dewey, invited to spend 2 years lecturing in China (1919–1921) about his pragmatic theories and practices (Lu 2001), heavily influenced several areas of Chinese thought, including early childhood education.

6.3.2 Birth of Preschool Education

Beginning in the 1880s, Western missionaries attempted to start some preschools and teacher-training schools. The Qing dynasty, though generally dysfunctional, supported early childhood education. In 1903, the first public preschool and kindergarten, Hubei *Meng Yang Yuan*, was established. A year later a government document, the *Guimao Educational System*, confirmed the dynasty's commitment to preschool and kindergarten as formal educational institutions for young children, and the government founded a small number of them, including the Beijing No. 1 Preschool and Kindergarten and the Fujian Public Preschool and Kindergarten. By 1907, there were 428 preschools with 4,893 children attending (Liang 2003).

At first, the new Republic of China followed the early childhood education system put in place by the Qing dynasty, but 10 years later, in 1922, the avant-garde government circulated a new document entitled the *Renshu Educational System*, that led to the founding of more and more public and private preschools. These included the famous Demonstration Preschool and Kindergarten of Nanjing Normal School, the Nanjing Gulou Preschool and Kindergarten, and the Xiamen Jimei Preschool and Kindergarten (Shi 1999).

Through the 1930s early childhood education was led by the central government. Drawing heavily from Western theory and research, great difficulties emerged in implementing the new systems and curriculum. Because China had so few teachers, the first hired were babysitters from other countries. Three Japanese babysitters, for instance, were employed as teachers in the first public preschool in Hubei province, and people grew unhappy about the foreigner-dominated system. Also, until 1920, almost all preschool teachers were trained by missionaries. Although Christianity was not permitted, schools devoted considerable time to religion. Finally, as Western early childhood education theory and practice began to dominate teacher training schools, the new teachers promoted the reading and understanding of Western children's stories and picture books rather than recitation from Chinese primers and learning to recognize characters.

By 1927, Heqin Chen (陈鹤琴, 1892–1982), considered the father of Chinese preschool education, reflected the growing concern that China had turned too strongly toward the West. He wrote in an educators' magazine:

> Now almost all the preschools and kindergartens in China are like those in the USA. The stories children listen to are American ones and the pictures they see are American …That's not to say, that what is from America should not be used. Rather, it should not be copied (or imitated completely) because the two countries are quite different. (Compilation Committee 1990, p. 148)

He and other educators, such as Zonglin Zhang (张宗麟, 1899–1978), Xuemen Zhang (张雪门, 1891–1973), and Xingzhi Tao (陶行知, 1891–1946), worked assiduously to combine modern Western concepts with traditional Chinese practices in early education. They had studied in the United States and believed Western research and practice could help move China away from the traditional education system, but they wanted to explore how to do this without rejecting Chinese culture.

In the United States, Heqin Chen learned from Edward Thorndike and studied with John Dewey at Teachers College, Columbia University. He was committed to developing a Chinese education system based on research and Western knowledge about the psychological development of the child. Dewey's pragmatic approach of grounding education in everyday life and in meaningful experiences for children was important to Chen's emerging curriculum, Reading Methods (He 1990).

Upon returning to China, Chen continued to develop curriculum that incorporated practical suggestions and tried his Living Education theory in preschools. Based on his and others' ideas, the first uniform government document on early education in China, *Early Childhood Education Standards*, was created and circulated in 1932 and revised 4 years later. Unlike previous documents that completely copied Western ones, it successfully integrated Western theories while maintaining a Chinese context. It included seven learning areas, such as language, math, music, and drawing, as well as project methods.

During this time (especially 1930–1940), scholars such as Heqin Chen and Xingzhi Tao developed the majority of ideas for early childhood education. They applied the theories and standards to actual conditions in China, and through careful observation of children, practice, and experimentation, they developed a Chinese system for preschool and childhood education, including early literacy education.

6.3.3 Pedagogy and Curriculum of Early Literacy

Although many still followed traditional pedagogical paths that resembled preparation for the Imperial exams (Cleverly 1985), new teaching and learning methods, as well as new content, sprang up as the purpose of education shifted towards developing Chinese men and women conversant with the modern world (Beijing Academic Society 1989).

In past centuries early literacy education, infused with morality, was the only component of early childhood education. In the new Republic it became one part of a diverse curriculum along with math, drawing, and other subjects. Children no longer spent long hours making exact copies of characters and reading them in isolation. Instead, literacy learning was embedded in reading, writing, listening, and speaking activities. Rhymes and story learning, observation and daily oral talk were encouraged (Zhao 2001). In *Government Guidelines of Education* (1904) of the Qing dynasty, curriculum domains included "play, songs and rhymes, oral talk, and manipulation skills" (Compilation Committee 1990, p. 9) The reworked *Preschool and Kindergarten Curriculum Standard* (1936), developed by the Ministry of Education of the Republic of China, stated in the section on "Stories and Rhymes" that children were to "read various pictures of stories," and teachers should ask them to talk about the pictures and create their own meaningful stories in simple Chinese (Compilation Committee 1990, p. 232). Even in Yan'an, the revolutionary area of the Communists in northern Shaanxi Province, that includes Xi'an and Yan'an, in the midst of war their No. 1 Child Care Center included early literacy education, such as reading newspapers and recognizing characters, as one of several curriculum areas (He 1990).

Another critical change was that children no longer had to read primers in the ancient Chinese language. Rather, they read stories and rhymes in vernacular Chinese, which meant the literacy learning process became much easier and more meaningful for them.

New story books became early childhood reading material, and the Confucian classics were abandoned. Traditional Chinese and Western translated folk stories, such as *Little Sparrow*, the *Race between the Tortoise and the Rabbit*, and selections about Monkey's adventures from *Journey to the West* were among these (Li et al. 2006). According to the standard for choosing texts in the Demonstration Preschool and Kindergarten of Nanjing Normal School where some curriculum was piloted, traditional and folk stories, historical stories, finger-play rhymes, and songs were to be included in the language curriculum. In addition, such picture books as *Introductory Physics* (物理引蒙) and *Children's Stories* (儿童故事) were to be available for youngsters to read in order to learn about natural science.

As the variety of children's textbooks increased, books translated from other languages appeared. *Peachy Clouds*, a play written by a Japanese author in 1921, *Little John*, a fairy tale by Eeden, a Dutch writer, in 1887, and *A Watch*, a fairy tale written by Panteleev, a Russian, in 1928 were translated by the well-known author Xun Lu (鲁迅; 1881–1936) and became outstanding reading material of the time (Yi 1994). The first children's magazines such as *Child Monthly* (小孩月报), *Child Pictorial* (成童画报), and *Children in Shanghai* (上海儿童) were launched. Books for recognizing characters, published by Business Affairs Press and Chinese Bookstore Press, included colorful pictures, and their style adhered to children's cognitive development (Beijing Academic Society 1989).

The methodological shift placed character learning in meaningful contexts. Children were taught to recognize words, such as their names or the character(s) for their favorite animal, which they would remember because they were connected to their personal lives. When teachers read stories, they showed children the pictures to help transmit word meaning and involve them in the story action. The scholar and reformer Youwei Kang (康有为, 1858–1927) said, "We should teach children to speak and read as they are able. Models and pictures are helpful for children's development of knowledge and skills, including recognizing characters" (Chen 1998, p. 265).

Heqin Chen's ideas about early literacy education were put into practice in the Nanjing Gulou Preschool and Kindergarten he founded in 1923 and later in other schools (Yi 1994). The core of Chen's Reading Methods was to engage children in reading picture-stories, to "draw" characters related to pictures, and to recognize them in daily life. To help children learn characters, Chen thought teachers should attend to the following principles:

i. Various materials, such as pictures, handiwork, stories, and rhymes should be used to interest children in imagining and recognizing characters.
ii. Reading material should come from children's daily life, and isolated drills should be avoided.
iii. What children learned to read and recognize should be connected with the content they were learning in other domains.
iv. Mistakes children made when reading or recognizing characters should be corrected at once. (He 1990, pp. 169–170)

Heqin Chen wrote in *Our Opinions* that teachers needed to use textbooks preschoolers could understand without struggling. If their attention wandered, they should change to a new activity. He also suggested teachers use pictures to help 3-year-olds identify characters, and 4-years-olds could learn characters when teachers read picture-story books to small groups or used slide shows (Beijing Academic Society 1989).

Some of the ideas from this period of early literacy learning are used in preschools today. For example, in teaching children to learn to recognize and write characters, teachers first tell a story with the help of pictures, so the youngsters become interested. Then they ask them to draw or color pictures about the story. Finally, they encourage the children to write some Chinese characters in their pictures that interest them.

Over the years, beginning with the opening of China to Western ideas in the early twentieth century, a paradigm shift was occurring in relation to the function of writing and the purpose of learning to write. Although the period from 1950 to 1980 wrought havoc in education, this paradigm shift held steady and grew to fruition after 1980.

6.4 Period 3. 1950 to 1980

6.4.1 Background

During ancient times, early literacy teaching ideas were drawn from Chinese culture. In the second period, during the first half of the twentieth century, teaching strategies were developed by integrating Western and Chinese ideas. From 1950 to 1980, however, the USSR became the source of teaching ideas for early childhood education. Beginning with the founding of the People's Republic of China on October 1, 1949, all social systems in China were copied from the Soviet Union, and the Soviet educational model became the foundation for China's schools. Traditional Chinese pedagogy, as well as Western ideas, were rejected. Even the Living Education and project methods of Heqin Chen and other scholars were abandoned. The widely accepted motto at the time was: "Reject everything from the old society" (Shi 1999).

For the first time in China's long history, universal education became a serious goal. Although it was not achieved in rural areas for many decades, in the cities all children, including girls, were required to attend school. In June 1960, however, a rift that had been growing between China and the USSR erupted. All Soviet advisers left, taking with them even the blueprints for in-process construction projects. Nevertheless, the Soviet-style education system continued because everything else had been discarded. Since China was closed to the outside world, the only education policies and models were those left behind by the USSR. Both research and pedagogy after 1960 followed the Russian model even though the Chinese did not want this and, for political reasons, did not mention it.

The Cultural Revolution followed from 1966 to 1976. Preschools and elementary schools remained open even when junior and senior high schools and universities were closed. Their curriculum mirrored the always-changing upheavals of political and pedagogical currents. This was the most limited of the four periods. In ancient times, although China was closed to the outside world, it had a rich cultural tradition to draw from that had developed over thousands of years. In the second period, China was open to the West, but during the third period, for 30 years she closed her door to everything except Russian thought.

6.4.2 Pedagogy and Curriculum

In the Soviet system, children began literacy education in elementary school. Preschool did not include reading instruction (Mou 2004), and from the 1950s to 1980s no documents disseminated by the Chinese government mentioned early literacy education (Zhou 2005).

Preschool children's reading skills were developed only through talking about pictures during language lessons (Textbook Editing Group 1982). Teachers could also read stories to children, repeat rhymes, and engage them in oral language play. Literacy training began when children reached first grade, with emphasis placed on pronunciation, learning the meaning of characters in isolation, and memorizing as many characters as possible, so they could read texts about other subjects. First-grade children were also taught *pinyin*, an alphabetic system that helps beginning readers identify the sound associated with characters.

Russian pedagogy held that knowledge is paramount and should be learned systematically, based on the teaching principles developed by Zankof, a Russian educator and psychologist. The pedagogy linked teaching to development, with difficult knowledge used to arouse special cognitive processes. In preschool different subjects required discrete types of knowledge that were often abstract and far removed from children's everyday life. Chinese educators seldom discussed Russian pedagogy during these years. Teachers just copied the Russian teaching style.

A debate persisted, however, about what was appropriate for young children to learn. The first draft of *Interim Provisions of Early Childhood Education*, sent to delegations attending the first national meeting on primary education in July 1951, included recommendations to teach older preschoolers to recognize Chinese characters encountered in daily life, such as their names and common articles like "chair." Apparently there was no agreement among officials or scholars, though, for when the final policy document was disseminated by the Ministry of Education in 1952, only oral language activities were included. Preschool teachers were forbidden to instruct children in writing or reading characters.

A second argument focused on whether preschoolers should be taught pinyin, which was considered the foundation for learning characters. Discussions and experiments in preschools were carried out in the 1950s, with some researchers and scholars believing 5- and 6-year-olds could learn pinyin while 6- and 7-year-olds could learn characters with the help of pinyin.

Such varied beliefs translated into mixed messages for practitioners. In spite of the ban on teaching characters, for instance, occasional directives said that "some children" could be taught pinyin and characters in preschool. In addition, government policy makers and educational scholars came to different conclusions about research results, leaving up in the air questions about when and what young children should be taught. The Ministry of Education and All-China Women's Federation suggested in a document July 1960, that preschools and kindergartens with the "right conditions" could teach the children pinyin, mathematics, and also Chinese characters. It urged that various methods and teaching aids be developed and used well, and recommended plays, rhymes and songs, stories, music, and gymnastics for high-quality early childhood education (CNSECE 1999, p. 112).

Interestingly, ignoring conflicting policies and disagreements, almost all parents taught their preschool-aged children to recognize and write individual characters they thought were important for elementary school. Even in rural areas where adult literacy was very low and universal schooling had not started, parents knew the importance of having their young children develop the ability to read and write. Literate or not, parents found others who knew how, neighbors or older children who attended school, and had them teach their children.

Although the arguments continued, toward the end of this period when the country was beginning to reestablish its educational institutions, experiments with early literacy in preschool and kindergarten showed positive results. For instance, Huang and Lu (1982) carried out several experiments between 1978 and 1982 that found preschoolers, even at age three, could recognize characters if appropriate methods were used. They also found that early literacy experiences positively affected children's achievement in Chinese language and math examinations at the end of grade one.

Because some preschools and kindergartens advocated and taught early literacy, a few rudimentary principles circulated among educators and researchers. For instance, to teach reading skills, teachers should use pictures meaningful to the children, and when they told children about something, they should point to it. When using several pictures, they should show them one by one to help children concentrate. In addition, they should ask age-appropriate, interesting questions (Textbook Editing Group 1982). To teach pinyin and characters, teachers, using a variety of aids, should ask children to recognize those useful in daily life and ensure they were having fun while learning (Mou 2004).

6.5 Period 4. 1980 to Present

6.5.1 Background

In 1978 China opened her door to other countries in order to pursue social and economic development, and found everything was new outside. After the Cultural Revolution, pursuit of a sound educational system was key to progress, but because high schools, universities, and normal schools had been closed for 10 years, the challenge was immense. Deng Xiaoping (邓小平, 1904–1997) understood it well :

> Education is the most fundamental undertaking of a nation. The realization of the *Four Modernizations* (i.e., modernization of agriculture, industry, national defense, and society and technology) depends on knowledge and skilled manpower. An error in policy can be rectified fairly easily, but knowledge cannot be acquired at once, nor can skilled manpower be trained in a few days. This is the reason why education must be conducted in real earnest, and started from early childhood. (Deng 1995, p. 140)

Between the late 1970s and the early 1980s China rebuilt the Soviet style education system (Shi 1999). Not only were many urban preschools and kindergartens restarted quickly, but a lot were set up in rural areas. Tasks and goals of early childhood education were affirmed in government documents (CNSECE 1999), but early literacy was essentially excluded. In the preliminary *Urban Preschool Regulations*, circulated for discussion by the Ministry of Education in 1979, for instance, the teachers' main task was to care for and educate children, with health and physical exercise, play and work, and moral lessons included in the curriculum, but not literacy. *Guidelines for Preschool Education* (Draft), distributed by the Ministry of Education in 1981, retained the 1951 Soviet structure and expanded curriculum considerably to healthy behaviors, physical exercise, moral lessons, language, general knowledge, math, music, and art, but in the language domain the only mention of early literacy education was that older children should be encouraged to enjoy reading and talking about books. However, in *Care and Education Guidelines for Children Under 3* (Draft), from the Ministry of Hygiene in 1981, literacy education was omitted. A draft or a trial document is distributed for testing its viability and for using experimentally.

Because schools and universities had been closed for so long, the whole country was in dire need of teachers, textbooks, and updated knowledge for the droves of students seeking high school and college certificates. Some qualified teachers returned to preschools and kindergartens, but there were not enough. Many untrained individuals were hired. However, immediately after 1978, normal schools for early childhood education were set up and 22 were operating within a year. By the 1990s, some preservice training programs for preschools were upgraded to universities, such as Beijing Normal University and Nanjing Normal University (Tian 2005).

International communication between China and the rest of the world was restored, and new theories and practices were introduced to early childhood education. Experts from different countries were invited to help fill the professional void caused by the Cultural Revolution, with many Westerners hired to teach in colleges and universities. Chinese scholars were sent abroad to study or interview experts. The foreign educational theories of Dewey, Montessori, Bronfenbrenner, Bruner, and especially Piaget and Vygotsky, began to spread throughout China (Zhu 2002), challenging the existing early childhood education system. Preschool textbooks were published according to government guidelines in 1982–1983, contributing greatly to the reconstruction of early childhood education.

Although research was sparse, even in the 1980s a few experiments on integrating Western and Chinese traditional experiences had begun in a few preschools. In 1983, researchers carried out an experiment at the Nanjing Experimental Preschool and Kindergarten on integrating curriculum areas, and in 1984, the China National Institute for Educational Research did a similar experiment in two Beijing preschools (Shi 1999).

6.5.2 Pedagogy and Curriculum

In this fourth period, China moved from copying or importing Western theory and practices to adapting them to local needs and exploring culturally relevant practices in early literacy learning and education. Early childhood curriculum reform began with spontaneous experiments in different parts of the country. For example, Jishi Zhao conducted research about Preschool Integrated Curriculum based on two important Western ideas. The first was Piaget's constructivism and the concept that children develop through direct interaction with people, objects, and events. The second was the proposition by Bronfenbrenner that development is a function of the interaction between the developing person and the changing environment (Zhao 2001). In 1989 *Preschool and Kindergarten Work Regulations and Procedures* (Trial Version) issued by the National Education Committee (the former Ministry of Education) accelerated research when it introduced progressive theories and practices to early childhood educators (Zhu and Zhang 2008).

Dynamic new research results taking root in the West deeply influenced Chinese early childhood education. The concepts of emergent literacy, early literacy, prereading, and early reading were opening new vistas in the U.S. and Britain. Research on invented spelling, use of environmental print, and emergent writing blossomed in preschool classrooms there and was coupled with the thrust to expose all children to books and print experiences at an early age in order to prevent reading difficulties (Snow et al. 1998). At the same time, in China, a paradigm shift related to the function of emergent reading and writing and methods of teaching preschool literacy was occurring. It had begun in the early twentieth century as Chinese educators like Heqin Chen tried to shake off the ancient model of memorization and isolated character learning. The impetus from new Western research in the 1980s and 1990s led to increased momentum to change the nature of preschool literacy instruction in China. However, when and how to teach literacy puzzled the teachers of young children. They were learning traditional teaching methods but knew these did not fit the new concepts.

Chinese scholars began to study curriculum needs and to carry out classroom research. By 1988, Jishi Zhao (1988) had recommended the teaching of literacy, including listening, speaking, and literature, in preschool, and her later research suggested young children would benefit from adults reading aloud to them and enlivening book characters, answering teachers' questions about the pictures, and reading enjoyable picture books themselves (Zhao and Lou 1993).

Jing Zhou's research suggested goals for early literacy education should focus on helping children become interested in written language and understanding the relationships between oral and written language, and early literacy education should include pre-reading, as well as pre-writing (Zhou 1995). In book reading activities, for example, children should be encouraged to recognize the characteristics of print, then understand and retell stories, and finally make their own picture books. In so doing they would learn the function and structure of characters and how to use different writing and drawing tools.

By the end of the 1990s, early literacy had gained considerable importance, a result of both research and new governmental directives. *Guidelines for Preschool and Kindergarten Education (Trial Version)*, publicized by the Ministry of Education in 2001, explicitly included early literacy goals. Teachers needed to interest children in reading picture books, encourage them to explore simple symbols and characters from daily life, and develop their pre-reading and pre-writing skills.

Since then, children's early literacy education has been recognized as important to overall development, and it has been generally accepted that teachers and parents should promote early literacy in the preschool years (Zhou 2007). Teachers have been encouraged to explore effective activities, and scholars have been asked to study and solve theoretical and practical problems.

Nevertheless, disagreement exists among teachers (Ouyang and Zhang 2003) and parents (Tang 2003) about what activities and strategies are appropriate and effective to support reading habits and children's interest in recognizing characters. Some have shown no understanding of early literacy. For example, many teachers, especially older ones, still think early literacy means primarily teaching children pinyin and recognizing and writing isolated characters (Ouyang and Zhang 2003). Changing these perspectives is a major challenge.

New types of activities have been introduced to develop young children's beginning literacy skills, and preschool teachers have begun to enjoy teaching with these activities (Yu 2005; Zhou 1995). So that children can casually learn the functions of written language, teachers now provide character-rich environments with signs such as "积木角" [block corner] beside the block area and "桌" [table] stuck to the table. They record children's stories and post them for all to enjoy. They help children read picture books and discuss plot and character roles in order to engage them in extended discourse (see Fig. 5.2). And in preschool, teachers now encourage children to communicate by using drawings and their own invented symbols, as well as conventional characters, as in Figs. 5.3 and 5.4.

6 Early Literacy Education in China: A Historical Overview 99

Fig. 5.2 Picture book sharing. A teacher shares a big picture book with several children and encourages them to talk about it (Photo by Zhenyou Yu)

Fig. 5.3 Writing sample produced by a 5-year-old girl. The child recorded her teachers' favorite sports. The "sentences" read:
Miss Boring's favorite sport is bowling
Miss Feng's favorite sport is swimming
Mr. Yu's favorite sport is playing basketball (Photo by Zhenyou Yu)

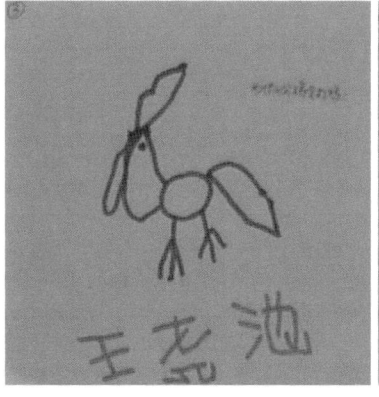

Fig. 5.4 Student-teacher joint writing. Two children drew a picture, their teachers recorded the questions they asked, and the children signed their names. On the *left*, Yaochi Wang (王尧池) asked, "Why does a cock crow?" On the *right*, Tuotuo's (拓拓) question was, "Why does a cock have a crest?"(All photos by Zhenyou Yu)

New strategies for early literacy instruction have spread among preschool teachers. Unlike the type of literacy teaching done at the beginning of elementary school—where children must adhere to strict instruction on how to write characters correctly and must comprehend and memorize whole texts—preschool teachers are beginning to help children learn to pre-read and pre-write in authentic contexts, using such items as newspaper advertisements and storybooks. They are learning that children can acquire Chinese characters casually in different activities, including play, picture book reading, and everyday life experiences. This is a completely different perspective from previous periods of early literacy teaching.

Picture books are now used widely in preschools. By 2008, at government request, almost all preschool classes had their own reading area where every child had access to many books (CNSECE 1999). Children are encouraged to read and enjoy them during their free time. Teachers also read them aloud to help youngsters understand what happened in a book, and encourage them to use reading strategies, such as commenting on character roles, speculating about how a story will develop, and comparing story events with their own experiences (Yu 2009).

However, a rift continues between modern theories and practices and parents' beliefs about what their only child needs (Tang 2003). Many parents continue to care more about how many characters their children learn than whether they can use literacy for multiple purposes. This tradition, dating back to ancient times, is ingrained in Chinese parents. They think the more characters a child knows, the brighter he or she is. Not only do they teach their children at home to recognize as many characters as possible, but also they put pressure on teachers to provide more traditional academic instruction, including teaching more characters. By doing this they believe they will provide their only child a fast start towards becoming economically successful in a future adulthood fraught with competition (Tobin et al. 2009).

6.5.3 Current Issues

In 2001, *Guidelines for Preschool and Kindergarten Education (Trial Version)* amplified the 1981 regulations, emphasizing meaningful and individualized early literacy learning, including children's rights and the promotion of independence and creativity. Activity theory, developed from work by Vygotsky (1896–1934) and Leontiev (1903–1979), provided a theoretical framework for the guidelines (Feng 1997). Even so, it has been difficult for practitioners to fully embrace this progressive ideology since powerful and deep-rooted Chinese cultural traditions run counter to modern scientific and democratic ideas (Wang and Mao 1996). Preschool teachers, for example, spend less time reading books to children or encouraging reading activities than they do on other classroom matters even though they understand their importance. They also still spend considerable time teaching children to recognize and write isolated characters even though it does not help increase their pre-reading and pre-writing skills (Yu 2006).

In addition, contemporary scholars such as Yan Liu and XiaoXia Feng (2005) have identified gaps in China's early childhood education reform: new top-down policies are disconnected from classroom practice, new theories conflict with embedded educational practice, and current educational realities are often distant from projected ideals. Different reasons have been suggested for these gaps. Zhu and Zhang (2008), for instance, argued the conflict between Western and Chinese cultures is the reason, with Chinese people considered more social unit-oriented and extrinsically motivated, and Westerners more individual-oriented and intrinsically motivated.

With the reform movement accelerating in China, Western ideology has continued to influence the development of early childhood education. Different curricula, such as the Project Approach, Reggio Emilia, and Montessori, have been widely adopted and localized in urban preschools. Some scholars warn outside theories such as these must be used carefully and must take into account traditional Chinese culture and social issues, such as the one-child policy, the disequilibrium of social and economic development in different parts of China, and the rifts between urban and rural populations and developed and developing areas (Li and Li 2003; Zhu 2008).

Many preschool teachers prefer traditional methods, such as drilling children to recognize and memorize characters in picture books they read to them, and some copy foreign activities without understanding their purpose and without integrating them into Chinese culture. This does not mean they do not understand the new approaches at all, but they are deeply influenced by Chinese traditional values and parental attitudes. The *Guidelines* of 2001 include specific requirements and content in different domains in order to ensure early childhood innovations contain Chinese characteristics. Many preschools are trying to adhere to these. Tobin et al. (2009) found some preschools incorporated storytelling and socio-dramatic play activities that in fact helped "children who would grow up to be socially minded and recognizably Chinese" (p. 227).

6.6 Conclusions and Implications

This chapter traces the development of early literacy education in China through an analysis of perceptions, concrete strategies, and important influences across 2,000 years from ancient times to the present. Perceptions and strategies held relatively steady for centuries, and then changed dramatically in the twentieth century under the influence of shifting social, economic, and cultural policies.

In recent years, greater attention has been given to the role of early childhood education programs. The preschool years are now considered a critical period for acquiring important early literacy skills. Researchers, practitioners, parents, and policy makers are increasingly coming to the conclusion that more effort needs to be given to strengthening the quality of child care programs across China, so children develop essential beginning literacy skills in the preschool years and are prepared for entering the formal primary school setting. While some teachers and parents are making major strides in promoting activities that build these skills in preschools or at home, a large number encounter confusion. They are trying to employ "new" child-centered strategies they have learned from different sources, but these frequently fail because they do not know how to implement them.

For observers from outside China, it is critical to understand the economic and political background when examining early literacy education in China. Before the twentieth century, education was based on Confucianism and was didactic, controlling, and teacher-centered. The only goal was to memorize Confucian classics and pass the Imperial exams in order to gain a higher rank, a government position, and uphold family honor. Young children were expected to begin by recognizing and remembering characters in the Confucian classics. During the second period, Confucianism became the target of the transformational New Culture Movement, and Western educational theory and practice had considerable influence. Preschool education became less didactic and more child-centered. At the beginning it was imported in its entirety, but was gradually localized. After the founding of the People's Republic of China, previous methods and traditions were thrown out, and the USSR education system was copied across the board. Academic-oriented preschool education became the norm in China, and even though the Chinese-Soviet collaboration ended abruptly in 1960, the Russian system continued to influence preschool education practice. In the 1980s economic and social reforms became the motivation to learn from Western education theory and practice, with growing attempts to blend them with Chinese culture. However, many difficulties persist in how to transform early literacy practices into modern perspectives.

For preschool teachers, it is important to realize Chinese traditional culture must be considered when teaching children early literacy. Confucian values, as well as Soviet socialist pedagogy, remain ingrained in Chinese people's everyday lives and cannot be erased. Even the radical attempt that Mao Zedong made to obliterate all the old traditions in China did not work. These previously used strategies continue in teachers' and parents' minds and habits when they are learning new instructional practices, such as including daily experiences in their teaching. Preschool teachers need to understand how to make good use of their own prior experiences while implementing new practices. Rather than applying "new strategies" mechanically regardless of their appropriateness for children, preschool teachers must be helped to comprehend new theoretical foundations and how they can be used in practice. Finally, it is imperative for preschool teachers to attempt to understand parents' perceptions and to develop realistic activities for them to use at home.

For researchers of early literacy education, it is urgent to conduct in-depth experimental research projects on early literacy development and education for Chinese preschool-aged children. Because the Chinese written language is very different from English, approaches that are fitting for native English-speaking children are not necessarily helpful to Chinese children. So far, little has been learned about how young Chinese children develop their pre-reading and pre-writing skills (Zhou 2007). Literacy experts also need to spend time in preschool classrooms and need to conduct action research collaboratively with preschool teachers. They need to convert theoretical ideas into concrete strategies that can be mastered in realistic settings. In addition, Chinese researchers and teachers need to forge a new approach to early childhood literacy education by fusing ingrained

Confucian values with the influx of new ideas (Tobin 2007; Tobin et al. 2009; Zhu and Zhang 2008).

For policy makers, sensitivity to Chinese culture is essential when developing new ideas. Without this consideration, new policies will not be implemented effectively. Documents that explain new concepts, such as pre-reading and pre-writing in *Guidelines for Preschool Education (Trial Version)*, need to be developed so preschool teachers can understand how to implement them. Government documents play an important role in the preschool experience. If they merely state preschool teachers should foster children's early literacy without explaining instructional strategies, teachers will be at a loss for what to do. To this end, the Beijing Society of Early Childhood Education has formulated an implementation document in which the requirements of early literacy are more concrete. For example, it explains 3- to 4-year-olds should be encouraged to become interested in listening to adults reading, to learn to turn book pages one by one, and to find and talk about persons or objects in books that interest them (Beijing Education Commission 2006). Much more of this needs to be done.

The professional development of teachers is also essential if they are to organize diverse early literacy activities. They need access to high-quality, age-appropriate picture books and other print material, and more in-depth training to provide them with the latest research-based information on how to teach children early literacy skills. Many preschool teachers are used to traditional, subject-based curriculum and teacher-centered pedagogy and will need considerable help implementing the new curriculum and pedagogies. Finally, urban preschools and their teachers receive more support to promote early literacy development than their rural counterparts. More attention needs to be focused on how teachers working in rural or remote areas can receive support and training that will assist them in their efforts to help children acquire essential early literacy skills.

Although many challenges lie ahead, the pedagogical and theoretical shifts that have occurred in China since the early 1900s are significant. In spite of massive twentieth century political and social upheavals, a paradigm shift has occurred in early literacy education in China during these years. It has moved, and continues to move, from didactic and teacher-centered to more open and child-oriented. A recent document from the Chinese State Council (2010) stresses the need to make preschool education available to all children in China in the next 10 years. Despite all the historical twists and turns, there is reason to believe early childhood education in China will continue to grow in a positive direction.

References

Beijing Academic Society for Education. (1989). 陈鹤琴全集第五卷 [*Corpora of Chen Heqin (Vol. 5)*]. Nanjing: Jiangsu Education Publishing House.

Beijing Education Commission. (2006). 北京市贯彻《幼儿园教育指导纲要(试行)》实施细则 [*Rules for the implementation of guidance for kindergarten education in Beijing*]. Beijing: Tongxin Press.

Chen, H. (1998). 中国古代幼儿教育 [*History of ancient Chinese early childhood education*]. Guangzhou: Guangdong High Educational Press.

Chinese National Society of Early Childhood Education (CNSECE). (1999). 中华人民共和国幼儿教育重要文献汇编 [*Collections of important literature of early childhood education in the Republic of China*]. Beijing: Beijing Normal University Press.

Chinese National Society of Early Childhood Education (CNSECE). (2003). 百年中国幼教 [*Early childhood of one hundred years in China (1903–2003)*]. Beijing: Educational Science Publishing House.

Chinese State Council. (2010). 国家中长期教育改革和发展规划纲要(2010–2020) [*State educational reform and development plans for medium and long-term programs (2010–2020)*]. Retrieved from http://www.gov.cn/jrzg/2010-07/29/content_1667143.htm

Cleverly, J. (1985). *The schooling of China: Tradition and modernity in Chinese education*. Sydney: George Allen & Unwin.

Compilation Commission of Historic Research of Chinese Early Childhood Education (Compilation Commission). (1990). 中国学前教育史资料选 [*A selection of historic research of Chinese early childhood education*]. Beijing: People's Educational Publishing House.

Deng, X. (1995). 邓小平文选 [*The thematic quotations of Deng Xiaoping*]. Beijing: People's Publishing House.

Feng, X. (1997). 以活动理论为基础建构幼儿园课程 [Building the preschool curriculum based on the activity theory]. 学前教育研究 [*Preschool Education Studies Journal*], *4*, 22–26.

Gao, S. (2007). 中国教育史论丛 [*On the history of Chinese education*]. Fuzhou: Fujian Educational Press.

Guo, Z. ed. & Trans. (2004). 汉英对照蒙学精品 (第二分册) [*A Chinese-English collection of the best Chinese traditional primers (Vol. 2)*]. Wuhan: Wuhan University Press.

Han, N. (1997). 明清塾师初探 [On private tutors in Dynasties Ming and Qing]. 中国社会经济史研究, *3*, 15–23.

He, X. (1990). 简明中国学前教育史 [*Introduction to the history of Chinese early childhood education*]. Beijing: Beijing Normal University Press.

Huang, R., & Lu, L. (1982). 幼儿园识字教学实验研究 [Experiments about teaching children to recognize characters in kindergartens]. 南京师范学院学报, *4*, 1–6.

Kinney, A. B. (1995). Dyed silk: Han notions of the moral development of children. In A. B. Kinney (Ed.), *Chinese views of childhood*. Honolulu: University of Hawai'i Press.

Leung, A. K. C. (1994). Elementary education in the Lower Yangtze Region in the seventeenth and eighteenth centuries. In B. A. Elman & A. Woodside (Eds.), *Education and society in late imperial China* (pp. 1600–1900). Berkeley: University of California Press.

Li, G. (1990). 清代前期教育论 [*A selection of education works in early Qing Dynasty*]. Beijing: People's Educational Publishing House.

Li, H., & Li, P. (2003). 幼教改革三思而后行–从蒙氏教育与瑞吉欧教育热说起 (上) [Lessons from implanting Reggio and Montessori curriculum in China]. 幼儿教育, *4*, 4–5.

Li, G., Qi, M., & Qian, M. (2006). 中国近现代教育史资料汇编 (普通教育) [*Collection of research on history of modern Chinese education (general education)*]. Shanghai: Shanghai Educational Publishing House.

Liang, J. (2003). *The historic development of Chinese early education of 100 years*. October: Chinese Educational Newspaper. 23.

Liao, Q. (2006). 中国幼儿教育史 [*The history of Chinese early childhood education*]. Taiyuan: Shanxi Educational Press.

Liu, J. T. C. (1985). The classical Chinese primer: Its three-character style and authorship. *Journal of the American Oriental Society*, *105*(2), 191–196.

Liu, Y., & Feng, X. (2005). Kindergarten educational reform during the past two decades in mainland China: Achievements and problems. *International Journal of Early Years Education*, *13*(2), 93–99.

Lu, J. (2001). On the indigenousness of Chinese pedagogy. In R. Hayhoe & J. Pan (Eds.), *Knowledge across cultures: A contribution to dialogue among civilizations* (pp. 249–253). Hong Kong: University of Hong Kong Press.

Mou, Y. (2004). 新中国幼儿教育变革与发展 [*The reformation and development of early childhood education in new China*]. Chongqing: Chongqing University Press.

Ouyang, X., & Zhang, L. (2003). 城市幼儿教师对早期阅读的调查 [An investigation on early literacy among urban preschool teachers]. *早期教育, 7*, 10–12.

Shi, Y. (1999). 学前教育课程论 [*Preschool curriculum*]. Beijing: Beijing Normal University Press.

Snow, C. E., Burns, M. S., & Griffin, P. (Eds.). (1998). *Preventing reading difficulties in young children*. Washington, DC: National Academies Press.

Tang, F. (2003). 儿童早期阅读能力培养的家庭调查分析 [*An investigation on early literacy education at home*]. 山东教育, *1–2*, 16–19.

Textbook Editing Group of Early Childhood Normal School. (1982). 幼儿师范学校幼儿园语言教学法(内部资料) [*Language teaching methods* (unpublished teaching materials)].

Tian, J. (2005). 中国幼儿师范教育的世纪回顾与前瞻 [Retrospect and prospect on Chinese preschool normal education]. *学前教育研究, 7–8*, 58–60.

Tobin, J. (2007). 从民族志研究视角看学前教育的质量 [An ethnographic perspective on quality in early childhood education]. In J. Zhu (Ed.), *国际视野下的学前教育* [*Global perspectives on early childhood education*] (pp. 131–143). Shanghai: East China Normal University Press.

Tobin, J., Hsueh, Y., & Karasawa, M. (2009). *Preschool in three cultures revisited*. Chicago: University of Chicago Press.

Tom, K. S. (1989). *Echoes from old China: Life, legends and lore of the Middle Kingdom*. Honolulu: University of Hawaii Press.

Wang, F. (2001). Meeting points of transcultural exchange – A Chinese view. In R. Hayhoe & J. Pan (Eds.), *Knowledge across cultures: A contribution to dialogue among civilizations* (pp. 295–300). Hong Kong: Comparative Research Center, University of Hong Kong.

Wang, J., & Mao, S. (1996). Culture and the kindergarten curriculum in the People's Republic of China. *Early Child Development and Care, 123*, 143–156.

Wu, P.-Y. (1995). Childhood remembered: Parents and children in China, 800 to 1700. In A. B. Kinney (Ed.), *Chinese views of childhood* (pp. 129–156). Honolulu: University of Hawai'i Press.

Yee, C. (1940). *My Chinese childhood*. New York: John Day.

Yi, H. (1994). 中国近现代学前教育史 [*History of modern early childhood education in China*]. Changchun: Northeast Normal University Press.

Yu, L. (2003). *A history of reading in late Imperial China, 1000–1800* (Unpublished doctoral dissertation). The Ohio State University. Retrieved from http://etd.ohiolink.edu/view.cgi?acc_num=osu1054655134

Yu, Z. (2005). 日常生活中的早期阅读指导 [How to guide infants to read in their daily life]. *学前教育研究, 1*, 31–34.

Yu, Z. (2006). 论早期读写的习得性 [On acquisition of early literacy]. *幼儿教育(教育科学版), 2*, 19–23.

Yu, Z. (2009). 早期阅读活动中师幼交往策略研究 [On teacher-child communicative strategies in early literacy activity]. *幼儿教育(教育科学版)* [*Early Childhood Education (Educational Sciences)*], *7*, 17–20.

Zhang, Q. (2004). *Traditional Chinese culture*. Beijing: Foreign Languages Press.

Zhao, J. (1988). 试论口头语言向书面语言的转换 [On the transition from oral to written language]. 学前教育研究, *2*, 34–37.

Zhao, J. (2001). 学前儿童语言教育 [*Language education in early childhood*]. Beijing: People's Educational Publishing House.

Zhao, J., & Lou, B. (1993). 学前儿童语言教育 [*Language education in early childhood*]. Beijing: People's Educational Publishing House.

Zhou, J. (1995). 幼儿园语言教育活动设计与组织 [*Designing and organizing language education in kindergartens*]. Beijing: People's Education Press.

Zhou, J. (2005). 学前儿童语言教育 [*Language education in early childhood*]. Nanjing: Nanjing Normal University Press.

Zhou, J. (2007). 早期阅读发展与教育研究 [*Research on early literacy development and education*]. Beijing: Educational Science Publishing House.

Zhu, J. (2002). *Early childhood care and education in P. R. China.* Paper presented at 2002 KEDI-UNESCO Bangkok Joint Seminar and Study Tour on Early Childhood Care and Education, Seoul, Korea.

Zhu, J. (2008). 西方学前教育思潮在中国大陆的实践和反思 [Implementation of and reflection on western thought in early childhood education in Mainland China]. *基础教育学报*, *17*(1), 3–16.

Zhu, J., & Zhang, J. (2008). Contemporary trends and developments in early childhood education in China. *Early Years: An International Journal of Research and Development, 28*(2), 173–182.

Chapter 7
Chinese Youth Literature: A Historical Overview

Minjie Chen

7.1 Introduction

This chapter chronicles the birth and development of Chinese youth literature within the dynamic social, political, and cultural context of modern China. Although Chinese language arts textbooks contain a significant amount of short-length children's stories, trade books for young readers have not been widely integrated into formal teaching practices in China. Nonetheless, for those Chinese families with access to youth literature either through ownership or borrowing, youth literature remains an important type of home literacy resource for young learners. As Zipes (2006) astutely reminded us, researchers must recognize the "complex historical transformation" that children's literature has gone through and avoid "simplistic assumptions about its role and meaning in different cultures throughout the world" (para. 3). In this historical overview of Chinese youth literature, close examination of notable titles will show how youth literature is both a medium for children's literacy acquisition and considered an end in itself—by being made a distinct bearer of changing ideas, values, and ideologies to be instilled in young minds. Although I fully agree with Zipes' (2006) statement that children's literature "is practically indefinable, limitless in its scope, and daunting in its achievements" (para. 1), in this chapter the term "Chinese youth literature" loosely refers to non-curriculum trade publications available in China and primarily intended for and read by two age groups, children and young adults.[1]

---

[1] In Chinese language it is still uncustomary to acknowledge the distinction between children's (age 0–12) and young adult (age 12–18) literature. The term *er tong wen xue* (literarily meaning "children's literature") is often inclusive of trade publications for all underage readers, whereas in English "youth literature" seems a more accurate term for that scope.

M. Chen (✉)
Cotsen Children's Library, Princeton University Library Rare Books Division,
Princeton University, Princeton, NJ, USA
e-mail: minjiec@gmail.com

7.2 The Historical Transformation of Chinese Youth Literature

Scholars of Chinese youth literature generally concur that literature published specifically for young readers did not take a solid shape in China until the early twentieth century. Prior to the introduction of youth literature in modern China, young learners had access to primers for literacy and moral instruction. Among the most familiar titles were *Qian Zi Wen* [千字文, or Thousand character classic] (sixth century), *San Zi Jing* [三字经, or Three character classic] (thirteenth century), and *Bai Jia Xing* [百家姓, or The hundred family surnames] (ca. tenth to eleventh century). As Scott's (1980) review of traditional Chinese popular culture points out, for amusement children made do with "what they could cull from the popular literature and entertainment" (p. 109) intended for a general audience.

The most prominent example of cross-age cultural consumption would be *Xi You Ji* [西游记, or Journey to the west] (sixteenth century). Having originated from oral culture and considered one of the four major Chinese classical titles, *Journey to the West* is a saga of a magic monkey's adventurous pilgrimage to India in order to obtain Buddhist scriptures. The story and its numerous adaptations and performances have captured the imagination of Chinese people for hundreds of years through oral storytelling, text and illustrations, puppet plays, operas—and, since the twentieth century—movies, anime, and television series. Although enjoyed by all ages in China, *Journey* has remained the favorite of generations of young people, thanks, perhaps, to its strong fantasy elements. Today, the story of the Monkey King, as well as other Chinese folktales, myths, and legends, has supplied youth literature with an inexhaustible source of reprints, retellings, fractured adaptations, and inspirations for original creations. It is worth noting that after Chinese authors started creating literature for children in the early twentieth century, Chinese youth still shared a great deal of popular reading materials with adults. Chapter 10 in this book, "Chinese *Lian Huan Hua* and Literacy," focuses on one type of popular format, roughly equivalent to illustrated story books and comics in Western countries, and further investigates the phenomenon of cross-age reading.

A heavy Western influence was characteristic of youth literature available in China, even before the birth of native Chinese works. An English-Chinese bilingual version of *Aesop's Fables* was published in 1840 in the late Qing Dynasty, apparently for children for their language training (Farquhar 1999, p. 20). Following China's defeat in the First Opium War (1939–1942) with the British, China was forced to open treaty ports to foreign trade and to accept unequal treaties, which allowed Western missionaries to "flood in" and establish modern movable type printing presses (Zhang et al. 1999). By 1876,[2] the Brooklyn, New York-based Foreign Sunday-school Association reportedly had helped to launch in China a child's paper, written in the "Mandarin dialect" and described as "a good family

---

[2] Sources vary on the exact year when *The Child Paper* was launched, but generally give a date between 1874 and 1876 (See, for example, Shen 2002, p. 82).

paper for grown-up children" ("The Sunday School," 1876, p. 6). Despite its Christian background, *The Child Paper* covered a wide range of topics and stories in addition to the Bible. The illustrations that accompanied the monthly publication, until it discontinued in 1915, are considered the earliest fine art produced specifically for young people in China (Xu 2004). The popular *Tong Hua* [Fairy tales] series edited by Yuxiu Sun[3] (孙毓修)—the first children's literature series in China—appeared in 1908 and featured many more works translated from Western countries than adaptations from Chinese historical stories (Zhu 2000, p. 27–28).

The patriotic May Fourth Movement of 1919 provided a major impetus to the development of indigenous Chinese youth literature. Initially a mass protest in Beijing against the unequal Treaty of Versailles after World War I, the event stimulated a New Culture Movement that was directed at "using some Western ideas to strengthen Chinese culture itself" (Palmowski 2008). Farquhar (1999) has traced how youth literature flourished as progressive Chinese intellectuals came to embrace changed concepts of childhood, education, and reading. The discovery of childhood as a stage with its own special characteristics and needs, contrasting with the traditional view of children as immature adults, and the notion of a child-centered education, which was disseminated in China through John Dewey's 1919–1920 lecture tour, provided the rationale for a distinctive children's literature in easily accessible vernacular language—as opposed to the dead, dull language found in classical Confucian canons taught to children (Farquhar 1999).

Chinese youth literature at its very beginning was placed firmly within the education field. The medium is regarded as "one of the educational tools for children" (Er tong wen xue 1990, p. 12; Wang 2000, p. 576) and even "life's first textbooks" (Jiang 2005, p. 190), whether the subject of acculturation is literacy, humanities, science, aesthetics, morality, or political ideology. Zuoren Zhou (周作人, 1885–1967), a translator and theorist of youth literature and one of the earliest advocates for a body of literature specifically for Chinese children, delivered a highly influential lecture in an experimental Peking Conte School in October 1920. In his talk, Zhou (1920/1988) coined the phrase "er tong de wen xue[4]" (children's literature) and equated the term with "literature for primary schools" (p. 3). Addressing teachers, he detailed guidelines for choosing age-appropriate and interesting "teaching materials" from poetry, fables, fairy tales, nature stories, realistic stories, etc. for the literature education of the age groups 3–6 (kindergarten), 6–10 (primary school), and 10–15 (middle school and adolescence) respectively.

Another of Zhou's main ideas, which would be misinterpreted and vehemently condemned in Communist China, shows that Zhou was not reducing children's literature to a dry didactic instrument. Espousing a child-centered approach, Zhou

---

[3] Most Chinese full names in this essay have been inverted to conform to the Western sequence of first and last names. In a few cases the original Chinese sequence is kept in respect to customary usage in English media.

[4] Later the phrase would be shortened into "er tong wen xue," omitting the character "de" which forms the possessive case but meaning "children's literature" all the same.

(1920/1988) argued that literature used as instructional materials in primary schools and its teaching must first "be for children" (p. 4); benefits to children—including the cultivation of interest in reading, intelligence, and imagination—should be a secondary concern, although Zhou seemed positive that these would be the natural "side effects" of providing children with literature. While his notion of "for children" is open to interpretations, Zhou took issue with the tendency of forcing "ideas or behaviors" (p. 4) upon children through literature regardless of their developmental needs, contending that it was wasteful of children's time and harmful to child life. Unfortunately, some of the ideologies that Zhou (1920/1988) considered unsuitable for children's literature, such as "improper hero worship and patriotism" (p. 8), would dominate works produced in Red China, contributing to the unpopularity of Zhou's theory.

As Jiang (2005) has pointed out, it was not until the 1980s that children's authors began to challenge the prevalent notion that children's literature is necessarily "an educational tool," arguing that it was sufficient for the literature to entertain children and bring them pleasure (p. 281). The outcome of the heated debated has been a more tolerant view of the multiple functions of youth literature, and a more sophisticated understanding of how the educational function should be achieved through literature (Jiang 2005, pp. 279–83). As we shall see, even though orthodox Chinese youth literature is never divorced from its educational role, the relationship between youth literature and China's formal schooling and teaching practices has been contested and at times difficult.

Researchers generally have divided the history of Chinese youth literature into at least four time periods (see, for example, Chen 2006a; Tang 2006): (i) from the May Fourth Movement of 1919 to the establishment of Communist China in 1949, (ii) the first 17 years of new China from 1949 to 1966, (iii) the Great Proletarian Cultural Revolution from 1966 to 1976, and (iv) from the end of the Cultural Revolution to the 1989 crackdown on protesters in Tiananmen Square. The most recent, or fifth, period runs from the 1990s to the present day. One can always identify finer dividing points within each time period. In her historical study of Chinese children's literature, Farquhar (1999) further differentiated the first period (1919–1949) into the years prior to the outbreak of the Sino-Japanese War in 1937 and the subsequent war periods of 1937–1949. These major segments, punctuated by significant events in modern Chinese history, suggest the intimate relationship between Chinese youth literature and the historical, political, and cultural dynamics in China.

7.2.1 From 1919 to 1949

Produced during the New Culture Movement, Shengtao Ye's (叶圣陶, 1894–1988) collection of fairy tales—*Dao Cao Ren* [A scarecrow] (1923)—and Xin Bing's (冰心, 1900–1999) letters to young readers (1923–1926) are widely recognized as two pioneer works of children's literature by Chinese writers. As early as 1921, Ye, a school teacher for 11- and 12-year-olds, wrote essays about his students' favorite texts, called for the creation of new literary works appropriate for children, and pointed out the dearth of children's magazines and an inadequacy of school library collections (Ye 1921/1988). When the Shanghai-based Commercial Press launched the children's magazine *Er Tong Shi Jie* [Children's world] in 1922, its editor Zhenduo Zheng (郑振铎) invited Ye to contribute and thus started his career as a children's literature writer (Zhu 2000, p. 180). (Another magazine *Xiao Peng You* [Little friends], launched in Shanghai the same year, has enjoyed an amazing longevity and remains the oldest Chinese children's magazine active today.) Bing started her *Ji Xiao Du Zhe* [Letters to young readers] the day after she learned about a new column—"Children's World"—opening in the *Morning Post*, where the letters were serialized (Bing 1923). Addressed to "little friends," her 29 letters recorded Bing's fond or melancholy childhood memories, journey to the United States, student life at Wellesley College, and homesickness.

The formative period of Chinese youth literature was disrupted by the Sino-Japanese War (1937–1945), partly because the Japanese had taken over the publishing centers on the eastern coast (Farquhar 1999, p. 7). Almost all Shanghai-based children's magazines were forced to discontinue (Er tong 1990, p. 205). The warfare and Japanese censorship posed double threats to the personal safety of Chinese literati. Paradoxically, the war also enriched Chinese youth literature. The military conflict between China and Imperial Japan, soldier and civilian heroes who resisted the Japanese aggression, choices between loyalty and betrayal, struggles for survival, and family separation and reunion were among the common life dramas in times of war. The 8-year Sino-Japanese War not only shaped the content of youth literature produced during the war, but also continued to inspire Chinese writers and artists and became the setting of some of the canonical titles of postwar Chinese youth literature. Wang's (2000) comprehensive overview of wartime Chinese youth literature confirms that the dominant topic was war, and the dominant theme patriotism.

The few issues of *Little Friends*, dated between the outbreak of full-scale war on July 7, 1937 and its publishing cessation, well illustrate the impact of the war on the subject matter of youth literature. A strong educational purpose is palpable in them. By virtue of its short publication cycle, the magazine united current affairs with language and reading, geography, history, and patriotic education in a swift responsiveness that would be unrealistic to achieve for school textbooks.

Starting from Issue No. 768, published on July 15, 1937, war-related news, informational texts, stories, children's own written responses to the current warfare, and photos of the Chinese military were increasingly present in the magazine. Even the craft section taught children to make a toy soldier (Fang 1937, pp. 24–25). Patriotic education for young readers was the prevalent agenda of these texts, which helped youth make sense of the war, urged them to share the nation's concern, and mobilized them to contribute what they could to the war effort. In the short story "Qing Ni Bu Yao Jiao Ao" [Please do not be smug] (Du 1937), an elder cousin, using a map of Nationalist China, teaches the younger one—as well as readers of the magazine—how much land China has lost to Japan following the annexation of Manchuria in 1931. The bigger boy does a good job of translating what could have been an abstract concept into transparent ideas: the lost territory is equivalent to one sixth of China's total area, and seven times as big as the Sichuan Province, or six times as big as Imperial Japan, etc. Ending with the smaller boy vowing to defeat the enemy and defend the land, the story is followed by five reading comprehension questions. It is laudable that the magazine also included an illustrated text on safety tips during an air raid (Wei 1937, pp. 13–14), although survival skills were a far less prioritized topic than war mobilization in these issues.

Some of the most memorable characters in Chinese youth literature were created during the war. The story of Erxiao, a young boy who guides Japanese soldiers to an ambush by Chinese guerrillas before his trickery is discovered and he is killed, was based on a true incident in the Hebei Province of North China. The boy's heroic sacrifice also inspired a melodious narrative song "The Cowherd Wang Erxiao" (1942). Both the popular song and the story (an early version I found, "Fang Niu Lang" [The cowherd], was dated 1947, 2nd edition) later appeared in elementary music and Chinese language textbooks,[5] ensuring that generations of Chinese youth were familiar with Erxiao. Two other household names of fictional boy heroes are Yulai and Haiwa. In "Yulai Mei You Si" [Yulai did not die, aka Little hero Yulai] (Guan 1948/1990), a quick-thinking and dauntless young boy rescues an underground messenger pursued by the Japanese and escapes the enemies' gunshot by faking death in the river. The plotline of "Ji Mao Xin" [Feather letter] (Hua 1949/1990) is reminiscent of "The Cowherd" except that Haiwa, a shepherd who deliberately leads Japanese aggressors astray, is rescued by guerrillas. Again, both "Little Hero Yulai" and "Feather Letter" were classical texts for primary schools in post-1949 China. According to the teacher's edition of a recent fourth grade textbook issued by China's major textbook publisher, People's Education Press, the goals and objectives of the lesson "Little Hero Yulai" include "to learn eight new characters," "to apply contextual reading strategies to figure out the deep meaning of sentences in the text," and "to learn about people's lives in times of war, to receive patriotic education from the young hero's bravery and resourcefulness" ("Xiao ying xiong Yulai," 2005). The text thus serves to teach basic literacy, reading skills, history, moral values, and patriotism.

7.2.2 From 1949 to 1966

After the Communist victory in the Chinese civil war (1946–1949) and the founding of the People's Republic of China (PRC) in October 1949, youth literature enjoyed what was hailed as its first "golden age," characterized by fast growth in the quantity of publications for youth, a wide variety of formats and genres in youth literature, an increasing number of children's authors, and the establishment of two publishing

---

[5] Despite the death of the young hero, in a current Chinese language textbook (Beijing, China: People's Education Press, 2001) a simplified and illustrated version of Erxiao's story is taught to first grade students.

houses for juvenile literature, as well as magazines and newspapers for different age groups of young people (Er tong 1990, pp. 220–235; Wang 2000, p. 162–168).

One document was widely credited for having boosted the production of Chinese youth literature in the 1950s. *People's Daily*, the official organ of the Chinese Communist Party (CCP), carried an editorial entitled "Greatly Increase the Creation, Publication, and Distribution of Reading Materials for Youth" on September 16, 1955. The editorial opens by stating that "[g]ood reading materials for children and adolescents are a forceful tool for the Communist education of youth," and further elaborates the two significant aspects of these age-appropriate publications: first, "literature and science reading materials" are part of young people's extra-curricular education, supplementing their formal schooling; second, those graduates who have either joined the labor force or are teaching themselves rely upon youth reading materials and other publications as the main source of knowledge ("'Ren min ri bao' she lun," 1955/1989, pp. 9–11). The editorial called for institutional support (which did materialize thereafter) from the Writers' Society, publishers, and bookstores to address issues including the inadequate quantity, low quality, and lack of diversity in youth literature. However, its designation of youth literature as a Communist education tool suggests the ruling party's increasing ideological control over reading materials for youth.

A critical article, published in a 1953 issue of *Wen Yi Yue Bao* [Literature and art monthly] and written by Jingtang Ding, who in the 1950s headed various offices in the Propaganda Department[6] of the Shanghai CCP Municipal Committee, exemplifies how the Party regulated the themes of youth literature, weeding out undesirable elements and exhorting Party-approved messages. In his "brief appraisal of children's literature published [from 1950 to 1953] in Shanghai," historically China's publication center and the hub of youth literature, Ding (1953) criticized titles which he deemed "poisonous" to youth. Some of the "erroneous and flawed" themes he found in the text and illustrations of children's books include a pessimistic portrayal of Chinese people, feudalistic and superstitious ideas, a crude distortion of serious political struggles, and an overemphasis on children's agency in the revolution to the effect of insulting the strength of adult peasants and the people's army (Ding 1953). The Party's censure carried genuine power. According to Ding (1953), children's author Jingshan Lu, together with his publisher, had to make a public admission of guilt after his book *Xiao Hei Ren* (1950) received harsh criticism from a CCP's newspaper (p. 26).

One title that Ding (1953) disapproved of was Zeren Xu's *Xi Jun he Xi Jun Zhan Zheng* [Bacteria and bacterial warfare]. Published in 1951 and in its third edition in 1953, *Bacteria* explains the concepts in bacteriology in vivid, jargon-free language, goes over the history of scientific discovery in microbiology beginning with Antony van Leeuwenhoek, and, in the second half of the book, introduces Japan's biological warfare in China, drawing data from confessions made by the Japanese Army

---

[6] As Hung clarifies, the Chinese word *xuan chuan*, or propaganda, "meaning to inform and to propagate, carries a more positive connotation than its English counterpart" (1994, p. 9).

men interrogated and tried by the Soviet Union in 1949–1950. *Bacteria* conveys timely and reasonably well-researched information at the interest and comprehension level of middle and high school students. Ding (1953), however, criticized *Bacteria*, among a few other titles, for "boosting the enemy's arrogance and dampening our own morale," most likely referring to the part where Xu (1953) recounts that Chinese POWs were tortured in human experiments and that civilians were the victims of biological weapon attacks. Ding argued:

> [These titles] describe how American and Japanese Imperialists murdered and bombed Chinese people, who are described as "obedient subjects"—weak-kneed, incompetent, and surrendering to the enemy's killing without any resistance.….This is an insult to Chinese people,…who have never been intimidated by the enemy and kowtowed to them.….[Such descriptions] will foster in children a sense of inferiority about their own people and sap their brave and strong will. (1953, p. 26)

The domination of the type of reasoning like Ding's accounts for the fact that after the early 1950s, literature (regardless of the targeted age group) devoted to Japanese war crimes and atrocities all but disappeared. Chinese wartime suffering and temporary setbacks were marginalized, or sketched in just enough detail to highlight the valor, ingenuity, and ultimate invincibility of Chinese people and of the CCP's military. During the same time period when the wartime experiences of European civilians, particularly Jewish people caught in the Holocaust, generated a long list of eminent works in postwar Western youth literature, in China a parallel topic was effectively closed, gradually forgotten, and did not receive renewed attention until the beginning of the twenty-first century.

The most important title produced during the first 17 years of the PRC is arguably *Xiao Bing Zhang Ga* [Little soldier Chang Ka-tse] (Xu 1964), one of the many Sino-Japanese War stories that have made the list of best Chinese youth literature of all time. Ka-tse, a 13-year-old orphan boy, is allowed to join a team of underground Communist fighters after his grandmother—his only guardian—is killed by the Japanese. Like the classical Canadian juvenile fiction *Anne of Green Gables* (1908) by L. M. Montgomery, Xu's novel is peppered with the amusing scrapes into which a cheerful, daring, yet often stubborn boy gets. Under the strict discipline of a loving Commander, Ka-tse grows into a worthy and mature member of the army, receives a handgun of which he has dreamed, and makes up his mind to join the Communist Party. The author Guangyao Xu (徐光耀), who joined the Communist Eighth Route Army in 1938 at age thirteen, created a convincing and likeable young character in a war story interlaced with affectionate relations, constant tribulations, and comic relief.

The touted golden age withered quickly. Even before the Cultural Revolution was launched in 1966, political commotion plagued Communist China. The Anti-Rightist Campaign of 1957 targeted intellectuals in particular, and many writers and artists were among the "rightists" whose reputations were tarnished and whose voices in the public media were lost. In his memoir Guangyao Xu revealed that writing the stories of a saucy Ka-tse was therapeutic for him when he was visited by suicidal thoughts while waiting for his verdict in early 1958. Xu finished the draft the same year,[7] shortly before he was accused as a "rightist," sent to a labor camp to be punished with other political outcasts, and survived (Xu 2001). Regardless of Xu's exceptional case, the overall effect of the Anti-Rightist Campaign on youth literature in China was harmful. Children's authors were either silenced, or could publish only didactic, formulaic, contrived stories that echoed whatever political doctrines were being propagated by the Party (Wang 2000, pp. 168–72).

7.2.3 From 1966 to 1976

Again, researchers concur that the Cultural Revolution was devastating to Chinese youth literature, as it was to virtually every aspect of Chinese society (Farquhar 1999; Wang 2000). Radical changes took place in China's schooling system, affecting the life course of millions of Chinese youth. The purpose and means of education were redefined, and even subverted. Mao Zedong had declared the dual standards of "red and expert" for the working class—"redness" referring to ideological and political orthodoxy, and "expert" meaning mastery of secular knowledge in science and technology—and seemingly treated both criteria as equally important (Mao 1958/1993). Over time, however, "redness" was increasingly emphasized over professional competence. For young students a political subscription to the Maoist doctrine was promoted through required participation in manual labor. According to Zhou (2004), over 17 million urban youth—mostly graduates from middle and high school and constituting "about one-third of the children of the Cultural Revolution"—were sent to labor in rural areas between 1967 and 1978 (p. 125), typically in the name of receiving re-education from "the poor peasants," in Mao's words (as cited p. 124). The recruitment of college students was largely based on politically oriented admission criteria, rather than academic credentials. Suspicion and contempt of academic competence culminated in the so-called "Tiesheng Zhang's blank exam paper" incident in July 1973. In his college entrance exam in physics and chemistry, Zhang, who would score 6 (out of 100), wrote a letter on the back of the test paper, stating that "close to 18 h' daily harsh labor and work" did not permit him to prepare for the test, and contrasting his collectivism with those "idle bookworms" who pursued their personal interests only (Liang 2000, p. 67). Zhang was subsequently recognized as a hero in official newspapers, admitted into the college as an exceptional student, and given important positions in the Party.

In Jiang's (2005) unflattering words, the 10-year Cultural Revolution was "a tragic era witnessing the near demise of children's literature in China" (p. 51). Particularly during the first 5 years of the turmoil, not only were there few new

---

[7] The first edition of *Little Soldier* was not published until 4 years later in 1962. During the first half of the 1960s, a series of corrective measures, sandwiched between the disastrous Great Leap Forward campaign (1958–1960) and the Cultural Revolution (1966–1976) were initiated by Chinese leaders, resulting in a brief swing to the right of the political tide.

publications for readers of all age groups, but old works were also banned and even destroyed in fire and wastepaper mills, on ideological grounds (Ho 2006). Aside from the children's magazine *Hong Xiao Bing* [Little red guard], and a small number of illustrated storybooks which were adaptations of Party-approved plays and biographical stories of Maoist role models, youth reading materials were scarce—even dictionaries were unavailable for elementary school children to purchase (Fang 1999, p. 13).

Little Red Guard was actually a common title adopted by at least 20 seemingly independent children's magazines published in various provinces during the 1970s. They were written at the reading level of primary school students, and often carried much coveted comic strips and color illustrations. Anecdotes suggest that some schools would subscribe to the magazine and make it available in classrooms for supplementary reading. *Little Red Guard* well illustrates the intertwining double mission of literacy acquisition and political socialization in Chinese youth literature. For example, *pinyin* exercises that drilled the crucial literacy skill of pronouncing phonetics spelled out political slogans.

Censorship relaxed slightly in the second half of the Cultural Revolution, and publication resumed on a restricted scale after 1970 (Zhang 1999; Yuan 2001). The one major juvenile fiction produced in this time period was *Shan Shan de Hong Xing* [Shining red star] by Xintian Li published in 1972. The novel, reaching a print run of three million the first year, immediately received significant approval from a *People's Daily* article by Zuoli Han, a high official of the Beijing Education Bureau, who praised it as "good teaching material for children's education" (Li 2005, para. 3). *Shining Red Star* was serialized in radio nationally, and its movie adaptation, released in 1974, also became an instant hit. The story spans from 1934 to 1949 and portrays the maturation of a 7-year-old boy, Dongzi, during the social and political turmoil in which he becomes involved. Born into a poor peasant's family, Dongzi is orphaned when his mother, a new Communist Party member, is tortured to death by the local landlord, and the boy is separated from his father, who has joined the Red Army. Homeless and pursued by the murderer of his mother, but helped by many poor people and Communist mentors, Dongzi survives, is socialized into Communist ideas, and joins the People's Liberation Army as China undergoes constant changes resulting from the rivalry between the CCP and Nationalist government before, during, and after Japan's invasion.

Red Star is an eloquently told story that creates a clear-cut dichotomous world, where evil and virtue strictly follow the class and party line—a typical fictional world in Chinese Communist revolutionary literature. Wealthy characters (landlords, rich businessmen) and those serving the Nationalist government (police chief, Nationalist army officers and soldiers) are without exception cruel hatchet men, greedy exploiters, and despicable traitors, who readily collaborate with the Japanese during World War II. All poor people selflessly help each other, including strangers, at the cost of their own safety, and support the Communist revolution with loyalty. Even the morals of child characters are solely determined by their family background: the son and daughter of rich men are snobbish bullies and selfish nuisances, and poor people's children are all gentle and sweet to each other and form lasting friendships. Whereas evil and virtue, rewards and punishments are common dichotomies in folktales, *Red Star* conflates evil with "class enemies" and members of the CCP's political rivals, and virtue with lower class people who are Communist sympathizers. *Red Star* is representative of the folktale-style characterization found in reading materials intended for adults and youth alike during the Cultural Revolution. The black-and-white fictional world of *Red Star*, set prior to the Communist victory in China, leaves no narrative space for liberal landlords and capitalists who were known to have participated in worthy missions, or patriotic Nationalist military officers and the rank and file who fought with bravery during World War II, or poor peasants and workers who were not noble. The world is religiously organized by rules written in the Communist rhetoric, rules that justified numerous punitive policies in Mao's era—such as the redistribution of arable land from more prosperous owners to other peasants, penalty for people who had served in the Nationalist government, and discrimination against a younger generation in their education and employment prospects if their family class and political background were found to be "dishonorable."

Narrated in first person by Dongzi, *Red Star* maintains a convincing child's point of view, respects his initial inability to fully comprehend a complex and changing political situation that affects every member of his family and rural hometown, allows his political consciousness to grow as the narrator comes of age, and all the while invites young readers to identify with a strong-willed boy who is able to fend for himself and accomplish great deeds in his adventurous journey to freedom and independence. Farquhar carried out a rare experiment in cross-cultural audience response in 1978 and attested to the captivating power of the story. She showed the movie *Shining Red Star* (with English subtitles) to Australian primary school children, who "sat enthralled throughout and then went outside to play 'Little Red Soldiers' in the playground" (1999, p. 287).

Folkloric storytelling, child-friendly perspective, tension-ridden plotline, and the final triumph of the young hero made *Red Star* an ideal story for the teaching of class struggle theory. Through text, illustration, radio broadcast, and film and its popular theme songs, Dongzi became the idol of countless Chinese youth, especially boys, growing up in the 1970s.

7.2.4 From 1976 to 1989

The time period from Mao's death in 1976, especially after Deng Xiaoping regained power and helped steer the priority of the nation from class struggle to economic development, until the end of the 1980s is considered a new "golden age" for Chinese youth literature. First, after what was metaphorically referred to as a 10-year "starvation" for the mind of both adults and youth, the fervor demonstrated by Chinese book buyers at the beginning of the post-Mao era was unprecedented. As Chinese publishing historian Houshu Fang (1999) writes, in 1977–1978 people would arrive at bookstores the night before book releases, queuing up for the limited supply of re-sanctioned works in reprints, and 150,000 copies of a children's book, *Shu Xue You Xi* [Mathematical games], were sold within two hours of its release in Beijing (p. 14). This was virtually a seller's market for books, except that China was running a planned economy, not a market economy.

Second, Deng Xiaoping restored the academic merit-based college entrance exam system in 1977, once again turning academic excellence into a ticket to upward social mobility. Compulsory Education Law of the People's Republic of China also took effect July 1, 1986. These national policies and legislation changes were conducive to an increased literacy rate among the young generation, and were likely to encourage the use of books as a source of knowledge and an aid to better learning outcomes. To be sure, in pursuit of young people's academic success, many parents and teachers have always perceived the tension between leisure reading and coursework, between "good" reading of serious, classical works and time "wasted" in reading light material. During the 1980s, however, these tensions, which we shall revisit in the next section, did not seem intense enough to prevent the youth literature industry from flourishing.

Third, the production of youth literature benefited from a relatively tolerant political climate and direct administrative support. Researchers credit the 1978 National Forum on Publishing for Youth—organized by China's National Publishing Administration, Department of Education, Department of Culture, and other central government agencies—with supporting the enrichment of youth reading materials and with helping "emancipate the thoughts" of children's publishers and editors from the ultra-Left constraints of the Cultural Revolution (Fang 1999, p. 14; Wang 2000, pp. 176–7). The Party never foregoes ideological control of any cultural artifacts, but the liberal spasm of the 1980s did have a noticeable impact upon the subject matter and theme of Chinese youth literature.

The 1980s enjoyed a proliferation of Chinese youth literature in quantity, publication format, genre, topic, and targeted age level. Pu (1990) reports a total of 26 children's and young adult literature publishing houses, a record number of about 200 titles of periodicals for youth, and a rich body of juvenile fiction surpassing the sum of productions from the first 27 years (1949–1976) of the PRC (pp. 30–32). Previously, the production of color picture books suitable for preschool and emergent readers had been severely restricted by cost, but now publishers were able to sell large-size, short-length, beautifully illustrated, and brightly printed paperback picture books to Chinese families, which, following the one child policy first announced in 1979, were shrinking in size and gaining purchasing power especially in urban areas. The two-volume *365 Ye* [365 nights] (Shanghai: Juvenile and Children's Publishing House, 1980) achieved great success in tapping the market of Post-Mao urban families who were paying more attention to preschoolers' intellectual development. A collection of 365 short tales, nursery rhymes, and children's riddles suitable for 4–6 year olds, the book provides young parents with 1 year's convenient supply of read-aloud stories for bedtime, and has remained in the fond memories of many Chinese who grew up in the 1980s.

Fairy tales, according to Pu (1989, pp. 27–28), were nearly extinct during the Cultural Revolution. The 1980s saw the rise of children's author Yuanjie

Zheng (郑渊洁), now dubbed China's "king of fairy tales." An incredibly prolific writer whose formal schooling ended at the fourth grade when the Cultural Revolution broke out, Zheng published his first fantasy novel in 1982 featuring a naughty boy Pipilu, created the children's magazine *Tong Hua Da Wang* [The king of fairy tales] in 1985, and has since remained the sole contributor to the commercially successful magazine. Pipilu, who debuts in Zheng's book at age 12 and is the central figure of numerous fantasy series, is found by X-ray inspection to have been born with an extra amount of "guts," and a medical operation has to be performed to spare some of them for his twin sister Luxixi, whose "guts" are close to invisible. A bold and energetic child who likes to speak his mind, Pipilu is a magnet for trouble. With black humor, Zheng criticizes the Chinese education system, which he perceives to be destroying independent thinkers and honoring obedient students who parrot teachers' words. In *Xun Tu Ji* [The taming of the bunny], Pipilu witnesses his classmates turning into long-eared, red-eyed, meek rabbits one after another, as they do whatever the teacher says and never challenge authority. Despite increasing pressure from the teacher, parents, and peers, Pipilu is unwilling and unable to transform because he cannot stop speaking his true thoughts and making up his own mind. Finally, out of sympathy for his hardworking teacher and her disabled son, the boy purchases a bunny suit to please everybody, but hopes that he will not have to wear this suffocating costume all his life.

What has won Zheng the title of fairy tale king in the first place is not embedded social commentary like this, but the great child appeal of his imaginative writing. Zheng's criticism and sarcasm may escape young readers, and some messages are more relevant to adult caregivers and educators than to children. Yet his storytelling prevails. For example, an 8-year-old girl posted her reading response to *The Taming* in a Weblog. She finds the story most entertaining, thinks the idea of all her classmates turning into rabbits is hilarious, and decides that she should be a cat instead of a rabbit because her favorite food is fish (Mimiyan 2009). *The Taming* is among Zheng's best tales that reward rereading at different ages. Zheng's works have attracted a huge fan group since the 1980s. Children eagerly spend their allowance on every new issue of *The King of Fairy Tales*, and many have followed his works from primary school, to high school, and even to college.

A relatively tolerant political and cultural climate led to a great expansion of themes in youth literature, including condemnation of the Cultural Revolution and exposure to contemporary social ills (Zhao 1985/2006; Pu 1990, pp. 33–36). The short story "Jin Ye Yue Er Ming" [The bright moonlight tonight] (1984) by Ahu Ding, published in the Shanghai-based magazine *Shao Nian Wen Yi* [Literature and art for adolescents], marked the birth of Chinese young adult fiction. Ding treats a crush that a middle school girl has on a boy as an understandable feeling, but a feeling that is inappropriate for her age and needs to be resolved. Still, the story aroused a storm of controversy because teenagers' sexuality had been a taboo topic in Chinese youth literature.

Finally, it is worth pointing out the great influx of translated youth literature in the 1980s. Previously, Communist countries, particularly the Soviet Union, were the dominant source of foreign publications introduced to China. After Deng

Xiaoping's "Open Door" policy, a large number of books published in Western developed countries and Japan were translated into Chinese. Imported youth literature enriched the choices of Chinese young readers and served as a window to diverse cultures of the world, as well as to a common nature that unites human beings across racial, ethnic, national, and ideological differences. In this time period, many time-tested youth literature titles were made available for the first time in eloquent translations for Chinese readers, including *Charlotte's Web* by E. B. White (Beijing: Ren Min Wen Xue Chu Ban She, 1979), *Lisa and Lottie* by Erich Kästner (Beijing: Zhongguo Shao Nian Er Tong Chu Ban She, 1981), *Pippi Longstocking* by Astrid Lindgren (Changsha, Hunan: Hunan Shao Nian Er Tong Chu Ban She, 1983), and *Anne of Green Gables* (Beijing: Zhongguo Wen Lian Chu Ban She, 1987).

7.2.5 From the 1990s Onward

Chinese youth literature did not fare well in the 1990s but has grown in sales since the turn of the century. Symptoms of the initial inactivity were manifold and interrelated. As researchers and publishers have noted, in the 1990s the print run of most youth literature titles dropped drastically (ranging from 3,000 to 5,000) and sold poorly; some high-quality works could not be published because bookstores did not place enough orders; publishers' heavy reliance upon reprints of canonical and translated titles in the public domain resulted in the dominance of a small number of essentially the same works in the book market; new authors decreased; and well-known children's authors stopped writing for youth, or stopped literary creation altogether (Jiang 2005; Wang 2000, p. 177; Li 2003, p. 96; Tang 2006, p. 22; Sun 2008, p. 10).

Researchers, journalists, and educators have cited many factors to explain the dispirited Chinese youth literature of the 1990s. Under the market economy introduced in 1992, Chinese publishing, once purely state-owned and subsidized by the government, now struggled for survival, transforming children's editors from midwives for literary products to bottom-line-driven businessmen (Jiang 2005, p. 41). Competition from foreign imports of popular reading materials, such as Japanese comic books, and from new media, such as television and video games (the ownership of TV Sets per 1,000 people leapt from 5.1 in 1980 to 155.2 in 1990 to 292.0 in 1999) (*Dian shi ji* 2001), was frequently blamed for drawing children's interest away from native Chinese youth literature. Incidentally, imported comics overwhelmingly were pirated copies sold in less reputable venues, and only a relatively small number of Chinese editions were legitimate (Liu 2009). After China implemented its first copyright law in 1991 and joined the Berne Convention and Universal Copyright Convention in 1992, the cost for legally publishing foreign titles rose in China, motivating the repetitive printing of such familiar collections as those by Hans Christian Andersen and the Grimm Brothers until the situation improved in the late 1990s. Rarely discussed is how the freedom of creating

Chinese youth literature might have been affected by the Tiananmen Square protests of 1989, still a taboo topic in mainland China, and the subsequent tightened thought control.

Ironically, another factor that is accused of being seriously responsible for a declining youth literature industry is China's education system. Since the late 1980s, the pressure for students to achieve academic success has mounted, resulting in multiple ramifications. Numerous surveys and reports blame heavy coursework and test pressure for eating away children's reading time, and frequently list it as the No. 1 reason "why today's kids don't read" (Chen 2006b, p. 451). While it is debatable whether or not youth read at all, depending on the definition of "reading" (popular genres, including kung fu novels, romance novels, and the rampant pirated comic books, as well as online texts are frequently dismissed by adults), high-stakes standardized testing clearly has influenced publishing for youth. The high profit of study aids, "how-to" guides on Chinese composition, and test preparation materials, as Jiang (2005, p. 41) and Lin (2003, pp. 104–5) point out, has been a big attraction to children's publishers, and their market seems to remain strong despite continuous education reforms intent upon reducing the pressure of entrance exams at all school levels. A quick scan in January 2010 of Amazon.com, the Chinese branch of the American-based electronic commerce company, found 23,190 non-test preparation books listed for youth, with about 87% designated for the age group 0–14 and 13% for teens in general; meanwhile, under a separate category of "test prep" were 20,366 items for the preparation of senior high school (33%) and college (67%) entrance exams. The proportion of youth leisure reading materials to those for test preparation—1.15:1—gives us a rough picture of Chinese young adults' reading choices.

Unlike students in Grade 6 and higher, younger Chinese children can engage in reading as a bigger part of their leisure life. Needless to say, the educational value of engaging books for pre-literate and beginning readers can be more intuitively understood by China's emerging middle-class parents, which are the best educated generation of fathers and mothers in Chinese history. In fact, a few amateur parent-reviewers have become the most active advocates for children's reading, particularly promoting picture books (Chen 2008). The decade since 2000 has seen a further growth of picture books, refreshed by a new influx of translated titles. As many as 600 or so picture books were imported in the year 2008 (Deng 2008). *Fu Mu Bi Du* [Parenting science], a magazine targeting parents of young children from birth to lower elementary school, released its first annual list of Top 10 best children's titles in 2005. Except for one Chinese fantasy title in 2005, the lists from 2005 to 2009 are dominated by picture books imported from the United States, Western European countries, and Japan. Works by renowned American authors Dr. Seuss, Eric Carle, Shel Silverstein, and William Steig have crossed the Pacific Ocean and been added to Chinese children's favorite readings.

Publishers and researchers also credit the *Harry Potter* series, which appeared in China in 2000, for having inaugurated an upward trend in the Chinese youth literature industry. According to Sun (2008), in addition to the *Harry Potter* series, foreign imports such as R. L. Stine's *Goosebumps* series and Austrian author Thomas Brezina's detective series *A Mystery for You and The Tiger Team* used to monopolize children's bestselling list, but since 2005, native Chinese works, the best-known being female writer Hongying Yang's (杨红樱) *Tao Qi Bao Ma Xiaotiao* [The mischievous boy Ma Xiaotiao] series, have made increasing gains in market share and competed with foreign titles as equal rivals (p. 10). Yang taught elementary Chinese classes for 7 years before she launched her creative writing career and rose to become China's top children's author of the 2000s. It is perhaps no accident that, like Yuanjie Zheng, Yang is an earnest critic of China's authoritarian and test-driven education system. Her criticism is embedded in the portrayal of unpopular teachers' hurtful handling of student disciplinary problems. Yang promotes her ideal educational model through sensitive teacher characters who understand children and respect their personalities. In fact, in her *Shen Mi de Nü Lao Shi* [The mysterious teacher lady] (2004), the eccentric teacher who makes learning a joyful experience for students is a fairy. For child readers, Yang's writing gives voice to their pain in facing a highly competitive, drill-based schooling environment and satisfies their wishful thinking. As Yang readily admits, she was sending messages to adults as well; even though she alone could not change the sorry situation of Chinese youth, she wished to influence parents and teachers through adult role models in her fiction (Wei 2004, p. 220).

One notable and controversial phenomenon in Chinese youth literature at the turn of the twenty-first century has been the rise of teenage writers who were born after 1980 and who first got published as early as their teenage years. Han Han (1982-), Yueran Zhang (1982-), Jingming Guo (1983-), and Fangzhou Jiang (1989-), who published her first book *Da Kai Tian Chuang* [Open the skylight] (2000) at age 11, are among those who were still active by the end of the first decade of the 2000s. Works by these precocious and prolific young authors have been popular among their peers, and Han, Zhang, and Guo are currently major writers of native literature for teens. Han's first novel *San Chong Men* [The third way] (Beijing: Zuo Jia Chu Ban She, 2000), contemporary realistic fiction set in a high school in Shanghai, was a huge commercial success and sold over one million copies within the first 6 years. Written before Han dropped out of school (he failed seven subjects twice in Grade 10, but simultaneously won first prize in an influential national essay contest for youth), *The Third Way* is another sharp critique of China's education system. For this reason, the adaptation of the novel for television drama did not survive government censorship, was banned for 3 years, and then was released in an abridged and bland version that softened the original criticism and soul of the book (Liu 2004).

7.3 Youth Literature and China's Formal Education System

Despite a long tradition of creating and using youth literature for educational purposes, the relationship between Chinese youth literature and the formal education system is anything but harmonious today. On one hand, the value of youth literature in literacy, aesthetics, science and humanities, morality, and ideological education is acknowledged and reflected in works of youth literature reprinted in school textbooks. According to Wei's (2009) statistics, of a total of 400 or so entries in current elementary Chinese language textbooks (Grades 1–5), there are 68 children's poems, 66 fairy tales and fables, 88 children's essays, 92 children's stories (including mythology and legend), and 19 children's informational texts on science—adding up to more than 80% of the total entries (p. 82). The curriculum goal set in the Compulsory Education Standards for Chinese Language, adopted by the Ministry of Education in 2001, states that in 9 years students should be exposed to no less than four million Chinese characters[8] in their extra-curricular reading; recommends a short list of fairy tales, fables, mythology, historical stories, folktales, poetry, essays, and classical titles and suggests that Chinese language teachers use book award lists and collaborate with other subject teachers on recommending reading materials to students ("Yu wen ke cheng" 2002).

On the other hand, youth literature is prevented from becoming a larger part of students' schooling experience, partly due to significant flaws in teacher training and school librarian training systems. As students proceed to middle and high schools, reading youth literature can be perceived by unappreciative teachers, as well as parents, as a distraction that works against academic excellence. Wang (2007) wrote a most articulate article that traces flaws in these training systems to national educational regulations that discourage faculty members and college students from pursuing the study of youth literature in China's higher education system. Fewer than 30 children's literature instructors are employed in the 100 or so Chinese teachers colleges, and, where children's literature courses are offered, they are never required for preservice teachers (Wei 2009, p. 81). The result is that, as Wang (2007) estimates, 99% of the teachers in primary and secondary schools have not received any training in youth literature. Most of these teachers are unlikely to be familiar with any high-quality youth literature titles besides the limited number of short pieces in the curriculum, are not prepared to incorporate extensive youth literature materials into classroom instruction, and do not understand the importance of youth literature for the intellectual, emotional, and moral growth of young people.

Similarly, the training of librarians serving youth in public and school libraries is largely absent in Chinese library and information science (LIS) schools that pride themselves in having jumped on the bandwagon of information and digital technology by offering such courses as "information management," "information systems," "information retrieval," and "digital libraries." The marginalization of youth services in Chinese LIS education explains why, when a group of American school and youth services delegates visited China in 1998, Chinese library school students were "baffled by the idea that anyone with a postgraduate degree would choose... 'babysitting' as a profession." One library director in Beijing even commented, "To work here [in a children's library] would be a waste of knowledge" (Kniffel 1998, p. 59). Lacking professionally trained youth services librarians means that even well-funded and well-stocked libraries can fall short on services

---

[8] The Chinese translation of *The Wind in the Willows* by Kenneth Grahame, for example, is about 40,000 characters—1% of four million.

that effectively bring together youth literature and young readers and that assist classroom teachers in selecting appropriate library materials for reaching curriculum goals.

The closer students approach the college entrance exam in grade 12, the more intense the tension between reading youth literature and formal schooling. As mentioned above, the tension has risen so high that China's education system is blamed for the tepid youth literature industry after 1990, and the inflexible education system is the key concern of several important authors for youth in their works of fiction since the 1980s. To resolve the unfortunate conflict, the state-controlled higher education system will need to increase financial, material, and human resources allocated to the areas of youth literature and library youth services; train teachers and librarians who are sophisticated in the evaluation, selection, promotion, and teaching of youth literature; and support scholarly endeavors that investigate youth literature in several disciplines including, but not restricted to, literature, arts, child development, education, and library and information science.

7.4 Summary

This chapter has reviewed the historical transformation of Chinese youth literature, which, rooted in Chinese oral and popular culture and heavily influenced by Western imports from time to time, began in the early twentieth century with an important educational mission. War, political upheaval, economic expansion, and educational reform have all had a visible impact on the content, style, format, genre, quantity, and quality of Chinese youth literature. Whereas it is ironic that a test-driven, merit-based education system should be identified as a barrier to the thriving of the youth literature industry, the market for publications for beginning readers and lower grade students is more encouraging than for young adult literature. Teacher and librarian training in youth literature, curriculum connections, and youth services, if implemented, should lead to increased support for students' leisure reading and incorporation of children's and young adult books in their formal educational experiences.

References

Bing, X. (1923, July 25). 寄小读者(之一) [Letters to young readers, no. 1]. 晨报. Retrieved February 25, 2010, from http://www.godpp.gov.cn/wmzh/2009-02/27/content_15814292.htm

Chen, D. (2006a). Trends in Chinese youth culture and literature. *Bookbird, 44*(3), 13–19.

Chen, M. (2006b). 推广阅读更新少儿图书服务理念与实践——来自明德英文图书馆的报告 [Reading promotion in apple tree libraries: Innovating youth services in Chinese public and school libraries]. In 管理创新与图书馆服务: 第三届上海国际图书馆论坛论文集 [*Management innovation & library services: The proceedings of the third Shanghai International Library Forum*], ed. Shanghai tu shu guan, (pp. 449–457). Shanghai: Shanghai Science and Technology Press.

Chen, X. (2008, January 23). 他们是中国儿童阅读推广人 [They are promoters of children's reading in China]. 中华读书报, 3. Retrieved from http://www.gmw.cn/01ds/2008-01/23/content_726674.htm

Deng, X. (2008, December 19). 优秀童书Top10中国作品又无缘 [List of top 10 children's books passes Chinese works again]. 北京青年报. Retrieved February 25, 2010, from http://bjyouth.ynet.com/article.jsp?oid=47156728

Dian shi ji he you xian dian shi pu ji lü 2001 nian [Penetration rates of TV sets and cable TV service, Year 2001]. Retrieved from http://www.stats.gov.cn/tjsj/qtsj/gjsj/2001/t20021113_402193335.htm

Ding, J. (1953, September). 简评上海出版的儿童文学作品 [A brief appraisal of children's literature published in Shanghai]. 文艺月报, 26–28.

Ding, A. (1984). 今夜月儿明 [The bright moonlight tonight]. 少年文艺, (1). 14–29.

Du, Y. (1937, July 15). 请你不要骄傲 [Please do not be smug]. 小朋友, 768, 8–15.

Er tong wen xue gai lun [*An introduction to children's literature*]. (1990). 成都: 四川少年儿童出版社.

Fang, H. (1937, October 28). 兵士 [Soldier]. 小朋友, 777–8, 24–25.

Fang, H. (1999). 新中国少儿读物出版50年 [Fifty years of publishing for youth in the new China]. 出版科学, 4, 10–15.

Farquhar, M. (1999). *Children's literature in China: From LU Xun to MAO Zedong*. Armonk: M. E. Sharpe.

Guan, H. (1990). 雨来没有死 [Yulai did not die]. In M. Pu (Ed.), 中国儿童文学大系. 一, 小说 (pp. 738–744). 太原: 希望出版社. (Original work published 1948)

Ho, D. D. (2006). To protect and preserve: Resisting the destroy the four olds campaign, 1966–1967. In J. Esherick, P. Pickowicz, & A. G. Walder (Eds.), *The Chinese cultural revolution as history* (pp. 64–95). Stanford: Stanford University Press.

Hua, S. (1990). 鸡毛信 [Feather letter]. In M. Pu (Ed.), 中国儿童文学大系. 一, 小说 (pp. 639–671). 太原: 希望出版社. (Original work published 1949)

Hung, C. (1994). *War and popular culture: Resistance in modern China, 1937–1945*. Berkeley: University of California Press.

Jiang, F. (2005). 蒋风儿童文学论文选 [Selected children's literature papers by Feng Jiang]. 南宁: 接力出版社.

Kniffel, L. (1998). The changing face of youth services in China. *American Libraries, 29*(11), 58–61.

Li, X. (1972). 闪闪的红星 [Shining red star]. 北京: 人民文学出版社.

Li, Y. (2003). A growing children's book publishing industry in China. In R. E. Baensch (Ed.), *The publishing industry in China* (pp. 85–99). New Brunswick: Transaction Publishers.

Li, X. (2005, October 12). 小说《闪闪的红星》(下) [On the novel *Shining Red Star*, part II]. 齐鲁晚报. Retrieved from http://www.qlwb.com.cn/display.asp?id=94342

Liang, Y. (2000). 民间语文资料: 书简034号 "白卷英雄"张铁生试卷 (1973) [Hero of the blank answer sheet: Tiesheng Zhang's exam paper of 1973]. 天涯, 6, 67.

Lin, C. (2003). A study of Chinese young adult reading and its market. In R. E. Baensch (Ed.), *The publishing industry in China* (pp. 101–112). New Brunswick: Transaction Publishers.

Liu, W. (2004). 《三重门》改编成电视剧 韩寒不满导演遗憾 [*The Third Way* in TV adaptation: To Han Han's dissatisfaction and director's regret]. Retrieved from http://ent.sina.com.cn/2004-12-16/0849601306.html

Liu, T. (2009, March 26). 中少社引进日本漫画遇到难题 [China children's press encounters challenge in importing Japanese manga]. 北京晨报, A13.

Mao, Z. (1993). 工作方法六十条(草案) [60-point work method, draft]. In 中共中央文献研究室 (Ed.), 毛泽东文集. 北京: 人民出版社. (Original work published 1958)

Mimiyan. (2009, June 10). 《皮皮鲁传》读后感 [Thoughts on reading *Pipilu*]. Retrieved February 25, 2010, from http://blog.wuhunews.cn/?uid-10602-action-viewspace-itemid-17245

Palmowski, J. (2008). May fourth movement. In *A dictionary of contemporary world history*. Oxford: Oxford University Press. Retrieved from http://www.oxfordreference.com/views/ENTRY.html?subview=Main&entry=t46.e1500

Pu, M. (1989). 导言 [Introduction]. In M. Pu (Ed.), 中国儿童文学大系. 童话 [*Chinese children's literature series: Fairy tales*] (pp. 1–39). 太原: 希望出版社.

Pu, M. (1990). 导言 [Introduction]. In M. Pu (Ed.), 中国儿童文学大系. 一, 小说 [*Chinese children's literature series: Fiction I*] (pp. 1–40). 太原: 希望出版社.

"Ren min ri bao" she lun. (1989). 大量创作、出版、发行少年儿童读物 [Greatly increase the creation, publication, and distribution of reading materials for youth]. In Z. Chen (Ed.), 论当代中国儿童文学 (pp. 9–12). 长沙: 湖南少年儿童出版社. (Original work published 1955)

Scott, D. H. (1980). *Chinese popular literature and the child*. Chicago: American Library Association.

Shen, J. (2002). 试论19世纪在华传教士的报刊活动 [On missionaries' publishing of newspapers and periodicals in China during the 19th century]. 华中师范大学学报 (人文社会科学版), 6, 78–86.

Sun, J. (2008). 从市场终端数据看少儿图书出版 [What market data reveals about juvenile publishing]. 中国出版, 6, 8–12.

Tang, R. (2006). Chinese children's literature in the 21st century. *Bookbird, 44*(3), 21–29.

The Sunday School. (1876, December 14). *The Independent*, pp. 6–7.

Wang, Q. (2000). 现代中国儿童文学主潮 [Main trends in modern Chinese children's literature]. 重庆: 重庆出版社.

Wang, Q. (2007, July 4). 学科级别·左右学术命运的指挥棒? [Are ranked disciplines controlling the destiny of academic studies?]. 中华读书报, 11. Retrieved from http://www.gmw.cn/01ds/2007-07/04/content_634051.htm

Wei, Y. (1937, October 28). 儿童防空常识图解 [Illustrated safety tips for children during an air raid]. 小朋友, 777–8, 13–14.

Wei, M. (2004, March 10). "孩子心里想什么,我的书里能找到" [Find in my books what children are thinking]. 中国新闻出版报.

Wei, H. (2009). 儿童文学在高师中的地位与小学语文教育的需求研究 [A study on children's literature in teacher's college education and the needs of elementary Chinese education]. 黑龙江高教研究, 8, 81–83.

Xiao ying xiong Yulai [Little hero Yulai]. 2005. In Y. Ji et al. (Eds.), 义务教育课程标准实验教科书 语文 四年级下册 教师教学用书. 北京: 人民教育出版社. Retrieved February 25, 2010, from http://www.pep.com.cn/xiaoyu/jiaoshi/tbjxzy/jiaocan/xy4x/200703/t20070311_314636.htm

Xu, Z. (1953). 细菌和细菌战争 [Bacteria and bacterial warfare] (3rd ed.). 上海: 商务印书馆.

Xu, G. (1964). 小兵张嘎 [Little soldier CHANG Ka-tse] (2nd ed). 北京: 中国少年儿童出版社.

Xu, G. (2001). 昨夜西风凋碧树 [Last night's west wind and a withered tree]. 北京: 北京十月文艺出版社.

Xu, C. (Ed.). (2004). 上海美术志 [Art history of Shanghai]. 上海: 上海书画出版社. Retrieved from http://www.shtong.gov.cn/node2/node2245/node73148/node73151/node73199/index.html

Yang, H. (2004). 神秘的女老师 [The mysterious teacher lady]. 北京: 作家出版社.

Ye, S. (1988). 文艺谈 [On literature and art]. In F. Jiang (Ed.), 中国儿童文学大系 (pp. 11–24). 太原: 希望出版社. (Reprinted from晨报, March 3-June 25, 1921).

Yu wen ke cheng biao zhun yan zhi zu. (2002). 全日制义务教育语文课程标准 (实验稿)第二部分 课程目标[Chinese curriculum standards for full-time compulsory education (experimental edition), part 2: course objectives]. Retrieved February 25, 2010, from http://www.pep.com.cn/peixun/xkpx/peixun/kbjd/jiedu/200804/t20080414_458858.htm

Yuan, L. (2001). 周恩来文革期间关心新闻出版工作纪事 [Zhou Enlai cared about news and publishing works during the Cultural Revolution]. 出版科学, 01, 57–62.

Zhang, Z. (1999). "文革"期间出版工作忆实 [A truthful recollection of publishing during the Cultural Revolution]. 新文化史料, 3, 42–46.

Zhang, S., Pang, D., & Zheng, R. (1999). 中华印刷通史 [A general history of printing in China]. 北京: 印刷工业出版社. Retrieved from http://www.cgan.net/book/books/print/g-history/gb_12/13_4.htm

Zhao, L. (2006). 八十年代儿童小说主题走向概观 [A broad overview of thematic trends in children's fiction during the 1980s]. In J. Hu, & Q. Sun (Eds.), *中国新时期儿童文学研究资* (pp. 74–78). 济南: 山东文艺出版社. (Reprinted from *Dang Dai Wen Yi Si Chao, 1985*(3)).

Zhou, Z. (1988). *儿童的文学* [Children's literature]. In F. Jiang (Ed.), *中国儿童文学大系* (pp. 3–10). 太原: 希望出版社. (Reprinted from *新青年* 8(4): October 1920).

Zhou, X. (2004). Children of the cultural revolution: The send-down episode. In *The state and life chances in urban China: Redistribution and stratification, 1949–1994* (pp. 124–153). New York: Cambridge University Press.

Zhu, Z. (2000). *中国儿童文学与现代化进程* [Chinese children's literature and modernization]. 杭州: 浙江少年儿童出版社.

Zipes, J. D. (2006). Introduction. In J. Zipes (Ed.), *The Oxford encyclopedia of children's literature*. Oxford: Oxford University Press.

Chapter 8
Primary School Chinese Language and Literacy Curriculum Reforms in China After 1949

Jiening Ruan and Lijun Jin

8.1 Introduction

Yuwen, also known as Chinese language and literacy, is one of the most critical school subjects in the Chinese education system at both primary and secondary levels. In this chapter, we present an overview of the various historical periods in the development of primary Chinese Yuwen education from the founding of the People's Republic of China in 1949 to 2000, as well as a brief review of the key content of the most critical curriculum documents that guided primary Chinese Yuwen education within each period. We then provide the background for the latest primary Yuwen curriculum reform and present the highlights of the 2011 *Primary Yuwen Curriculum Standards for Full-Day Compulsory Education*. Finally, we discuss the impact and challenges of this most recent Yuwen curriculum reform. Implications for primary Yuwen education are also drawn.

8.2 Historical Development of Primary Yuwen Curriculum from 1949 to 2000

The Chinese education system has gone through several education reforms since 1949, usually following major political and social movements. Such reforms were carried out through the government's initiatives to develop and implement new curriculum guidelines in the form of teaching syllabi or curriculum standards for all

J. Ruan (✉)
Reading/Literacy Education, University of Oklahoma, Norman, OK, USA
e-mail: jruan@ou.edu

L. Jin
Elementary Education, Towson University, Towson, MD, USA

school subjects, with Yuwen at the center of each reform movement. Each reform has left its mark on history. In this section, we draw on the work of Wu and Yu (2009a, b) and Jin (n.d.) in our review of historical periods and highlight key curriculum documents for each period.

8.2.1 From 1949 to 1957

This period marked an end to the use of the old terminology *Guoyu (national language)* and *Guowen (national writing)*. Yuwen was a new term coined to refer to the subject of Chinese language and literacy and to more accurately reflect the major mission of the subject—to develop student knowledge and skills in both oral and written communications (Guo 2005). In 1950, the Ministry of Education (MOE) promulgated *Primary Yuwen Curriculum Temporary Standards (Draft)* and stipulated that the goal of Yuwen instruction was to teach listening, speaking, reading, and writing and to apply these skills in acquiring knowledge in other subject areas, including patriotic and civic responsibilities.

In 1956, the Ministry of Education published *Primary Yuwen Teaching Syllabus (Draft)* to replace the 1950 draft and its revised version (1952) and to initiate the first primary Yuwen reform in China. This document set specific expectations for the teaching of Chinese language and required primary schools to offer two periods of Chinese language per week. Primary students were expected to recognize between 3,000 and 3,500 high frequency Chinese characters, and reading was to be taught through the use of literature and detailed analysis of literary texts. As New China's first primary school Yuwen curriculum document, this document was heavily influenced by the Soviet Union's language teaching system and Kairov's pedagogy. The impact of such a move towards Yuwen instruction was long lasting and can still be found in today's Yuwen instruction in China.

8.2.2 From 1958 to 1976

With the Great Leap Forward Movement in 1958, Yuwen instruction deviated from its original purpose and focused on political and moral indoctrination. To reset the course for Yuwen instruction, the Ministry of Education published *Full-Day Primary Yuwen Teaching Syllabus (Draft)* in 1963. The document, for the first time ever, clearly defined Yuwen as an essential tool for knowledge acquisition and job performance. It also emphasized the importance of providing primary students with training in "double basics" (i.e., basic knowledge and basic skills in Yuwen). The teaching syllabus also stipulated that primary students should master 3,500 high frequency Chinese characters, and Yuwen teaching should address the teaching of Chinese spoken and written language, as well as transmitting political ideology sanctioned by the government.

Unfortunately, the reform was derailed when the Cultural Revolution began in 1966. In the 10 years that followed, all previous reform efforts were abandoned.

The sole purpose of Yuwen curriculum and instruction during that period was to advance political ideology and indoctrination.

8.2.3 From 1978 to 1991

China opened its door to the rest of the world in 1978. The demand for Yuwen reform was widespread. Western educational philosophies and pedagogies—such as Bruner's inquiry learning, Bloom's taxonomy, and Sukhomlynsky's aesthetic approach to learning—flourished in China. Various teaching methods were explored to promote students' language and communication competencies. These methods included contextualized learning and reading-writing connections. A teaching sequence was established to help students move from focused character recognition to extensive reading to step-by-step exercises to prepare for standardized tests (Cui 2010).

In 1978, the Ministry of Education issued *Full-Day Ten-Year Primary School Yuwen Teaching Syllabus (Draft – Trial Version)*. This teaching syllabus was the first one published after the Cultural Revolution. It restored the function of Yuwen as defined in the 1963 Syllabus, noting it should be a basic tool for all learning. The major task of this reform was to improve the quality of teaching and learning of Yuwen by developing students' language competence in comprehension and communication. Unprecedentedly, it proposed an end to the traditional spoon-feeding method of Yuwen teaching and emphasized the importance of helping students develop independent learning skills by teaching them learning methods. It pointed out that student acquisition of Yuwen knowledge and development of Yuwen skills should be accomplished through teachers providing students with basic training in Chinese language and literacy. The syllabus required primary students to recognize 3,000 characters and to achieve full mastery of 2,500 of those characters. It placed high expectations on using Yuwen education to support student learning of government-sanctioned ideologies. This teaching syllabus was revised in 1986, but the content of the revised syllabus was very similar to its original version. Some important changes in the 1986 version included a new emphasis on the importance of rigorous training in listening, speaking, reading, and writing, as well as developing students' good learning habits.

In 1986, the *Compulsory Education Law of the People's Republic of China* was passed. Compulsory education in China covers grades 1–9 and requires that all children receive basic education in those grades. To support the full implementation of the law, the Education Commission was in charge of developing teaching syllabi for all school subjects for both basic education (grades 1–9) and high school education (grades 10–12).

8.2.4 From 1992 to 2000

In 1992, *Nine-Year Compulsory Education Full-Day Primary School Yuwen Teaching Syllabus (Trial Version)* was published. The syllabus reflected the government's agenda to promote quality education and identified objectives related to supporting students' Yuwen learning, as well as their cognitive, moral, and ethical development. To accommodate all students, the syllabus lowered expectations for the amount of characters primary students had to master, reducing the number to 2,500 characters. Specific requirements were set for teaching at each grade level in the areas of Chinese pinyin, character recognition and character writing, listening and speaking, reading, and composition. The 1992 syllabus also contained a new section on extracurricular activities, so that while following the same teaching syllabus, schools could choose to adopt different textbooks to meet their own needs. The syllabus was instrumental in guiding the various primary Yuwen curriculum reform initiatives underway during this period. Another noteworthy aspect of this document was that for the first time ever it included Yuwen education as part of the nation's strategic plan for improving the overall quality of the entire nation. In 1993, the Central Committee of the Chinese Communist Party and the State Council jointly issued *China Education Reform and Development Guidelines* that also called for a shift from examination-oriented education to quality education for the betterment of the nation.

The changes in this period reflected a desire to promote the quality of students' language acquisition through systematic training in listening, speaking, reading and writing (Wu and Yu 2009b). The aforementioned reforms beginning in 1950 do not substantially differ much from each other in that they all focused on a teacher-centered, knowledge-based, and skills-oriented paradigm, devoid of the spirit of independent and critical thinking. Yuwen education was mainly seen as an indoctrination tool, with its main purpose to cultivate a populace devoted to the causes of the Communist Party and the central government (Jin et al. 2007). It also served as a vehicle for promoting and achieving social uniformity and conformity (Hu 2004).

8.3 Primary Yuwen Curriculum Reform from 2001 to the Present Time

The new millennium has ushered in dramatic changes on all fronts. Economically, China has become more market-oriented. Politically, China is less centralized and more locally governed. Globally, China has become a major political and economic force. In addition, new technologies have brought about an information explosion, and people have gained unprecedented access to a large amount of information at their fingertips. With all these changes happening to the Chinese society, the old rigid knowledge-based, skills-oriented school curricula were no long adequate. Consequently, there was a public outcry for a new education reform to prepare the country for the demands of the new times.

In response, the Chinese government began its most recent education reform at the turn of the twenty-first century to support the central government's Quality Education Initiative. This initiative aims at promoting students' intellectual development, aesthetic appreciation, morality, and physical fitness, while fostering creativity, originality, and hands-on skills. The ultimate goal is to educate productive future citizens who can contribute to China's economic development and cope with the challenges brought about by the new millennium. Curriculum reform is at the forefront of the education reform because curriculum is the "carrier of Quality Education" (Yu 2010, p. 35), and Yuwen curriculum reform is at the front and center of the full reform movement.

In 2001, the Chinese Ministry of Education published *Yuwen Curriculum Standards for Full-Day Compulsory Education (Trial Version)*, a key document to guide the reform of Yuwen curriculum for grades 1 to 9, which covers primary school (grades 1–6) as well as junior high school (grades 7–9). This is the most comprehensive curriculum document developed since 1949.

In the following 10 years, the document was put under intense examination while it was being implemented. The MOE sought input and feedback from Yuwen experts, schools, and Yuwen teachers. In 2011, the finalized *Yuwen Curriculum Standards for Full-Day Compulsory Education* was published (hereafter referred to as *Standards*). Except for some minor changes, the structure and content of the two versions are very similar. A major revision involved reducing the number of Chinese characters students in lower grades (1–4) are expected to recognize and write, so that the number is more manageable for younger primary students. There is also an increase in the number of classical Chinese poems primary and junior high students are required to memorize and recite to strengthen their understanding of and appreciation for Chinese language and traditional Chinese culture. Six more poems were added to the primary list while 14 were added to the list for the 7th to 9th grade band. The 2011 revised version also added a new requirement for student learning of Chinese calligraphy, another effort to strengthen students' understanding of and appreciation for traditional Chinese language and culture.

The *Standards* reconceptualizes the subject of Yuwen not only as a critical discipline but as the foundation for student success in all other subject areas. It defines Yuwen as the most important tool of communication, a carrier of information, and a critical component of human culture. Yuwen plays an important role in Chinese 9-year compulsory education. The *Standards* highlights four guiding principles for the Yuwen curriculum reform: (a) fully develop students' fundamental competencies in and positive dispositions towards learning Chinese language and culture; (b) properly understand the characteristics unique to Yuwen education; (c) actively promote independent learning, collaborative learning, and inquiry-based learning; and (d) strive to build openness and vitality into Yuwen curriculum. These guiding principles are reflected throughout the whole document.

The *Standards* points out that Yuwen curriculum and instruction should focus on knowledge and skills, process and methods, and dispositions in five major areas: character recognition and character writing, reading, writing (composition), oral communication, and integrated learning. Specific objectives are set for students at various developmental levels. For example, students in the 5th to 6th grade band are expected to recognize 3,000 characters and write 2,500 of them, write Chinese calligraphy with a brush, read with fluency in Mandarin Chinese (*Putonghua*), understand the main outline of narrative texts and key points in expository texts, compose simple realistic and creative writing, complete about 16 compositions in class, read more than one million characters in out-of-school reading, communicate with others through oral and written language, and conduct research through various information channels to solve real-life problems.

In terms of recommended practices, the *Standards* suggests that schools should give full play to the creativity and innovation of teachers and students in the process of teaching and learning. It redefines the roles of students and teachers in Yuwen teaching and learning and emphasizes the importance of independent learning, aesthetic response to literature, collaboration, and inquiry-based learning. Students are to be given ownership of learning. Yuwen instruction should stimulate student interest in learning, create an environment for independent learning, cultivate students' awareness and habit of independent learning, and encourage students to draw on their own learning styles when learning Yuwen. Teachers are the facilitators and guides in student learning and should promote student interests, motivation, and positive dispositions towards Yuwen learning, as well as engage students in inquiry- and discussion-based learning.

The *Standards* recognizes that traditional paper pencil exams provide only one method of assessment and evaluation. It stipulates the purposes and functions of assessment and evaluation. In other words, assessment and evaluation not only should focus on whether students meet the curriculum goals and objectives, but also should be used to examine the effectiveness of teaching, enhance student learning, improve curriculum design, and perfect instructional processes. It is recommended that both formative and summative assessments take into consideration student overall performance in various areas of knowledge and skills, process and method, emotions and attitudes, as well as values. The document also recommends that student self-evaluation and peer evaluation be an integral part of teacher and parent evaluation to respect individual differences and promote the healthy development of every student.

8.4 Analysis of the Current Primary Yuwen Curriculum Reform

Unlike previous curriculum reforms, it is noteworthy that the current Yuwen curriculum reform is future-oriented and heavily influenced by Western educational philosophy (Chen 2010). Instead of placing heavy emphasis on the function of language and literacy as a tool for ideological and political causes as it was in the past, the new curriculum establishes that Yuwen is the carrier and transmitter of Chinese culture and the foundation for personal life-long success, and that Yuwen education should gear itself toward modernism, the world, and the future. Creativity, innovation, and problem-solving abilities also seem to weigh heavily in the current reform. Such an orientation aligns closely with the Chinese government's overall vision for the country to embrace the challenges of the twenty-first century while preserving and revitalizing traditional Chinese culture.

The new primary Yuwen curriculum recognizes the importance of affective factors in student learning and supports the development of interest and positive attitudes towards Chinese language and literacy learning. It values personal experiences and individuals' responses to and appreciation of literature. For the first time, a concept similar to the term "dispositions" used in the U.S. context is proposed to expand the goal of Chinese language and literacy education beyond the acquisition of knowledge and skills to develop student motivation and positive attitudes toward Yuwen learning and competencies in inquiry and decision-making. Compared with previous curriculum documents, the new curriculum places less emphasis on the acquisition of knowledge and skills for primary students. Instead, helping students experience the pleasure of reading and to construct personal meanings becomes an important goal of Yuwen instruction. For example, isolated grammatical knowledge was considered essential in the old curricula, but not in the new curriculum. Prior to the reform, there was only one way to interpret a text, and students had to match their answers to the ones prescribed in the teachers' guide, but the new curriculum encourages personal responses. The new curriculum still describes memorization and recitation of outstanding classical literature as an important means to develop students' sense of the Chinese language and culture, but it also gives much attention to students' personal and emotional responses to literature.

Regarding methods of delivery, the new curriculum promotes collaboration, independent learning, and inquiry-based learning (Zheng 2003). It encourages student learning through dialogue between students and teachers and between peers. Teachers are asked to encourage students to explore different learning methods and to engage in independent learning. This counters the traditional notion of Chinese instruction as teacher-directed and textbook-centered practices. It is also the first time in recent literacy education history that extensive after-school reading is mandated in curriculum guides (Zheng 2003). It is expected that students will develop their reading abilities through both intensive reading of textbooks and extensive, self-selected after-school readings. This new addition to the *Standards* supports the call for more extensive reading recommended by Wu, Li, and Anderson (1999) in their review of Chinese reading curriculum and instruction.

The most significant change brought about by the latest reform is the redefinition of the roles of teachers and students under a new curriculum that strives to be student-centered and developmentally appropriate. The new Standards document acknowledges students as the main agent in the learning process and encourages them to take initiative and ownership of their own learning. Teachers become facilitators and guides instead of authoritative figures who possess all the knowledge and spoon-feed their students.

Another major departure from previous curricular reforms is the new perspective on assessment and evaluation. Chinese education has long been a test-driven enterprise and is well known for its test-oriented paradigm. The new Standards document mandates that assessments and evaluation should be used to promote student growth, teacher development, and improvement of instructional practices. Shifting the purpose of assessments from ranking and selection to promoting student growth, teacher development, and improvement of instructional practices resembles the perspectives on literacy assessments proposed by many Western educators (see Afflerbach 2007; Caldwell 2009).

8.5 Issues and Challenges of the Current Primary Yuwen Curriculum Reform

Because of its profound impact on how Chinese language and literacy teaching and learning should move forward in China, the reform has been under intense scrutiny and heated debate (Chen 2010). However, it is indisputable that this reform has already left an indelible mark on Chinese education.

The new primary Yuwen curriculum reform marks a significant departure from any previous curriculum reforms (Feng 2006; Yu 2010; Zheng 2003) and has generated controversy among Yuwen teachers and educators. Some primary Yuwen teachers have wholeheartedly embraced the reform and implemented new ways of teaching, and they encourage student learning through exploration and social interaction in a low-risk learning environment (Xiao 2008). However, changes are difficult for many others. It is not surprising that several issues and challenges exist that prevent the new curriculum standards from being fully and effectively implemented.

When one examines the *Standards*, it is not difficult to notice that many similarities exist between some of the ideas promoted in the *Standards* and Western philosophy and practices of literacy education. In particular, the paradigm shift from teacher-centered instruction to student-centered learning is hard for many teachers to make within a short period of time. The shifting of the teachers' role from an authoritative figure to a facilitator and guide also contradicts the traditional view of teachers in Chinese culture. According to Confucius, a teacher's job is to "transmit wisdom, teach knowledge, and resolve confusion." In this sense, the current curriculum reform is more than a reform of education. It is a reform of the Chinese culture of education. This reform can only be successful if teachers change their view of the teacher-student relationship in the learning process.

The new Yuwen curriculum standards for primary grades (1–6) have a decreased emphasis on the acquisition of knowledge and skills, especially knowledge of Chinese grammar, but there is an increased focus on encouraging students to experience the joy of reading and to respond to texts through inquiry-based, collaborative, and independent learning. Some educators and teachers feel the new curriculum does not pay adequate attention to skills instruction. Therefore, they call for a return to the basics in teaching and learning Chinese (Chen 2010; Song 2006; Xiao 2007; Zhang and Liu 2009).

The current reform places a higher demand on teacher quality, teacher knowledge, and teacher expertise in order for them to implement new standards in their teaching. The number of new ideas for teachers introduced in the *Standards* is overwhelming for teachers to process (Yu 2010). Some complaints from primary Yuwen teachers include a lack of instructional time due to having to spend more time on discussion and exploration, as well as students' inability to collaborate and learn through inquiry due to their previous spoon-fed schooling experiences. In addition, teachers have to improve their own knowledge base in all subject areas because of the need for integrated learning (Chen 2010; Xiao 2007).

Another important issue to address is the relatively small amount of writing mandated in the curriculum Standards document. The literacy field in the West has long recognized the symbiotic relationship between reading and writing development (Kucer 2009). Strengthening writing instruction and increasing the amount of writing, both in class and after school, can further improve the quality of Chinese literacy teaching and learning.

Other issues include inequality in student access to reading materials since extensive after-school reading is mandated. Students from disadvantaged socio-economic backgrounds, as well as those in poor regions, will have less access to reading materials. Access to information technologies is also problematic for teachers and students in poor schools.

While progress is being made and individual responses are encouraged, the meaning of critical reading and critical thinking has not yet been fully explained in the Standards document. Since Chinese teachers and students have been conditioned to accept the traditional skills-oriented teaching, much effort should be provided related to professional development for teachers on how to engage students in critical reading and creative thinking if China wants to have future generations who are truly creative and innovative.

Currently, several textbook companies in China are eligible to publish Yuwen textbooks. Schools can choose which textbook series to use. Therefore, finding a series that fits local needs is also a challenge.

8.6 Implications for Primary Yuwen Education Practices and Policies

The Ministry of Education understands that the current curriculum reform is an exploratory process due to its scope and depth (Yu 2010). A major reason behind the resistance from some schools and teachers is the inability of teachers to make the paradigm shift and their lack of preparation and training for its successful implementation. Since this is a top-down reform, in order to ensure the reform is successful, systematic efforts have to be made to effectively address the clash between traditional and current views of Yuwen instruction and to bring schools and teachers on board to support the reform.

Even though it is helpful to borrow ideas from Western literacy educational philosophies and practices, primary Yuwen instruction should also maintain some of its traditional practices that have endured the test of time, such as oral recitation and repeated reading of classical texts for fluency and better comprehension. The Chinese language is a carrier of Chinese culture and has its own unique characteristics. It is important to find a balance between Western pedagogical practices and Chinese traditional teaching methods that are rooted in the special nature and characteristics of the Chinese language. In addition to learning Western philosophies and pedagogical practices, Chinese teachers need to increase their knowledge and understanding of traditional Chinese culture and Chinese teaching to integrate the two (Song 2006).

Inservice teacher training and preservice teacher preparation should be strengthened in order for teachers to fulfill their new roles (Zhong and Liao 2008). In addition, teachers should also be encouraged to take on the role of researcher to achieve new thinking and adopt new practices (Zhang 2004; Zhong and Liao 2008). Teacher education institutions and universities need to restructure their goals and objectives, programs, curriculum structure, and instructional approaches to reflect the new reform and provide leadership in moving the reform forward.

To ensure the success of the new curriculum, the test-driven Chinese society and teacher accountability issues have to be addressed. Chinese teachers have to grapple with the tension between implementing the new curriculum standards that are more student-centered, experience- and inquiry-based and handling the societal pressure for increasing student test scores. Although in primary schools, the pressure for standardized high-stakes testing has been decreasing dramatically in recent years due to the elimination of middle school entrance exams in most places in China, teachers are still facing the pressure of having their students' test scores compared to those of students from other classes in the same school or across different school districts. As a result, many teachers are still teaching to the test.

The issue of providing students with equal access to technologies and reading materials should be addressed. In addition, teacher education needs to address how technologies can be used to effectively facilitate Yuwen instruction. It is critical that technologies be used to support literacy instruction but not drive literacy instruction.

8.7 Summary

Since 1949, primary school language and literacy education in China has gone through five major stages of development characterized by the various reform efforts associated with the unique social and historical contexts of the country during those times. The current primary Yuwen curriculum reform initiated in 2001 is the Chinese government's response to the dramatic changes the country has experienced in global and domestic arenas and aims at meeting the demands of the information age, globalization, and individualization. It has expanded teachers' perspectives and enriched Yuwen instruction (Chen 2010) by pushing teachers to think and reflect on their existing practices and find innovative ways to prepare a new generation of students in the age of technology. However, it is also important to understand that the reform has encountered opposition from old-school Yuwen educators and teachers. Although facing mounting challenges, the current literacy reform is moving in the right direction towards engaging students in mind, heart, and hands.

While embracing many of the ideas in the new curriculum standards that strive to provide a more student-centered curriculum, many primary Yuwen teachers have to deal with the cultural clashes between their traditional views of Yuwen education and Western ideas. The reality is that traditional approaches to Yuwen instruction are deep-rooted and still are much favored and practiced by many Yuwen teachers in China. Finding a balance between teacher-directed, knowledge-based, skills-oriented, test-driven teaching and more student-centered, collaborative, inquiry-based learning remains a pressing issue to be solved in the foreseeable future. The paradigm shift cannot be achieved overnight. Teacher preparation and teacher training need to catch up with the demands of the new curriculum standards. Furthermore, the test-driven culture has to be continuously challenged and changed to accomplish the new curriculum goals and objectives.

References

Afflerbach, P. (2007). *Understanding and using reading assessment, K-12*. Newark: International Reading Association.

Caldwell, J. (2009). *Reading assessment: A primer for reading teachers and coaches* (2nd ed.). New York: Guilford Press.

Central Committee of the Chinese Communist Party & State Council. (1993). 中国教育改革和发展纲要 [*China education reform and development guidelines*]. Retrieved from http://www.edu.cn/zong_he_870/20100719/t20100719_497964.shtml

Chen, Y. (2010). 在中国小学语文教学改革的折点上: 周一贯老师访谈录. [At the turning point of primary school Chinese teaching reform in China: An interview with Teacher Yiguan Zhou]. 教学月刊小学版, *1*, 4–9.

Chinese Ministry of Education. (1950). 小学语文课程暂行标准 (草案) [*Primary school Yuwen curriculum temporary standards (draft)*]. Beijing: Chinese Ministry of Education.

Chinese Ministry of Education. (1952). 小学语文课程暂行标准(修订草案) [*Primary school Yuwen curriculum temporary standards (revised draft)*]. Beijing: Chinese Ministry of Education.

Chinese Ministry of Education. (1956). 小学语文教学大纲 (草案) [*Primary school Yuwen teaching syllabus (draft)*]. Beijing: Chinese Ministry of Education.

Chinese Ministry of Education. (1963). 全日制小学语文教学大纲 (草案) [*Full-day primary school Yuwen teaching syllabus (draft)*]. Beijing: Chinese Ministry of Education.

Chinese Ministry of Education. (1978). 全日制十年制学校小学语文教学大纲 (试行草案) [*Full-day ten-year school primary school Yuwen teaching syllabus (draft – trial version)*]. Beijing: Chinese Ministry of Education.

Chinese Ministry of Education. (1986). 全日制小学语文大纲 [*Full-day primary school teaching syllabus*]. Beijing: Chinese Ministry of Education.

Chinese Ministry of Education. (1992). 九年义务教育全日制小学语文教学大纲 (试用) [*Nine-year compulsory education full-day primary school Yuwen teaching syllabus (trial version)*]. Beijing: Chinese Ministry of Education.

Chinese Ministry of Education. (2001). 全日制义务教育语文课程标准 (实验稿) [*Yuwen curriculum standards for full-day compulsory education (trial version)*]. Beijing: Beijing Normal University Publishing House.

Chinese Ministry of Education. (2011). 全日制义务教育语文课程标准 [*Yuwen curriculum standards for full-day compulsory education*]. Beijing: Chinese Ministry of Education.

Cui, R. (Ed.). (2010). 新中国中小学教材建设史1949-2000研究丛书小学语文卷 [*The history of the development of primary school and middle school textbooks 1949–2000: Research series on primary Yuwen*]. Beijing: People's Education Press.

Feng, D. (2006). China's recent curriculum reform: Progress and problems. *Planning and Changing, 37*(1 & 2), 131–144.

Guo, G. (2005). 从教学大纲的历史变迁看中学语文教 改的发展 [Views of the development of middle school Yuwen education reforms through the examination of the historical changes in the teaching syllabi]. 山东教育 (中学刊), *35*, 17–18.

Hu, Y. (2004). The cultural significance of reading instruction in China. *The Reading Teacher, 57*, 634–639.

Jin, N. (n.d.) 小学语文教学大纲 [*Primary Yuwen teaching syllabi*]. Retrieved from http://student.zjzk.cn/course_ware/web-xxyw/index.html

Jin, L., Ruan, J., & Liu, X. (2007, December). *Chinese education reform*. Poster session presented at the National Reading Conference 57th Annual Meeting, Austin, TX.

Kucer, S. (2009). *Dimensions of literacy: A conceptual base for teaching reading and writing in school settings* (3rd ed.). New York: Routledge.

Song, X. (2006). 语文课改: 要避免三个误区 [Yuwen curriculum reform: Three pitfalls to avoid]. 中学语文教学, *1*, 77–78.

Wu, Z., & Yu, L. (2009a). 新中国60年小学语文教学改革(上) [Reform of primary school Chinese teaching in sixty years of New China (part 1)]. 语文教学通讯, *9*(1), 10–14.

Wu, Z., & Yu, L. (2009b). 新中国60年小学语文教学改革(下) [Reform of primary school Chinese teaching in sixty years of New China (part 2)]. 语文教学通讯, *9*(2), 15–18.

Wu, X., Li, W., & Anderson, R. (1999). Reading instruction in China. *Journal of Curriculum Studies, 31*, 571–586.

Xiao, Z. (2007). 小语教学的困惑与对策 [Confusion over teaching Chinese in primary schools and problem-solving strategies]. 中小学电教, *11*, 9.

Xiao, Y. (2008). 新理念指导下的识字教学 [Teaching character recognition under the guidance of new perspectives]. 新课程, *Z1*, 29.

Yu, H. (2010). 深化课程改革系列1 给素质教育一个现实的画像-访教育部基础教育课程教材发展中心副主任曹志祥. ["Deepening curriculum reform" series I: Painting a realistic picture of quality education – An interview with Zhixiang Cao, Associate Director of Basic Education Curriculum and Textbook Development Center of Ministry of Education]. 人民教育, *5*, 35–37.

Zhang, G. (2004). 课改带动科研 科研促进课改 – 简谈教师与课改同步成长 [The curriculum reform drives the scientific research while the research promotes the reform]. 学科教育, *4*, 12–15, 27.

Zhang, H., & Liu, P. (2009). 小学语文教学改革存在的问题和对策 [Existing problems in the reform of primary school Chinese teaching and problem-solving strategies]. 教学与管理, *30*, 60–61.

Zheng, G. (2003). 小学语文低年级阅读教学的改革 [The reform of Chinese reading in the first phase of primary school]. 学科教育, *4*, 4–10.

Zhong, J., & Liao, W. (2008). 课程改革因理性而精彩 [Using a rational attitude toward curriculum reform to achieve excellence]. 语文建设, *3*, 38–40.

Chapter 9
High School Chinese Language and Literacy Curriculum Reforms

Jiening Ruan and Guomin Zheng

9.1 Introduction

Even though compulsory education in China only covers grades 1-9, high school education (10th-12th grades) has become increasingly more accessible to a wider youth population. The most recent reform of high school Chinese language and literacy (Yuwen) education was initiated in 2000 when *Full-Day Common High School Yuwen Teaching Syllabus (Revised Trial Version)* was published by the Chinese Ministry of Education (MOE 2000). This document and its subsequent revised version (MOE 2002) served as a transitional curriculum guide for the subject of Yuwen while the new curriculum standards were being developed. In 2003, *Full-Day Common High School Yuwen Curriculum Standards* (hereafter referred to as the *Standards*) was published as the formal document of the latest Yuwen curriculum reform (MOE 2003). Noticeably different from previous education reforms, which were mostly politically motivated, the current high school Yuwen curriculum reform is a direct response to the desire of the country to become a modern nation that can compete globally in the twenty-first century, the demand of the society for a more well-rounded workforce with the ability to think creatively and innovatively, and the need of students for greater freedom and individualism (Guo 2004; Qin 2004).

This chapter traces the historical development of Chinese Yuwen curriculum with a particular focus on various efforts to reform the curriculum since 1949, the year when the People's Republic of China was founded. This is followed by a discussion of how Chinese political and social factors have shaped the curriculum and reform efforts. Major highlights of the latest high school Yuwen curriculum reform are discussed, and the current and previous Yuwen curricula compared.

J. Ruan (✉)
Reading/Literacy Education, University of Oklahoma, Norman, OK, USA
e-mail: jruan@ou.edu

G. Zheng
Chinese Reading Education, Beijing Normal University, Beijing, China

The chapter concludes with a discussion of issues and challenges arising from the latest reform, as well as recommendations for continued improvement of the high school Yuwen curriculum.

9.2 Historical Development of High School Chinese Language and Literacy Curriculum

9.2.1 *High School Curriculum Standards Before the 1950s*

The earliest curriculum standards for Chinese high school education date back to 1904 when the Qing government issued *Zouding Xuetang Zhangchen (奏定学堂章程)*, a landmark document that prescribed the rules and regulations for schools in China. Schools were required to offer two subjects: the Classics and Chinese literature. At that time, the Classics was considered a distinct subject area concerning the reading and discussion of the Four Books (四书) and Five Classics (五经), authoritative books on Confucianism. The Four Books include *The Great Learning* (大学), *The Analects of Confucius* (论语), *The Doctrine of the Mean* (中庸), and *Mencius* (孟子) while the Five Classics include *The Book of Songs* (诗经), *The Book of History* (书经), *The Book of Rites* (礼记), *The Book of Changes* (易经), and *The Spring and Autumn Annals* (春秋). The subject of Chinese literature covered reading, writing, practicing Chinese characters, and Chinese literary history (cited in Jin 2006; Zheng 2003a). This document and its implementation established Chinese as a critical school subject and laid the foundation for the development of Chinese curriculum and instruction in modern and contemporary China.

The New Culture Movement began in 1919 and brought a flood of Western ideas to China, along with a call for educational reform (refer to Chap. 3 for more discussion on the impact of the New Culture Movement on Chinese literacy education). In 1923, *Required Public National Language Subject Curriculum Syllabus* (公共必修科国语科学程纲要) was published. The syllabus contained specific goals related to contemporary Chinese language and writing, ancient Chinese language and writing, arguments, and informational texts. Another important curriculum document entitled *Required Specialized Chinese Language Subject Curriculum Syllabus for Senior High School* (高级中学必修科特设国文科学程纲要) was also published in the same year (cited in Jin 2006). This Syllabus identified language and literature as two important components of Chinese as a school subject. These two standards documents were built upon a subject-centered and teacher-centered educational philosophy and have left an indelible mark on the teaching and learning of Chinese. In terms of instructional practice, the five-step instructional sequence (preparing, prompting, making comparisons, summarizing, and applying) developed by the German educator Johann Friedrich Herbart was introduced to China and became popular among Chinese teachers. This instructional sequence is still seen in many Chinese classrooms (Jin 2006).

In 1932, *Senior High School National Language Curriculum Standards* (高级中学国文课程标准) was published. This document called for a change in curriculum goals from the acquisition of subject knowledge to the cultivation of students' ability to use the Chinese language. Such a change was influenced by John Dewey, who had visited China from 1919 to 1921. The document, however, did not result in significant changes to the existing practices of Chinese teaching in place at that time (Jin 2006). In the subsequent two decades, China experienced an 8-year long resistance war against Japanese invasion and a civil war. During those two decades, curriculum standards were influenced by the ideologies promoted by the ruling Chinese Nationalist Party, and political goals were added to the curriculum goals. No substantial effort in curriculum reform was made during those two decades (Jin 2006).

9.2.2 High School Curriculum Standards from 1950 – 2000

A watershed moment in Chinese modern history was the founding of the People's Republic of China in 1949. The country went through a period of dramatic changes, politically and socially, and China's educational system changed dramatically. In 1950, the Chinese central government published *General Understanding of Editing* (编辑大意) to accompany two textbooks developed for middle and high schools. This was the first time the term Yuwen (语文) was coined to replace previously used terms such as Guoyu (国语 – national language) and Guowen (国文 – national script/writing) to better reflect the nature of the subject area. The document defines Yuwen as the following: "Speaking is Yu (语 – language) and writing is Wen (文 – writing). Spoken language and written language cannot be separated" (Guo 2005). In other words, spoken language is Yu and written language is Wen. When they are combined together, the term becomes Yuwen.

Traditionally, the main focus of Chinese education was on written language, with little attention paid to spoken language. The document *General Understanding of Editing* is groundbreaking because it moved the discipline away from its previous narrow emphasis on written language and re-conceptualized the subject matter of Chinese to include listening, speaking, reading, and writing (Guo 2005). The term Yuwen reflected the new thinking that overall competence in communication is the most important goal of teaching Chinese. Yuwen as a term for the subject matter has been used ever since. Based on this definition, the most appropriate English translation for Yuwen is Chinese language and literacy. The document, however, had a strong political orientation and treated Yuwen as a course to educate students on politics and the Chinese Communist Party's ideologies.

Between 1950 and 1996, there were five major high school Yuwen curriculum reforms. Table 9.1 summarizes the changes that occurred in the curriculum during this time and the highlights of each based on the work of scholars of educational reforms in China (e.g., Guo 2005; Hou 2010; Jin 2006). It is important to mention that in China, for a long period of time, schools were organized as primary schools

Table 9.1 Major junior and senior middle school (junior and senior high school) Yuwen curriculum reforms and changes, 1950–1996

Year	Curriculum reform documents	Major highlights
1956	(a) Junior Middle School Chinese Language Teaching Syllabus – Draft 初级中学汉语教学大纲(草案) (b) Junior and Senior Middle School Literature Teaching Syllabus 初、高中文学教学大纲 (c) Initial Plan for Teaching Middle School Composition – Draft 中学作文教学初步方案(草案)	• The first nationwide standardized subject syllabi used to standardize the teaching of Yuwen • Divided Yuwen instruction into two separate focus areas: language instruction and literature instruction • The instructional focus for high school was on literature instruction, building on the language instruction students received in middle school • Major high school instructional content for literature included important literary works by Chinese writers and foreign writers; classics of literature and basic knowledge of literary theories and history of Chinese literature; language features of works in different historical eras in China • Curriculum goals for language included the development of students' reading ability and ability to understand archaic forms of Chinese (文言文) and to solidify their interest in and habit of frequent reading of literary works • Writing instruction focused on developing students' ability to observe, think, and imagine in addition to their ability to use spoken and written language to express their ideas, and to solidify the knowledge and skills previously obtained from their language and literature courses • The curriculum was influenced by the ruling party's ideology. Major mission included cultivating students' socialist political orientation, communist morals and ethics, patriotism, and collectivism • The syllabi for language and literature instruction were valuable attempts at treating Yuwen systematically and scientifically • The syllabi were short-lived and abolished in 1958. The government concluded that the syllabi did not align with the then dominant "class struggle" ideology and therefore did not serve the political agenda of the government

(continued)

Table 9.1 (continued)

Year	Curriculum reform documents	Major highlights
1963	Full-Day Middle School Yuwen Teaching Syllabus – Draft 全日制中学语文教学大纲(草案)	• It was initiated and implemented in the aftermath of the Great Leap Forward Movement (1958–1961) to remediate the damages done to Chinese Yuwen education. Yuwen classes had been turned into politics classes and as a result significantly decreased the quality of Chinese language and literacy instruction • It stated that Yuwen is the basic tool for learning, communicating, and work • The goal was to teach students to correctly understand and apply Chinese spoken and written language and to help them acquire the ability to read and write modern Chinese • It argued that Yuwen should not be taught as a politics class or a literature class and Yuwen instruction should return to the teaching of reading and writing • Selections in textbooks should have both positive thoughts and high literary qualities
1978	Full-Day Ten-Year School Chinese Teaching Syllabus – Trial Version Draft 全日制十年制学校教学大纲(试行草案)	• It was developed to bring Yuwen education out of the state of utter confusion and chaos created by the decade-long Cultural Revolution • It recognized the primacy of Marxist ideology in the curriculum • It reflected the consensus that politics could guide Chinese language and literacy instruction but should not replace it • It established the understanding that Yuwen instruction had its own unique mission, which is to cultivate students' ability to master and apply spoken and written language • It reinstated the position made in the 1963 Syllabus that the basic nature of Yuwen should be a tool for learning, communicating, and work
1986	Full-Day Yuwen Teaching Syllabus – Trial Version Draft 全日制语文教学大纲(试行草案)	• It placed the acquisition of basic skills ahead of basic knowledge as the main purpose of Yuwen teaching • It recognized the function of Yuwen was to promote quality education and cultivate productive citizens • Testing should focus only on skills questions instead of knowledge questions and not require rote memorization • It deleted the previous requirement of universal textbook development so multiple textbooks issued by different publishing houses could be available for local textbook adoption decisions

(continued)

Table 9.1 (continued)

Year	Curriculum reform documents	Major highlights
		• Yuwen began to regain its status as a separate discipline instead of a tool to serve political purposes
1995	Nine-Year Compulsory Education Middle School Yuwen Teaching Syllabus – Trial Version 九年义务教育全日制初级中学语文教学大纲(试用)	• It was the first time when junior middle school and senior middle school had their own separate Yuwen curricula
		• Curriculum for junior middle school emphasized the development of basic language and literacy competence and included the development of listening, speaking, reading, and writing
		• It was the first time the objective of cultivating good learning habits was added to the curriculum. This object has become a part of subsequent curriculum documents
		• It emphasized the development of students' intelligence and imagination and their use of comparison, analysis, induction, and deduction for observation, memorization, and thinking
		• It provided specific guidance for Yuwen instruction to promote student development of listening, speaking, reading, and writing abilities
		• It was the first time after-school reading was added to the syllabus as a requirement
1996	Nine-Year Compulsory Education Senior Middle School [High School] Yuwen Teaching Syllabus – Trial Version 九年义务教育全日制高级中学语文教学大纲(试用)	• It established the notion that Yuwen is the most important communication tool and carrier of culture
		• It proposed six major principles for the teaching of Yuwen: the integration of Yuwen training and moral education; the symbiotic relationship between Yuwen training and cognitive training; the close connection between knowledge instruction and skills training; the comprehensive training of listening, speaking, reading and writing; teacher guidance and student personal initiative, and the integration of in-class and after-school reading
		• It specified that high school Yuwen curriculum should consist of three types of courses: required, electives, and free choice to allow greater student choice but it did not provide specific guidelines on how to do so
		• Information on assessment and evaluation and on instructional resources was added

and middle schools. The term "middle school" is comparable to the concept of secondary school in the United States and included junior middle school and senior middle school. Senior middle school is the equivalent of high school in the United States. Oftentimes, school curricula for Chinese middle schools covered both junior middle school and senior middle school until the 1995 Yuwen reform. Unless pointed out otherwise, the term middle school in this chapter applies to both junior middle school and high school.

9.3 High School Yuwen Curriculum Reform in the New Millennium

9.3.1 Social and Political Background of the Current Curriculum Reform

High school Yuwen curriculum reform is an important part of the government's reform initiatives to improve Chinese education. The central goal of the most recent education reform is to provide "quality education" and create well-rounded, creative, and innovative citizens of the twenty-first century (Hou 2010; Yu 2010). The current education reform is a direct response to globalization, an increasingly diverse population, a young generation that demands more freedom of choice, and advances in information technology.

Politically, for the past two decades the Chinese government has gradually moved from a Marxist political ideology with a focus on class struggle to a focus on maintaining social stability and improving China's economy. Joining the World Trade Organization in 2001 also has served as a strong catalyst for China to be further integrated into the world community. In order for China to compete successfully with other nations in the global economy, its future citizens must be equipped with new knowledge and skills that were not adequately supported in the old school curriculum. The government has also realized the importance of creativity and innovation, so China can continue to sustain its current economic growth.

On the other hand, China has become an increasingly diverse society. With major improvements in transportation and its infrastructure, the Chinese people have gained unprecedented mobility within the country. This also has created challenges because people from different social and ethnic backgrounds must be able to communicate with each other effectively. Technological advances have brought a new set of challenges. People are bombarded daily with a vast amount of information generated in various media, including the Internet. The ability to search for relevant information and process and analyze that information has become a critical skill of the twenty-first century.

Socially, due to the One Child policy a substantial number of young people have been given great personal freedom and choices at home. They are more independent and willful in their thinking and decision making compared with their parents' generation. As such, the long-held traditional teacher-centered philosophy of teaching and learning is no longer adequate for this new student population. Furthermore, since the 1980s, the Chinese government has sent a significant number of scholars to receive training in Western countries. These scholars have brought back with them a constructivist, student-centered educational philosophy. Such an influence can be found in the new curriculum standards for all subject areas, especially in the Yuwen standards.

All these changes and challenges have a direct bearing on Yuwen education because of its critical role in schooling. Under such a backdrop, starting in 1997, a heated debate surrounding the current status and future direction of Yuwen education took place across the nation. Specifically, major concerns included the following: the amount of content was too overwhelming and too difficult for students to learn; the curriculum was isolated and not integrated with other subject areas; the major mode of teaching and learning was drill and skill; too much emphasis was placed on grades and using assessments as a tool for differentiating good students from poor students; and curriculum management was one-size-fits-all and prescriptive (Hou 2010). Yuwen educators and government education decision-makers came to a consensus that the old Yuwen curriculum, including its content, goals, and implementation, was out-of-date and no longer adequate for the conditions and goals of the country (Task Force 2003). As a result, the Ministry of Education organized a group of Yuwen experts and charged them with the task of researching and developing a new set of curriculum standards. In 2000, *Full-Day Common High School Yuwen Teaching Syllabus (Revised Trial Version)* was published as a transitional document while the new curriculum standards were being fully developed. The document was further revised in 2002. In 2003, *Full-Day Common High School Yuwen Curriculum Standards* for grades 10–12 was formally unveiled, and the piloting of the standards began. Almost concurrently, a separate curriculum standards document was developed to guide the Yuwen curriculum reform for grades 1–9.

9.3.2 Implementation Timeline

The implementation of the new curriculum reform has been a long and deliberate process (Hou 2010; Task Force 2003). In order to achieve success, the MOE developed a three-stage timeline and gradually rolled out the new standards in one region of the country at a time.

The period from 2000 to 2003 was the preparation stage. In 2000, *Full-Day Common High School Yuwen Teaching Syllabus Revised (Trial Version)* was published to initiate the curriculum reform. It was a precursor of the *Standards*. Still, the teaching syllabus was teacher-centered and prescriptive. It focused on the scope and sequence of instruction, as well as the types of instructional activities and the amount of time to be allocated for each teaching objective. In 2002, *Full-Day Common High School Yuwen Teaching Syllabus* was published. Then, *Full-Day Common High School Yuwen Curriculum Standards (Trial Version)* was published in 2003 to replace the teaching Syllabus. The 2003 *Standards* officially marked the beginning of the latest high school Yuwen curriculum reform.

The piloting stage, from 2004 to 2008, began in four provinces in 2004 and expanded to ten provinces by 2006, 15 provinces and regions by 2007, and 21 provinces and regions by 2008.

After the piloting stage came the full implementation stage. The new curriculum standards were set to be implemented in all provinces and regions by 2010. Currently, the new curriculum standards have been implemented in all provinces in China except in the Guangxi Zhuang Autonomous Region. This region is populated with numerous ethnic minority peoples. The complexity of the languages and cultures present in the region make it a challenge for the *Standards* to be implemented at the same pace as in the rest of the country.

During each stage of implementation, the MOE conducted rigorous, extensive research. However, the focus of such research was not on revising the *Standards* but on identifying the issues and problems (e.g., logistics and resources) that prevented the *Standards* from being fully implemented in a particular stage and on avoiding similar problems in the upcoming stages. The research results were also used to help the MOE, regional and local education bureaus, and schools to develop effective professional development programs for teachers, so they would be able to make a successful transition to teaching the new standards. As of this date, the *Standards* have not been modified.

9.3.3 Major Content of the New Full-Day Common High School Yuwen Curriculum Standards

The *Standards* published in 2003 by the MOE defines the nature of Yuwen as "the most important tool of communication and a critical component of human culture. The fundamental characteristic of Yuwen curriculum is the integration of its utility and humanity" (p. 3). The document serves as a guide to the current high school Yuwen curriculum reform and posits that high school Yuwen curriculum should lead to further improvement in students' competence in language and literacy, knowledge application, aesthetic understanding, inquiry, and life-long learning.

Five major curriculum goals are identified in the *Standards*: (a) **accumulation and integration** (Students will strengthen their knowledge of the Chinese language and develop individualized learning methods.); (b) **experience and appreciation** (When reading exemplary literary works, students will consider authors' use of language, experience the beauty of the artistic craft, and develop their imagination and literary appreciation. Students will possess a good sense of modern Chinese language and gradually develop understanding of the archaic form of Chinese.); (c) **thinking and understanding** (Students will select classics and other exemplary literature to read based on their own learning objectives, and will establish positive goals for their lives, strengthen their sense of cultural mission and social responsibility, and develop the habits of independent thinking, questioning, inquiry, and critical thinking.); (d) **application and extension** (Students will be able to accurately, skillfully, and effectively apply the Chinese language in life and in their studies.); and (e) **discovery and innovation** (Students will carefully observe linguistic, literary, and cultural phenomena both within the country and abroad and will cultivate an awareness of inquiry and discovery.).

The *Standards* proposes a new structure for the high school Yuwen curriculum with five required core modules (courses) and five elective series. Specific objectives are provided for each module and series. The core modules focus on two main areas of Chinese language and literacy: (a) reading and appreciation and (b) expression and communication. Common core courses provide students with basic knowledge of Chinese language and literacy skills in reading and writing Chinese accurately, proficiently, and effectively, laying a solid foundation for their future learning. The elective series are designed to allow students to exercise personal choices for individualized development, and schools can offer multiple elective modules within each elective series (e.g., poetry and prose, fiction and drama, news and biography, language application, and research and reading on cultural works).

Guidelines recommend teachers actively promote independent, collaborative, and inquiry-based learning. Teachers should establish a positive learning environment and help students take ownership of their learning. In addition, teachers should flexibly use various teaching strategies and creatively use textbooks and other curriculum materials. Textbooks should promote Chinese culture and an understanding of and respect for diverse cultures and should be conducive to the development of hands-on skills and an innovative spirit. Textbook content should be open and flexible to allow local governments, schools, teachers, and students room for self-development and choice. The fundamental purpose of assessment and evaluation should be to promote students' overall language and literacy competence. Assessments should not be used for tracking students but to identify students' strengths and weaknesses and to improve teaching.

9.4 Comparison Between the Current and Previous High School Yuwen Curricula

Nine-Year Compulsory Education High School Yuwen Teaching Syllabus (Trial Version) published in 1996 was the guiding document for high school Yuwen curriculum across China until *Full-Day Common High School Yuwen Curriculum Standards (Trial Version)* was formally published in 2003 and subsequently implemented. The documents are similar in some respects, but there are a number of major differences in the two documents.

9.4.1 Similarities

Both curriculum documents emphasize the importance of carrying out education policies set by the Chinese government. In addition, both require Yuwen teachers to pay particular attention to the unique nature and characteristics of the Chinese language, both spoken and written, and to follow important principles for the teaching and learning of a first language. Both documents consider applying knowledge and skills of Chinese language and literacy to real life situations an important goal of high school Yuwen education. Other common goals include the development of students' patriotic spirit, aesthetic appreciation, communicative competence in listening, speaking, reading, and writing, and a love of the Chinese language and culture (Zheng 2003b).

9.4.2 Differences

The 1996 curriculum (MOE 1996) heavily emphasized knowledge and skills. The new curriculum, however, is more complex and multi-dimensional than the previous curriculum. In addition to knowledge and skills, the new curriculum covers learning processes and methods, as well as emotions and attitudes.

One of the most noticeable differences between the two curricula is the curriculum focus. The 2003 Yuwen curriculum focuses on students and their learning while the 1996 curriculum focused on teachers and their teaching. The new *Standards* changes the role of teachers and students in the learning process. Teachers are expected to be facilitators and guides, and students are owners of their learning. Learning is to take place through dialogue instead of spoon-feeding or passive learning. The old curriculum was teacher-centered. It carefully laid out the scope and sequence of teaching and suggested instructional activities to accomplish various instructional goals for teachers to follow. The amount of time to be spent on the teaching of specific content and skills was also prescribed. There was mention of the student's role in the process of teaching and learning.

The new curriculum reform initiates an unprecedented curriculum structure that provides students with more choices based on personal interests and academic goals. Although the older curriculum document also recommended schools offer core, elective, and free choice courses, the recommendation was only briefly mentioned, and no specific guidelines were offered. Therefore, most schools did not follow this recommendation. The new curriculum document clearly stipulates schools must implement a new curriculum structure that consists of core modules (courses) and elective modules (Zheng 2003c). Under the new curriculum, high school students are required to take five modules (ten credit hours) of common core courses in order to graduate. They are encouraged to further develop their own personal interests in specific areas of language and literacy through selecting elective modules from the elective series. The inclusion of both common core and elective modules in the high school Yuwen curriculum reflects a more flexible, student-centered curriculum that allows for a more individualized high school Yuwen learning experience than provided in previous curricula.

In alignment with its goal to prepare students for the twenty-first century, the new *Standards* adds a technology component that was not included in previous curricula requirements. The *Standards* recommends students use modern information technology to present their writing, use computers for editing and interface design, and use email for communication. Teachers are also encouraged to use technology to support instruction.

Finally, the area of assessment and evaluation in the new curriculum emphasizes the use of multiple and ongoing measures to assess student learning and to inform teaching. Assessments should not only focus on the product but also the process of learning. In addition, assessment and evaluation should promote student motivation and positive attitudes towards learning. These recommendations about assessment and evaluation, in fact, are similar to Western views on the role and function of assessment and evaluation in teaching and learning (International Reading Association 2009). In comparison, the old curriculum primarily used assessment as a measure of student learning.

The new curriculum clearly signals a different orientation from the previous one. It is more student-centered and aims to promote collaborative, inquiry-based, and lifelong learning.

9.5 Impact of Current High School Yuwen Curriculum Reform

The new high school Yuwen curriculum reform is an extension and continuation of the curriculum reform for grades 1–9 (Task Force 2003; Zheng 2003c). The current high school Yuwen curriculum reform has created a positive impact on the quality of teaching and learning of Chinese language and literacy in many high schools in China. In 2009, Chinese students from Shanghai participated in the highly recognized Programme of International Student Assessment (PISA) for the first time in the program's history and ranked number one in the subject of reading, as well as in math and science (OECD 2011). Their performance shocked the international education community. Such results to a certain extent reflect the success of the latest Yuwen curriculum reform.

Significant progress has been made in several areas. First of all, a shift has occurred in teachers' thinking of Yuwen teaching. The traditional knowledge- and skills-oriented teaching is no longer a highly regarded mode of instruction among high school teachers of Chinese. Communicative competence, creativity, inquiry, problem-solving, and lifelong learning are topics of increasing interest among teachers. Second, teacher and student roles are redefined. More teachers have begun to view themselves as facilitators and guides, and they see their students as the main agent in the learning process. Teachers and students have become partners in educational dialogues. Third, Yuwen learning has become more individualized.

Students are given more freedom and flexibility in selecting elective reading modules that fit their personal interests. As a result, they are more motivated to learn Chinese. Fourth, group learning and cooperative learning activities are more popular now among teachers and students. Furthermore, an increasing number of schools and teachers have adopted student-centered, diverse, integrated assessment practices to improve their teaching (Zheng and Yin 2005).

9.6 Issues, Challenges, and Implications for Chinese Literacy Practices and Policies

A review of literature on Chinese Yuwen curriculum reforms suggests changes to the Chinese Yuwen curriculum have been closely tied to political movements. The changes also mirrored the social and cultural conditions of the country and the main agenda of the government and its ruling party. Yuwen was often treated as a political tool of the Chinese government and its ruling party to carry out their ideological agenda and to indoctrinate students. It is not surprising that during the Great Leap Forward and the Cultural Revolution, Yuwen courses were treated and taught as courses in politics (Wang 2005; Zheng 2003a). In the new *Standards*, even though there is still occasional reference to the ideological aspect of the curriculum, the function of Yuwen is redefined as a tool for lifelong learning and a carrier of culture and humanity (Zheng 2003a; Zhu and Liu 2005). This can be viewed as progress in curriculum reform. However, in order for Yuwen to grow into a true academic discipline, it is important to continue to further minimize the influence of political ideologies on the curriculum.

It is easy to detect the influence of Western educational philosophies on the new curriculum standards. In particular, views on the role of teachers and students and the need for more student-centered and individualized personal interpretation of texts come very close to Western educational beliefs. Furthermore, in multiple places throughout the *Standards*, there is a repeated call for critical reading and individualized interpretation of texts. This has the potential to change political and social conditions when students grow up and become independent and critical thinkers. This curriculum reform can hopefully lead to a society that is more open to individualism and diverse perspectives.

The current reform, however, has generated heated debate among educators and teachers and has even encountered resistance from some local governments, as well as teachers. Teacher resistance has been found to be a problem that impedes full implementation of the new *Standards* (Hou 2010; Wang 2007). Such resistance comes from the top-down nature of the reform, drastic changes in educational philosophy and beliefs, lack of a coordinated teacher evaluation system, and lack of inservice education. First and foremost, this reform is a top-down effort to transform Chinese language and literacy education (Wang 2007). Schools and teachers do not have ownership of the reform initiative, and some have strong feelings about the new curriculum being imposed on them when they are not ready to implement it.

The dramatic shift from a teacher-centered curriculum to a student-centered curriculum is a steep learning curve for many teachers. Furthermore, such a shift in teaching philosophy also involves changes in instructional practices that teachers have had no experience with or exposure to previously. In order to implement Yuwen instruction that truly integrates knowledge, skills, learning processes and methods, and affective factors, teacher quality and teacher education need to be addressed. In fact, the *Standards* recognizes this need and calls for teacher professional development.

Second, schools and teachers are confronted with the dilemma of implementing the new reading curriculum versus teaching to the college entrance examination, which has been a longtime tradition of high school Yuwen education. The evaluation of teacher effectiveness and high school quality are largely based on how well their students do on exams, college entrance exams in particular. In order to successfully implement the curriculum reform, a systemic approach should be taken, and the existing system for college admissions should be changed simultaneously. Reform of the college entrance exam is needed, as well as a fundamental change to the testing culture so deeply rooted in the Chinese education system (Sang 2005; Wang 2007).

A key feature of the new curriculum is its requirement to provide core courses and electives to high school students for a more individualized curriculum. However, several issues prevent this goal from becoming a reality or from being fully implemented (Wang 2009b). First of all, in order for students to do well on the college entrance exam, many schools only offer electives that contain content related to the exam. Second, schools that are limited in resources cannot afford to hire additional teachers to offer additional electives. Therefore, the good intentions behind this change to the curriculum are in danger of not becoming a reality in many schools. For the reform to be successful, schools should carefully examine their own resources and develop elective modules that are both connected to local conditions and fit student needs and interests (Zhu 2005).

Inequality in Yuwen education between urban and rural areas is also a challenge. Major concerns include textbooks that are not connected to the real life experiences of students in rural areas, poor teacher quality in rural schools, and a lack of educational resources to implement the changes (Hou 2010; Huang 2009). The Chinese government should take action to ensure such inequality is addressed.

Under the new curriculum, high school teachers struggle to achieve a balance between teacher explicit instruction of critical knowledge and skills and student-centered, inquiry-based instruction, between effective Chinese traditional instructional approaches and Western approaches to the teaching of Chinese Yuwen (Sang 2005; Wang 2009a). In addition to providing teachers with high quality professional development, teacher reflection and teacher action research may be a powerful way to help teachers become successful in implementing the new standards.

9.7 Summary

This chapter describes the current high school Yuwen curriculum reform from historical, political, and sociocultural perspectives. Several important themes that guide the implementation of the curriculum reform are identified in the new curriculum document. The reform is encouraging and moving in a positive direction. However, the reform has also brought about several challenges and issues that need to be addressed. Teacher paradigm shift perhaps is the most difficult obstacle to overcome in order to successfully implement the reform. Professional development has to keep up with the reform, and supports have to be provided to teachers making the transition. The testing culture and the college entrance exam also need to be reformed to align with the new curriculum. Curriculum reform is a long, exploratory process. However, the current Yuwen reform is a worthy effort to align high school curriculum with the demands of Chinese society and individual students. It will have a lasting impact on Chinese Yuwen education.

References

Chinese Ministry of Education. (1996). 九年义务教育全日制高级中学语文教学大纲 (试用) [*Nine-year compulsory education senior middle school/high school Yuwen teaching syllabus (trial version)*]. Beijing: Ministry of Education.

Chinese Ministry of Education. (2000). 教育部关于使用《全日制普通高级中学语文教学大纲 (试验修订版)》的通知 [The announcement of Ministry of Education on the implementation of Full-day common high school Yuwen teaching syllabus (revised trial version)]. 教育部政报, 3,128.

Chinese Ministry of Education. (2002). 全日制高级中学语文教学大纲 [*Full-day high school Yuwen teaching syllabus*]. Beijing: Ministry of Education.

Chinese Ministry of Education. (2003). 普通高中语文课程标准 (试用) [*Common high school Yuwen curriculum standards (trial version)*]. Beijing: Ministry of Education.

Guo, G. (2004). 高中语文课程标准产生的背景 [The background of high school curriculum reform]. 山东教育(中学刊), Z2, 30–33.

Guo, G. (2005). 从教学大纲的历史变迁看中学语文教改的发展 [Views of the development of middle school Yuwen education reforms through the examination of the historical changes in the teaching syllabi]. 山东教育 (中学刊), 35, 17–18.

Hou, X. (2010). 我国基础教育新课程改革的回顾与前瞻 [Reflection on and vision of basic education reform in our nation]. 湖南师范大学教育科学学报, 9(4), 74–79.

Huang, T. (2009). 谁来挽救农村普通高中的语文教育 [Who will save rural common high school Yuwen education?]. 作文教学研究, 4, 34–35.

International Reading Association and National Council of Teachers of English. (2009). *Standards for the assessment of reading and writing* (Rev. ed.). Newark: International Reading Association.

Jin, J. (2006). 高中语文课程标准的百年变迁 [The evolution of high school Yuwen curriculum standards within the last century]. 甘肃联合大学学报社会科学版, 6, 117–120.

Organization for Economic Co-operation and Development (OECD). (2011). *PISA 2009 scores and rankings*. Retrieved from http://www.oecd.org/document/61/0,3746,en_32252351_32235731_46567613_1_1_1_1,00.html

Qin, X. (2004). 课程改革前的高中语文教学 [High school Yuwen instruction before the curriculum reform]. 中学语文, 13, 8–9.

Sang, Z. (2005). 高中语文课程改革中应关注的几个问题 [Issues for attention related to high school Yuwen curriculum reform]. 中学语文教学, 8, 9–11.

Task Force for the Development of Common High School Yuwen Curriculum Standards. (2003). 关于《普通高中语文课程标准 (实验)》研制工作的说明 [The explanation on the task of developing common high school Yuwen curriculum standards – trial version], 语文建设, 9, 10–11.

Wang, N. (2005). 新课程的理念与新教材的教学 [New beliefs about curriculum and teaching with new textbooks]. 现代语文, 3, 54–55.

Wang, Z. (2007). 新课程改革遭遇教师冷漠态度的文化审视 [An examination of the culture of teachers' cold attitude toward new curriculum reform]. 教育探究, 2(4), 16–19.

Wang, B. (2009a). 高中语文课程改革的若干要点及需要注意的问题 [Several key issues related to high school curriculum reform that require attention]. 中学语文, Z1, 7–11.

Wang, P. (2009b). 语文选修课的困境与未来走向 [The dilemma of Yuwen electives and future directions]. 吉林省教育学院学报, 25(3), 1–3.

Yu, H. (2010). 深化课程改革系列1 给素质教育一个现实的画像-访教育部基础教育课程材发展中心副主任曹志祥 [Deepening curriculum reform series I: Painting a realistic picture of quality education – an interview with Zhixiang Cao, Associate Director of basic education curriculum and textbook development center of Ministry of Education]. 人民教育, 5, 35–37.

Zheng, G. (2003a). 侧重展示阅读的过程与方法,强调个性化的体验与理解 [Highlighting the demonstration of reading process and methods, emphasizing individualized experience and understanding]. 语文教学通讯, 3, 5–7.

Zheng, G. (2003b). 高中语文课程目标的表述 [Representations of high school Yuwen curriculum goals]. 中学语文教学, 8, 3–4.

Zheng, G. (2003c). 高中语文新课标,新在那里? [New high school Yuwen curriculum standards, where's the newness?] 中学语文教学, 8, 3–4.

Zheng, G., & Yin, X. (2005). 高中语文选修课程实施存在的问题及思考 [High school Yuwen elective courses: Issues and reflections]. 语文建设, 11, 4–6.

Zhu, Z. (2005). 领悟要旨,开拓思路,促进教改 [Understand the essence, expand perspectives, promote curriculum reform]. 宁夏教育科研, 1, 18–20.

Zhu, L., & Liu, H. (2005). 对《普通高中语文课程标准 (实验)》的三点思考. [Three thoughts regarding common high school Yuwen curriculum standards – trial version.] 渝西学院学报, 4(3), 76–96.

Chapter 10
Chinese *Lian Huan Hua* and Literacy: Popular Culture Meets Youth Literature

Minjie Chen

10.1 Introduction

An overview of Chinese youth literature, as given in Chap. 7, is incomplete without examining *lian huan hua* (连环画, hereafter LHH), a unique type of visual publication that partially overlaps with children's and young adult reading material. Arguably the most widespread and popular reading format among Chinese young people during much of the twentieth century, LHH has barely received scholarly attention from education researchers—as was often the case of popular culture—unless occasionally being "noticed" as a distraction from classroom learning in students' discipline problems. Youth literature researchers largely bypassed LHH as a legitimate subject of academic inquiry, and, until the recent expansion of picture books in China after 2000, scholarly works have focused on text-oriented juvenile publications. Like youth literature, the format was rarely incorporated into Chinese classroom instruction. Literary criticism of LHH works, pedagogical discussions on using them in an educational setting, and theoretical inquiries on the format from the perspective of youth literature are woefully lacking.

This chapter traces the trajectory of Chinese LHH in the twentieth century, a turbulent time period when China transformed from a semi-colonial feudal dynasty to a Communist state embracing market economy and capitalism. In a country dominated by an illiterate population until the latter half of the twentieth century, the content, format, readership, and perceived functions of LHH shifted as China underwent drastic political, social, and cultural changes. Based on a historical understanding of the relationship between LHH and literacy in China, a final section will propose future research questions that explore approaches to employ this format of reading material for literacy education and learning.

M. Chen (✉)
Cotsen Children's Library, Princeton University Library Rare Books Division, Princeton University, Princeton, NJ, USA
e-mail: minjiec@gmail.com

It is a tricky business to define the connotation and scope of the term "lian huan hua." Literally meaning "linked images" or "serial pictures" in Chinese, LHH has been used as a loose umbrella term for nearly all books with sequential narrative images on every page, including but not limited to illustrated story books, comic books, picture books, and movie spin-offs that are created from movie stills with accompanying captions. In addition to books, illustrated stories of varying length and comic strips are also published or serialized in newspapers and magazines, the most influential one being the semimonthly *Lian Huan Hua Bao* [Picture stories paper] launched in 1951. LHH may or may not be reprinted in book format, depending on length, popularity, and the significance of the creators. The focus of this chapter is on LHH available in book form.

There is a great diversity in format, page size, and text-image layout among LHH works produced from different time periods. In its heyday LHH typically appeared palm-sized, measuring about 4 by 5 in., and the length of each volume varied from a dozen pages to over a hundred. The great majority of LHH were illustrated story books, printed in black and white, usually with one image on every page and short text on the top, bottom, or right side of the page. Some applied conversation balloons within the illustrations (Fig. 10.1).

After 1990 when native LHH works lost their market to foreign imports of comic books, the earlier palm-sized booklets all but retired, except for some titles with a limited print run for LHH connoisseurs and nostalgic fans. The subcategories of *man hua* books (漫画书, equivalent to what are commonly known as comic books, manga, and graphic novels in the United States) and picture books (by the latest fashion also known as *hui ben*, a term borrowed from the Japanese word 絵本) have been increasingly aligned with format standards familiar in Japan and Western countries. However, LHH is still a widely accepted inclusive term for these visual narrative publications. I will use LHH in this sense in this chapter.

There is much to understand about how the seed of LHH germinated in the colonial city of Shanghai by the end of the Qing Dynasty (1644–1911). Chinese-language scholarship tends to stress the continuity of the LHH format—from illustrations found in age-old Buddhist murals, Confucian biographical texts, and popular novels—and downplays Western influences. According to this scholarship, LHH was inspired by illustrated news stories first appearing in Shanghai in the late nineteenth century, then took the shape of booklets in the 1910s, and started to develop in earnest after 1920[1] (Huang et al. 1999; Jie 2004). The earliest LHH was dominated by traditional opera stories and adaptations of pre-twentieth century Chinese popular literature, particularly supernatural and kung fu stories (Aying 1957; Huang et al. 1999). The format obtained its formal name in 1925 when the Shanghai-based publisher Shi Jie Shu Ju [The World Book] issued the first of a series of illustrated booklets and named them *lian huan tu hua* (later shortened to

---

[1] The early history of how LHH came into being between the turn of the twentieth century and the 1920s is still murky, and researchers have provided inconsistent title and date information, making slightly different claims. I have decided to make my statements broad enough to accommodate most researchers' findings.

10 Chinese *Lian Huan Hua* and Literacy: Popular Culture Meets Youth Literature

Fig. 10.1 Sample LHH pages. (**a**) *Bai Mao Nü* [The white-haired girl]/text by Yiqun Fang (Most Chinese full names in this essay have been inverted to conform to the Western sequence of first and last names. In the few cases where the original Chinese sequence is kept in respect to customary usage in English media, last names will appear in small caps to avoid confusion.); illustrated by Sanchuan Hua. Shanghai, China: Shao Nian Er Tong Chu Ban She 1964. LHH works with colorful illustrations were much less affordable and rare before 1985 in China. Used with kind permission from Cartoonwin.com. (**b**) *Xiao Bing Zhang Ga* [Little soldier Chang Ka-tse]/by Guangyao Xu; adapted by Yingxi Hu; illustrated by Pincao Zhang. New 1st ed. Shanghai, China: Shanghai Ren Min Chu Ban She, 1972. Used with kind permission from Cartoonwin.com. (**c**) *Hai Di Mi Gong Fu Mie Ji* [The destruction of the labyrinth on the seafloor]/by Peikun Wang. Shijiazhuang, China: Hebei Mei Shu Chu Ban She, 1984. Used with kind permission from Cartoonwin.com

lian huan hua) (Gu 1999). According to Shen (2001), at almost the same time that these pictorial story booklets took shape, periodicals in Shanghai started carrying comic strips, the artistic style and satirical or humorous content of which suggested an emulation of Western comics and cartoons. Comic strips published or reprinted in book format remained a small portion of indigenous Chinese LHH output, but still attracted noteworthy artists and titles.

Contrary to common misconception, LHH was not born as youth literature, even though the format appealed to young readers from day 1. Hoping to reach the widest possible audience, the World Book Company printed on the cover of its *lian huan tu hua* series "Nan nü lao you, yu le da guan" (男女老幼 娱乐大观), roughly meaning "for the entertainment of men and women, young and old" (Fig. 10.2). Gradually, the LHH market segmented into broad audience groups. In their introduction to major LHH artists during the 1930s and 1940s in Shanghai, which remained the

Fig. 10.2 Cover image of an early LHH title *The Records of the Three Kingdoms* (Shanghai: Shanghai Shi Jie Shu Ju, 1927. 2nd ed.). Reprinted in *Lao Lian Huan Hua*, 1999. The eight characters on the top—"Nan nü lao you, yu le da guan"— roughly means "for the entertainment of men and women, young and old."

center for the LHH publishing industry in China, Wang and Li (1999) note that Xiaodai Qian's (钱笑呆, 1912–1965) illustration of female characters from traditional opera stories won him a large number of housewife readers; Guangyi Chen's (陈光镒, 1919–1991) funny LHH stories, often featuring young protagonists, attracted child readers the most and gained national fame; and the works of two other artists, Manyun Shen (沈曼云, 1911–1978) and Hongben Zhao (赵宏本, 1915–2000), focusing on kung fu and hero stories, appealed to both adult and young audiences.

School-age children and young adults soon formed the largest patron group of LHH, according to surveys and observations of rental bookstalls, the main venue where readers obtained the booklets (see, for example, Mao 1932/1989 and Fang 1999 about Shanghai in the early 1930s and 1950s respectively; "Zhong yang," 1955/2004 about a survey in eight major cities). This explained why in the dialects of many regions LHH were misleadingly called kids' books. The dual audience for this format, however, persisted. Italian author Gino Nebiolo witnessed the popularity of LHH among Chinese grown-ups during the Cultural Revolution. Traveling in China on a night train, every passenger, including Nebiolo, received LHH along with hot tea from the stewardess, and he observed his companions—workers, petty officials, and peasants—"all completely absorbed in their reading" (1973, p. viii) (Fig. 10.3).

The dual audience could be attributed to two factors that fed each other. First, LHH as a popular reading material was compatible with the characteristics and needs of readers from a wide age range. Second, publishers and interest groups that saw LHH as a medium for mass communication, in pursuing profits or their agendas, were sensitive to the preferences of the market. China's illiteracy rate was estimated to be 85–90% of the total population at the turn of the twentieth century. That figure remained virtually unchanged for 50 years, until the Communist Party took over China in 1949 and through mass literacy campaigns reversed that rate to 15.88% in 1990 and 6.72% in 2000 (Ross 2005). LHH, with its rich

Fig. 10.3 An open-air LHH rental stall that attracts patrons from toddler to adult, male and female. It also sells tobacco. Possible location and date: Shanghai, 1949

illustrations and brief texts, as well as cheap rental fees, became the most accessible and affordable format of popular culture when other visual media, such as television and movies, either did not exist or were not widely available. A 1950 survey of rental stalls in Beijing finds that movie spin-offs were housewife patrons' favorite LHH because they could not afford going to the theatre (Bai 1950). Children's author Guangyao Xu, born into a poor family in 1925 and reared in rural Hebei Province where print materials were scarce, fondly recalls LHH as a great source of entertainment in his childhood. Despite being unable to read well, his peasant father could tell a few LHH stories to mesmerize the boy and his sister (Xu 2001). As we shall see, the Nationalist government, the Chinese Communist Party (CCP), and some intellectuals all tried using the format of LHH to get political messages across to the poorly educated public, achieving varying degrees of success.

10.2 From the 1920s to 1937: The Growth of Lian Huan Hua

The development of LHH falls into five periods. The first period from the 1920s to the eve of the Sino-Japanese War (1937–1945) saw the gradual convergence of page size and layout in LHH, the adoption of conversation balloons (said to be influenced by the first Chinese sound film released circa 1930), the prevalence of renting rather than selling LHH, and the increase of LHH illustrators (Aying 1957). After 1928, the print run of each title rose rapidly from a few hundred to around 2,000, and Shanghai publishers managed to extend their distribution network to inland China and Southeast Asia (Huang et al. 1999).

Not only were LHH publications ephemeral like many other popular culture artifacts, but also works published before 1949 are hard to locate because of repeated purging campaigns of the Chinese Communist Party (CCP). One of the Chinese intellectuals who paid early attention to the popular LHH and left us with precious historical records was Dun Mao (1896–1981), a novelist and cultural critic.

> Numerous small bookstalls are densely stationed like sentries in the streets and alleys of Shanghai....Whoever spends two coppers can sit on that stool, renting and reading 20–30 booklets; if you are a "regular," it is even possible that you may rent 40–50.
> These booklets are the so-called "*lian huan tu hua* novels." These small bookstalls have virtually become the most popular mobile libraries for the public of Shanghai, and are also the most powerful and widespread tool for "the education of the populace." (Mao 1932/1989, p. 650)

The majority of LHH readers that Mao witnessed were youth between 10 and 16 years old across class hierarchies, including school-age *sons* of laborers, sons and daughters of small business owners and affluent capitalists, as well as many 15- or 16-year-old apprentices and occasional adult laborers[2] (emphasis mine, 1932/1989). Mao was keenly aware of the relationship between this heavily visual reading material and literacy development. According to his analysis, two-thirds of the space on one LHH page was image, and one-third was occupied by text (in addition to conversation balloons in the picture), which matched the sequential pictures and could also stand alone as an abridged novel. Therefore, he argued that LHH could serve as one step on the reading "ladder" by "luring" with pictures those who could not read very well, and by helping them gradually make sense of the text (Mao 1932/1989, p. 652). This was perhaps true at the time of Mao's observation. As anecdotal evidence, in his memoir Shen (1999), a lifelong LHH fan, claims that his parents could barely read but entertained themselves with LHH. 7-year-old Shen had not learned to read at all but was fascinated by the pictures while listening in on what adults were saying about the stories.

Another of Mao's comments concerns the relationship between LHH and children's literature. The fact that so many primary school children liked LHH novels, Mao (1932/1989) said, indicated an inadequacy of reading material for children. His assertion was accurate, but also limited. Lacking literature defined as specifically produced for a young audience, Chinese youth throughout history had entertained themselves with what they could appreciate from popular culture intended for a general audience. Cross-age shared reading persisted after Chinese youth literature developed through translations, adaptations, and creations by

---

[2] One way that class difference manifested themselves here was that, as Mao (1932/1989) suggested, poor people tended to read LHH at the bookstall, while richer families could afford to carry them home with a higher rental fee. In the childhood memory of Shen (1999), born in 1924 and son of a successful businessman, LHH were brought home and shared among parents, brothers and sisters, and hired laborers.

Gender was an equally weighty factor that influenced the readership of LHH. Mao's careful note indicates that females from poor families were more likely to be denied education and access to LHH. The "apprentices" and "adult laborers" Mao mentioned were by default male.

Chinese authors, likely because what was strictly considered "youth literature" failed to satisfy young readers' need for quality, quantity, diversity of targeted age groups, etc. However, LHH differed from traditional folk culture and performance in that a small portion was indeed produced with young readers in mind and was suitable for them, even though youth often read beyond that. Mao's slight of LHH as a sub par replacement for, rather than a form of, youth literature continued, allowing scholarly investigation of the format to fall through disciplinary cracks.

Mao (1932/1989) disapproved of the subject matter of most LHH stories, calling them "poisonous" (p. 652). The market clamored for supernatural, kung fu, adventure, and romance novels, but news and realistic stories were small in quantity and unpopular. Research by Hung (1994) and Shen (2001) shows that some comics in early twentieth century Shanghai were works of political satire and social commentary, but their main readers at the time were the more educated urban middle-class who could afford newspapers and magazines. Lu Xun (1881–1936), a left-wing writer and critic, was among the earliest Chinese intellectuals to attempt to employ the popular format for the political socialization of the masses. In " 'Lian Huan Tu Hua' Bian Hu" [A defense of LHH], Lu argued against critic Wen Su's idea that LHH was lowbrow and that the format was inherently hopeless in terms of literary and artistic standing. Lu (1932/1973) pointed out that sequential narrative art was commonly found in both Western and Eastern religious sites for the purpose of *xuan chuan* [propaganda],[3] and he introduced Chinese readers to sample Western works of woodcut, metal plate, and lithography that used a series of continuous pictures to explore radical and Marxist themes. Intending to inspire Chinese LHH creators on artistic and thematic innovations, the Shanghai-based Liang You Book Company published four titles of European woodcut LHH stories, including Belgian artist Frans Masereel's 25-image *Die Passion eines Menschen* [One man's passion], originally a wordless pictorial novel, later with Chinese text provided by Lu Xun (Zhao 1979/1987).

Lu and the Liang You Book Company's early experiments saw no immediate impact. Displayed behind bookstore windows, portraying foreign topics, and presented in block prints with heavy dark shading, their books were distant from the populace who appreciated unpretentious neighborhood bookstalls, cheap rental fees, lucid line drawings—the dominant style employed by Chinese creators—and exciting page-turners. Liang You's attempt to collaborate with local LHH illustrators was thwarted by hostile industry owners who were wary of potential competitors (Zhao 1979/1987). Young woodcut artists who had aspired to follow Western works introduced by Lu Xun were quickly suppressed by the Nationalist government because of their revolutionary affiliation and the radical and subversive content of their art (Hung 1994). Lu's vision in conveying serious, progressive messages to the masses through LHH would be realized after his death, but it took a world war as the catalyst.

---

[3] The Chinese phrase *xuan chuan*, or propaganda, is a neutral term meaning disseminating messages, not necessarily with a negative connotation.

10.3 From 1937 to 1949: The "Metamorphosis" of Lian Huan Hua

The most important change in Chinese LHH of the twentieth century took place during the Sino-Japanese War and the subsequent civil war (1946–1949), which facilitated the use of the format as a tool for war and political causes. Six years after Imperial Japan annexed and colonized Northeast China, a full-scale war broke out between the two countries on July 7, 1937, followed by the fall of China's most industrialized cities on the east coast, including the capital city Nanjing, by the end of that year. In times of national crisis, individuals (regardless of their party affiliation), the government, and CCP[4] unanimously resorted to popular culture for war propaganda and mobilization. Even though wartime publishing was highly contingent on the personal safety of producers, supply of printing equipment and materials, and consumer potential of residents and refugees, LHH was one of the visual publications whose potential many interest groups hoped to mine.

10.3.1 *The Politicization of Lian Huan Hua in Nationalist-Controlled Areas*

In the preface of *Zhan Di En Chou Ji* [Friends and foes in the battlefield] (1943), Huang articulated the idea of capitalizing on the immense appeal and persuasive power of LHH for war mobilization:

> In order to serve the needs of the Anti-Japanese War, pictures have become a forceful weapon for propaganda and education. LHH enjoys a sizable output and a wide penetration among the folk. The format has been employed to satisfactory effect....My motivation for creating LHH stories comes from the needs of the war. (Huang 1943, n. p.)

The "needs of the war" encompassed informing the Chinese populace of Japanese brutality, encouraging men and women to contribute to the war effort, and keeping up morale through highlights of military victories and war heroes. Occasionally, the Japanese military and people were also the targeted audiences of Chinese propaganda materials, made available in the Japanese language and carrying anti-Fascism content. In fact, among the LHH that was directly sponsored by the Education Department of the Nationalist government were *San Xiong Di Yong Yue Cong Jun* [Three brothers eagerly join the army] (1944a), a thinly disguised recruitment advertisement containing 54 woodcut images, and *Rong Yu Jun Ren* [The disabled veteran] (1944b), a didactic story about how a disabled veteran becomes a leader in the agricultural, industrial, commercial, and cultural development of his hometown, partly for the goal of sustaining the war against Japan.

---

[4] In addition, extant library materials show that the Japanese occupation force also officially sponsored the publication of Chinese-language LHH works.

Huang's *Friends and Foes*, a realistic work of fiction, chronicles a Nationalist soldier's life from his abused childhood to his turmoil during the Sino-Japanese War, tracing his drastic identity shifts from a soldier fighting against Japan, to a POW surviving the fall of Nanjing, to a pawn coerced into the Japanese puppet army, and back to a Chinese resister after a successful revolt he leads among fellow puppet soldiers. This is one of the earliest LHH titles that cover the infamous Nanjing Massacre of December 1937. From crude woodcuts printed on flimsy paper, we can identify airplanes, explosions, fire, people or bodies in a river, and a Japanese soldier taking aim to shoot. The text gives "over 100,000" (p. 22) as the death toll of the Chinese military and civilians (Huang 1943).

The thematic transformation of Leping Zhang's (张乐平, 1910–1992) *Sanmao* series is the best example of how the war sensitized Chinese LHH creators to political issues and social conflict. Zhang's comic strips featuring Sanmao, a boy with three characteristic hairs standing on his nearly bald head, were first serialized in *Chen Bao* [Morning post] in 1935, and later collected in monographs. When Sanmao debuted in Zhang's nearly wordless comic world, the character amused the Shanghai public with his childish innocence, mischievous tricks, and slapstick humor. Sanmao's sexual innocence, for example, is the source of comedy in several strips. In one panel, the boy is seen, eyes shut tight, approaching a Cupid statue, intending to cover the angel's naked body with a long jacket (Zhang 2005, p. 3). China's class conflict and suspenseful social context of the late 1930s are occasionally present, but only as settings for comic relief, not as topics to be confronted. Sanmao of this time period lives in a middle-class family with an electronic fan and refrigerator at home, enjoys toys and snacks, and spends lots of leisure time with peers. When beggars appear in the story, Sanmao and his family are donators of money and clothing, but poverty is not the theme of concern in these early works. In one episode Sanmao encounters a beggar of his age, who has three locks of hair on his head just like himself. Sanmao fetches money and scissors from home right away, gives the boy money, and cuts off his three hairs, apparently disliking the resemblance (Zhang 2005, p. 67).

Zhang's *Sanmao* series was suspended shortly after the Japanese invasion. From 1937 to 1942, Zhang was a leading artist in Jiu Wan Man Hua Xuan Chuan Dui [The National Salvation Comics Propaganda Corps], which received modest financial support from the Military Affairs Commission of the Nationalist government. From the disbandment of the Corps in spring 1942 to the Japanese surrender, Zhang continued creating, publishing, and exhibiting propaganda comics with war themes (Qiu and Zhang 2007). As a patriotic artist, his single- and multiple-panel comics, appearing in newspapers, magazines, flyers, posters, fabric, and street walls, sent war mobilization messages to soldiers and civilians. While traveling widely to cities and rural areas as a Corps leader and later as a refugee himself, Zhang was exposed to hero stories, Chinese treachery, Japanese atrocities, civilian suffering, and Nationalist oppression. These first-hand experiences and observations not only inspired Zhang's art works for propaganda purposes, but also continued to provide substance to his postwar creations.

Resuming in 1946, the *Sanmao* series adopted a political thrust heavily influenced by Zhang's wartime experiences. In *Sanmao Cong Jun Ji* [Sanmao joins the army], first serialized in 1946 and published in monograph in 1947, an underage Sanmao joins the Nationalist army to fight the Japanese. Sanmao's cherished three hairs, tiny body size, and childish simple-mindedness are the source of light humor in many panels. However, two other themes are conveyed in some of these new "funnies." First, Zhang portrays a resourceful and resilient young soldier who is doing his part for the country. Second, Zhang takes a stab at the Nationalist army, contrasting the selfless Sanmao, who has been used as cannon fodder, with brutal higher-ranking officers, who never sacrifice personal comfort during the war.

Zhang's next series *Sanmao Liu Lang Ji* [Sanmao the vagrant], first serialized in 1947 and published in monograph in 1948, was a far cry from his prewar works. *The Vagrant* was inspired by the homeless youth with whom Zhang became acquainted in the streets of Shanghai, a city plagued by inflation, speculation, and bureaucratic capitalism after the Japanese defeat and thwarted by the ensuing civil war in an attempt at economic revival. Sanmao is an orphan boy who leaves his rural hometown to seek a livelihood in Shanghai. Except when gentle-hearted people temporarily take Sanmao in, the boy's honest hard work is barely rewarded, and instead he is often "bullied, tricked, robbed, and beaten by adults" (Mo and Shen 2006, p. 275). In one episode, Sanmao tries in vain to sell himself into slavery, only to discover that a well-to-do family pays for a doll at a price ten times as much as he asks for himself in the sale (Zhang 2006, p. 28). One farcical episode is sarcastic about the pecking order in semi-colonial Shanghai. An evil-looking man, in his attempt to hit Sanmao, accidentally hits someone who is dressed like a government official. While the man hurriedly makes his apology, the arrogant official tries to retaliate with his walking stick but hits a tall American soldier by mistake. The soldier, whose race and nationality have granted him a high social status and undue privileges in China, kicks at the official and spits at both men, now bowing subserviently to the foreigner to the dismay of Sanmao, who eyes the scene (Zhang 2006, pp. 72–73). Another episode might be a subtle allusion to Sanmao's socialization to pro-Communist ideas.[5] He is arrested and put into the same cell with a political prisoner, whose instruction gives Sanmao a hopeful dream about "a bright world," where he and another boy inmate are welcomed, cleaned, fed, and enrolled in a school to study and play (Zhang 2006, pp. 210–215). Sanmao's survival story and unfulfilled dreams, expressing the misery of poor people, is a bold confrontation with widespread poverty, social injustice, and class conflict of the 1940s in China.

---

[5] Biographical information indicates that in their wartime journey Leping Zhang's propaganda corps purchased works by progressive writers such as Lu Xun, Maxim Gorky, and Leo Tolstoy, as well as a book on materialism, to the resentment of the Nationalist authority (Qiu and Zhang 2007).

10.3.2 Lian Huan Hua as Art for Politics' Sake in Communist-Controlled Areas

In North and Central China, where the Communists gained partial control during the Sino-Japanese War, the ideological principles of literature and art were consolidated by Mao Zedong's influential talks delivered at a forum in Yan'an, May 1942. Mao (1942/2004, Conclusion, Sections III & IV) stated that there was no such thing as "art for art's sake…or art that is detached from or independent of politics," and considered it the fundamental task of revolutionary writers and artists to expose "all the dark forces harming the masses of the people" and to extol "all the revolutionary struggles of the masses of the people." Hung (1994) identifies three main functions served by the popular culture campaign in Communist regions. In addition to war propaganda, a common function shared with the Nationalist government, the CCP was more intent on using popular culture to win public support over its political rival (the Nationalists) and to spread revolutionary ideas and socialist reforms, which proved vital in the subsequent victory of the CCP in 1949.

Hung's (1994) point is confirmed by two of the most important LHH titles produced by Communist artists in this time period: *Langya Shan Wu Zhuang Shi* [Five heroes at the Langya Mountain] (1945) by Shan Hua and Han Yan (see 1951 ed.) and *Tie Fo Si* [*Iron Buddha Temple*] (1943) by Pu Mo, Meng Lü, and Jun Ya (see 1984 ed.) both illustrated with woodcuts. *Five Heroes* recounts the true story of five Eighth Route Army soldiers who, after holding back the enemy's progress to make retreat time for the main unit, committed suicide by jumping off a cliff to avoid Japanese capture and humiliation. Two of the soldiers survived the suicide attempt. After 1949, the story was reprinted in Chinese elementary school textbooks, and the loyalty, bravery, and altruism of Communist army soldiers became familiar to generations of young children. *Iron Buddha Temple*, likewise based on a true incident in the Anhui Province during the summer of 1942, focuses on a different theme. Although the Sino-Japanese War is the backdrop of the story, the villain is not Japanese aggressors but Desheng Wang—a rich land owner, a former neighborhood head under the Nationalist regime, and a notorious leader of local gangsters. Having tricked the Communist New Fourth Army and been appointed commander of the guerrillas, Wang seeks an opportunity to serve two masters. He gets in touch with his old boss Kaiyuan Liu, a former Nationalist township militia leader who has betrayed the Chinese and become a regimental commander of the Japanese puppet army. Soon Wang's evildoing escalates from looting local peasants to two assassinations (with Liu's military aid). The story ends with the murder case cracked by village cadres and Wang arrested. *Iron Buddha Temple* portrays no strong hero figures, but the identity of the enemy is firmly aligned with people of wealth or Nationalist affiliation, a stereotype that would be reinforced in the literature and art of Communist China until the end of the Cultural Revolution in the late 1970s.

To sum up, the war period facilitated the metamorphosis of LHH from apolitical popular reading material to a tool consciously constructed by intellectuals and politicians for promoting social change. A detailed analysis of how LHH artists adapted foreign styles of comics and woodcutting to the preference and understanding of a poorly educated rural audience can be found in Hung's (1994) research. He's (1947a, b, c) overview of 110 titles from a LHH exhibition held in Shanghai also indicates that the subject matter of LHH greatly expanded from traditional stories to a pleasant diverse range. Novels with progressive themes by LU Xun, who called for but did not live to see the change, a biography of Franklin D. Roosevelt, and Pearl S. Buck's *Dragon Seed* (1942), a war novel based on the fall of Nanjing, all found their way into illustrated story books (He 1947a, b).

10.4 From 1949 to 1976: Lian Huan Hua in the Mao Era

During the eventful period from the CCP's military victory in the civil war in 1949 to the end of the Cultural Revolution in 1976, it was imperative for the Party to stabilize its newborn state, which it perceived to be under the threats of the Nationalist Party, the Cold War, and a capricious relationship with the Soviet Union. The CCP continued to appreciate the potential of LHH in the political socialization of the Chinese populace. The first step it took in ensuring the intended use of LHH was a reform campaign launched in the first half of the 1950s against the immensely popular "poisonous" and "harmful" LHH works, mostly published under the Nationalist regime. Through organizational control of publishers and rental stalls, critical control of individual titles, and direct training of LHH artists, the Party successfully weeded works which were considered to be without "a correct political orientation" from the LHH market (Farquhar 1999; "Shanghai Lian Huan Hua" 1999).

The influential, semi-official magazine *Wen Yi Bao* published a public admission of guilt by Gan Xu (1951), giving us one example of the shaping power of critical control. Xu wrote the text of *Bao Wei Er Tong* [Protecting the children], a LHH adaptation of the short story *Guan Lian Zhang* [Company commander Guan] by Ding Zhu published in 1949. As the story was made into a movie in 1951 and attracted media and critical attentions, both the popular movie and the original work came under attack. Set on the eve of the Communist military victory in Shanghai, Zhu's short story features Commander Guan, who discovers that the enemy has used a school as its headquarters, trapping children inside. The situation forces Guan to adopt cautious offensive tactics, bringing more risk to the company for the maximum safety of the children. The enemy is defeated, the children are unharmed, but Guan dies in the battle. The story and movie were criticized by the Party mouthpiece *People's Daily*, as well as *Wen Yi Bao*, for "having seriously tarnished the image of the People's Liberation Army" and for representing "petty bourgeoisie's banal humanitarianism" (Zhang and Sun 1999, p. 33). Following mounting defamation, LHH writer Xu (1951) admitted having made a wrong choice, pledged to raise his political awareness in making future LHH adaptations, and reported that he had asked the publisher to withdraw *Protecting the Children*. Evidently, the publisher did so. My search in multiple bibliographical sources failed to find the work.

Weeding LHH works with an undesirable political framework was conducted simultaneously with the creation of new titles for a hungry LHH market. The earliest works approved by the authorities, however, were disliked by readers. Another *Wen Yi Bao* article "Duo Qu Jiu Xiao Ren Shu Zhen Di" [Seizing the territory held by old LHH] (Bai 1950) highlights how the low literacy rate and the poverty of the Chinese shaped the market preference for the style of LHH. The title suggests how the Party viewed the format as an ideological battleground it must occupy to reinforce Communist subjugation. As Bai (1950) reports, new LHH titles failed to meet the needs of average readers in many respects. Some of them contained too much text and too few images, while the vast number of illiterate and semi-illiterate readers relied heavily on sequential pictures to make sense of the story. Most new LHH were too short, thus not only offering fewer visuals to entertain readers but also far less financial competition than old titles from the previous Nationalist regime, because patrons were charged by the number of volumes in the rental business. Apparently, the LHH reform campaign took these complaints seriously and used them to inform later publications, helping to sustain the popularity of the format. A LHH title published in the People's Republic of China (PRC) averages more than 100 images, and two or three shorter stories may be bound in one volume as a strategy to reach the preferred length.

An enormous number of new LHH titles were released under the Communist regime. Wang's (2003b) incomplete bibliography listed more than 36,000 titles of LHH published from 1949 through 1994. He provided an estimated 50,000 post-1949 titles. In order to reach beyond the Mandarin-speaking population, some LHH titles were made available in languages used by China's minority ethnic groups—mainly Mongolian, Kazakh, Uyghur, Tibetan, and Korean—and in more than a dozen foreign languages, including Esperanto.

The use of LHH as an educational tool for "the masses of the people" can be exemplified by *Hun Yin Fa Tu Jie Tong Su Ben* [The marriage law in illustration: A popularized edition] (1951). Covering marriage licenses, divorce, bigamy, name change, women's and children's rights, and legal responsibilities, this is one of quite a few LHH works published to help the uneducated Chinese population understand the Marriage Law promulgated in 1950. To explain Article 18, that the husband may not file for divorce when the wife is pregnant, the image shows a woman with a pregnant belly and a man in front of a judge, who stretches out his arm to give the man a firm gesture of denial (p. 80). A strong concern for the literacy status of readers is also manifested in the text, which paraphrases each article in plain language and even provides pronunciation guides and definitions for difficult words. LHH on parenting, agricultural science, and other useful topics were also published to help popularize knowledge among adults.

A larger number of LHH works, however, served for the political socialization of the masses. My own study found hundreds of fiction, nonfiction, and biographical works set during the Sino-Japanese War, thematically focused on the victorious Communist leadership of the resistance against Imperial Japan. The publication of these works was a way to render legitimacy to the current ruling party, at the expense of canceling

Nationalist contributions and sacrifice to the war and the significant role that the U.S. ally played during the Pacific War. In fact, the Nationalist army is often portrayed as ineffective fighters, cowardly traitors, and bullies of Chinese civilians. *Shaziling Ji Chang* [Shaziling Airport] (1971) presents a deeply distorted history of the military collaboration between the United States and the Nationalist government. The construction of Shaziling Airport in Suichuan, Jiangxi Province for U.S. fighter pilots who aided China during the war against Japan's invasion, admiringly known by the Chinese as "American Flying Tigers," is described as part of America's colonization scheme. A devilish American military backed by Nationalist authority is shown committing cruelties and crimes against local residents and construction workers.

LHH publishing did not escape the devastating effect of the Cultural Revolution (1966–1976) on all aspects of Chinese society. From 1966 to 1970, the LHH industry, as did all book publishing in China, nearly froze. In fact, many LHH editors and creators had to stop working when they were sent to labor camps to be punished (Jiang 1986). Under Chinese Premier Zhou Enlai's intervention, LHH was among the earliest leisure reading material that resumed publication after 1970. Under stifling censorship control over content and style, LHH served as an intensive tool of ideological indoctrination (Jiang 2002). Titles from the 1970s received the most scholarly attention in the United States, thanks partly to the U.S.-China rapprochement in 1972. As multiple studies have shown, common topics and themes found in LHH works available in this period include hero worship for Chairman Mao Zedong and other Communist role models, celebration of CCP's leadership, superiority of China's Communist society, class struggle, collectivism, and revolutionary movements in other countries (see Blumenthal 1976; Chang 1979; Hwang 1978; "People's Republic of China" 1974).

10.5 From 1976 to 1989: The "Last" Golden Period and Decline

After the Cultural Revolution, the native LHH industry at first expanded quickly but then started to decline from the mid-1980s until a final "retreat" at the end of the decade. Although LHH was never allowed to challenge Party leadership and Party-approved ideology, the format was liberated from being a sheer propaganda tool, which often resulted in one-dimensional characters and formulaic stories. The subject matter of LHH works diversified as numerous taboos were lifted. Traditional stories set in ancient China, criticized in the 1960s for featuring royal and upper-class protagonists rather than contemporary proletarians, reappeared in LHH works. Folktales, fantasy, and fables—genres suppressed during the Cultural Revolution for reasons ranging from superstition to preaching feudalism, capitalism, and revisionism (Pu 1989, p. 27)—came back to entertain young readers. LHH renditions of translated literature, previously highly restricted to revolutionary content, such as stories about the Paris Commune and Vladimir Lenin, works by Maxim Gorky, and Nikolai Ostrovsky's fictionalized autobiography *How the Steel Was Tempered*, expanded to include titles from Western Europe.

For a brief time period from 1977 to 1979, LHH even provided an outlet for intellectuals to voice their pain and trauma about the Cultural Revolution, joining what is called "shang hen wen xue" [scar literature] that rose meteorically in China's literary landscape. The most influential title and a highly controversial one is *Feng* [Maple leaves] (Chen et al. 1981) (first published in the *Lian Huan Hua Bao* magazine in 1979), which is a rough version of *Romeo and Juliet*. Set during the chaotic Cultural Revolution, it is a tragedy about a young couple who find themselves in two opposing political factions. Both put loyalty to their political faith above love for each other and die as a meaningless sacrifice to the political turmoil orchestrated by powers from the central government. The biggest controversy revolves around artists' boldly realistic depiction of the "villains" Mao Zedong's wife JIANG Qing and Marshall LIN Biao, who were made by Mao's successors to shoulder the full blame of the Cultural Revolution—in a frontal view, breaking the taboo that villains are not worthy of highlights in artistic works unless in caricature (Chi 1979/1987).

Scar literature and art represented a deviation from China's Communist literary tradition shaped by Mao's 1942 talk in Yan'an. Even though anti-Cultural Revolution literature restrained its criticism within the rhetoric of the Party line, writers were preoccupied not with educating the masses about socialist ideology, but as Chen (1996) pointed out, with exploring humanism and human nature. The passionate reception of *Maple* suggested that the format of LHH was a double-edged sword for the Communist regime, which had benefited from its popularity and persuasive power, but which could also be undermined by exposure of the Party's dark history through authentic stories and visuals that struck a cord with the masses. A political climate amenable to scar literature did not last long, and the genre disappeared unceremoniously from LHH publishing,[6] as well as from Chinese literature in general. Although *Maple* won the first prize in the national fine arts show held in 1980, it remained, as Wang (2003a) lamented, the last shining piece of "scar art" (p. 11) intent on exposing the raw wounds and bloody ills of the Cultural Revolution.

The early 1980s saw a shift of LHH from popular reading material for the poorly educated populace to a format perceived as being mainly for youth. Chunguang Bian, head of the National Publishing Administration of the CCP's Propaganda Department, directed the shift from the top down when he spoke at a LHH publishing conference organized by the Administration in March 1982. Bian (1982) instructed that LHH should target children and young adults as the main audience; even works produced specifically for adults should be wholesome and wary of possible "poisonous effects" (p. 6) upon young readers who were not capable of critical reading; for late adolescents and older readers, LHH publications

---

[6] An editor from the Liaoning Fine Arts Publishing House, for example, specifically mentioned withdrawing scar literature from LHH on the grounds of undesirable "social impact," giving "political allegiance to the Party Central Committee" as the essential criterion for thematic appropriateness (Zhang 1982/1987, p. 586).

were not adequate to help them become "socialist-minded, educated" (p. 7) workers. These instructions, given after the enormous impact of adult-oriented works like *Maple*—read and discussed by people from factory workers to school teachers—are intriguing. Could it be that, by directing LHH publishers to focus on child-friendly works, the Chinese authority was steering them away from politically sensitive topics and themes that would promise great appeal to adults who had been disillusioned by the Cultural Revolution?

Prior to Bian's talk, some publishers had already increased their LHH publications for youth. Pilai Wang, editor of the influential People's Fine Arts Publishing House, perhaps represented a bottom-up push for the shift. Wang (1982/1987) argued that for children in the fourth grade and under, LHH was virtually their only extracurricular reading. For older adolescents and adults, however, the format was only one of their reading choices. He pointed out the discrepancy between the content of LHH and its readership. LHH in the market remained overwhelmingly oriented towards a general, cross-age audience, with little consideration given to the interest and reading level of young readers, particularly preschoolers and lower grade readers. Interestingly, he was also a pioneer voice proposing that LHH for beginning readers should be published in a large size (Wang 1982/1987), suggesting a transformation into picture books.

While the political socialization of youth remained the highest mission emphasized by the Party, LHH publications in the 1980s did lose some of their political edge and came to embrace a wider range of goals, including "intellectual development" and education in "science and culture" for young people (Bian 1982, p. 6). In a rare record of LHH being used by classroom teachers, Qian (1982/1987) confirmed that the *Zhongguo Cheng Yu Gu Shi* [Chinese idiom stories] series helped students learn classical Chinese and history, Chinese idioms, and moral values. Again using *Chinese Idiom Stories* (Vol. 1–15, 1979–1980)—winner of the first prize in the 1980 national LHH award for text—as an example, Jiang (1981/1987) stressed that the language of LHH was highly influential for the literacy development and literary refinement of young learners. Wu (1982/1987) reviewed the great commercial success (in the year 1981) of biographical stories about Chinese and world scientists, writers, and historical figures, published in order to convey information, as well as to encourage young readers to emulate biographees' scholarly assiduousness, and academic integrity. These LHH works were aligned with Chinese youth literature, with which the format overlapped but never fully merged. As we shall see, despite the high quality of many individual works, the transition of LHH from popular reading to youth literature in the 1980s was not successful enough to stop the decline of the industry.

Post-Cultural Revolution years first saw an exponential growth in the quantity of LHH works. In Wang's (2003b) incomplete bibliography, the number of listed LHH titles doubled from 1977 to 1979, and nearly doubled again in 1981. According to Xu (1986), LHH and children's books were nearly sold out after June 1, 1981, the International Children's Day celebrated in China and an important gift day for young people, prompting publishers to greatly increase LHH titles and print runs. In the peak years of 1982 and 1983, the total impression of LHH approached 1.5 billion, or one quarter of the book publishing in China (Jiang 1986). However, the industry met its downfall in 1985. More than 3,000 titles were printed that year with a total of 8.1 billion copies, but they sold poorly, marking the beginning of LHH's gradual retirement from being the most prominent popular reading material for "men and women, young and old" of twentieth century China. In 1991, the industry shrank to 350 titles in several million copies (Lin 1997).

It is beyond the scope of this chapter to offer a satisfactory answer to what caused the decline of Chinese LHH, a multifaceted question considered in numerous articles by laymen and researchers alike. Commonly cited factors include poor works released by unqualified publishers lured into the business, readers' changing tastes and value systems, a narrow thematic scope, rising production cost, and competition from television and other new media (See, for example, Yi 1987; Lin 1997; Zhong 2004). Since Japanese manga replaced native LHH works as the most popular graphic reading material for youth after 1990, some studies sought answers by comparing the two in content and style. Shi and Hu (2008) suggest that Chinese LHH stories lack the originality and appeal found in successful Japanese imports, whose visual art is not necessarily as refined as that of Chinese works but is highly integrated with the text for effective and dynamic storytelling. Seldom discussed is the responsibility of government censorship, which led to prevalent self-censorship, in constraining the range of topics and themes that could have helped sustain the interest of a wide audience. In a self-congratulatory piece, editor Daxin Qian wrote about how the Shanghai People's Fine Arts Publishing House cautiously decided against adapting a well-received play *Jia Ru Wo Shi Zhen De* [What if I were real] (written by Yexin Sha in 1979 and banned later) that criticizes the privileges abused by senior Party cadres (Qian 1982/1987). Like the short-lived scar literature, exposure to the Party's contemporary ills enjoyed a liberal political space only during the immediate Post-Cultural Revolution years.

Another neglected issue is how Chinese LHH has adapted to a Chinese population celebrating a greatly improved rate of schooling and literacy. Various sources indicate that the illiteracy rate in China dropped to 22–25% by 1982 (Ross 2005). Traditionally, LHH readers demanded a strong explanatory function from visuals, which were the main appeal of this format. As the vast majority of the Chinese population could now read, however, visuals that simply repeated the same message in the text, while still serving pre-literate and beginning young readers well, became redundant. Starting from the 1970s, it became increasingly common for Chinese LHH to do away with conversation balloons—which were thought to ruin the integrity of the pictures (Fei 1982/1987)—seriously diminishing the need for readers to look at image panels for extra information. Renowned LHH artist Youzhi He (贺友直) was dismayed that most of the readers he observed skipped the illustrations and had eyes on the text only (Duan 2000). My examination of *Lie Huo Jin Gang* [Steel meets fire] (Vol. 1, 1984), a title that appeared in both the traditional LHH and Japanese manga style, shows that this reading pattern is highly possible, if not true for all readers.

11　史更新正说着，忽听外边响起枪声和嘈杂的喊声，敌人已到跟前了。他忙让赵大爷快跑，赵大爷把史更新推进草堆里，又在他身上盖了许多草，才转身出了牛棚。

Fig. 10.4 *Lie Huo Jin Gang* [Steel meets fire] 1984 edition by Liu Liu; adapted by Ying Dai; illustrated by Yongzhi Li. Shenyang: Liaoning Mei Shu Chu Ban She. Used with kind permission from Liaoning Fine Art Publishing House, China

The 178-page volume [Steel meets fire] contains about 10,000 characters of text, which is continuous from page to page and makes up a complete story. A child finishing the third grade in elementary school would have learned nearly all the characters used in this book, which targets a general audience. For a fluent reader who needs no visual aid to comprehend the text, taking time to view images on every page might break the flow of reading. What role do images play in this LHH? Contrary to conventional expectation, not all images are a mere literal rendition of the text. Set during the Sino-Japanese War, the story begins with Shi Gengxin, an injured platoon leader of the Communist Eighth Route Army, seeking shelter from a peasant named Zhao. On page 11 is a paragraph of 71 Chinese characters (Fig. 10.4).

> Shi Gengxin's words were interrupted by sudden gunshots and noisy shouts from the outside. The enemies had come close. Shi urged Uncle Zhao to leave immediately. Zhao, however, pushed Shi into the haystack and covered his body with more grass before exiting the stable.

The image above the text shows the frontal portrait of an old northern Chinese peasant standing still, his weather-beaten face looking determined. A darkish background with curvy lines resembling stormy waves conveys a sense of impending danger. This is a carefully executed portrait intending not to capture the actions described in the text, but to highlight the heroic nature of the peasant in a perilous circumstance. A piece of interpretive rather than explanatory illustration, it may unfortunately be skipped by fluent readers just the same. In fact, artwork like this would have attracted more attention if offered in an infrequently illustrated chapter book.

10 Chinese *Lian Huan Hua* and Literacy: Popular Culture Meets Youth Literature

Fig. 10.5 *Lie Huo Jin Gang* [Steel meets fire] 1998 edition by Liu Liu; adapted and illustrated by Nanping Zhou. Shenzhen: Hai Tian Chu Ban She. Used with kind permission from Hai Tian Press (Shenzhen, China) and from creator Nanping Zhou

The dispensability of visuals in the 1984 edition contrasts sharply with a 1998 edition of the same story, which, illustrated in the style of *man hua*, adopts the vocabulary and grammar of narrative art found in Japanese manga and Western comic books. The same segment mentioned above is expanded into three panels (Fig. 10.5), one showing the coming noise and shouts, and two showing the peasant's successive actions—first hiding the soldier under the grass and then leaving the stable (p. 5). The length of text is cut by half, all of it appearing in conversation balloons except the onomatopoeia character "啪" (pa), written in the image to represent gunshot. These changes break the continuity of the text, which can no longer stand alone to form a complete story, and reduce the overlap of information between text and images, as a result forcing readers—regardless of their educational level—to put both together to make sense of the story.

My analysis of *Steel Meets Fire* suggests that traditional Chinese LHH, dominated by illustrated story books, lessened the significance of visuals for an increasingly literate Chinese population even as LHH creators were striving to perfect the artistic standard and expressive depth of individual panels. The "decline of Chinese LHH" after 1985 was partly the collapse of a "one-format-fits-all" model having prevailed in China since the 1920s, as different age groups were now attracted to other formats of reading and entertainment media, each with some competitive edge over the old LHH. As discussed in Chap. 7, the 1980s saw a fast growth of Chinese youth literature, boasting a plethora of high-quality works in diverse genres and formats tailored to different age levels. The bright side was that seeds for the diversification and specialization of Chinese LHH had long been planted. A small number of brief children's LHH stories with simple language and colorful illustrations, clearly taking very young readers' comprehension level and interest into consideration, seemed ready to morph into large-size picture books. A minority of LHH works were comic books relying heavily upon visuals for storytelling, the most famous titles being Leping Zhang's nearly wordless *Sanmao* series. Peikun Wang's fantasy and science fiction series *Xiao Jing Ling* [The little elf] (first issued in 1982), winner of the second prize in the fourth national LHH award given in December 1991, is an early and skillful adopter of the *man hua* style. The sad fact, however, was that these promising seeds failed to help revive the Chinese LHH industry in the latter half of the 1980s and became dormant in the 1990s when Chinese youth literature, too, suffered decade-long inactivity.

10.6 From 1990 to the Present

LHH broadly defined as sequential narrative art did not disappear from Chinese publications after the 1990s, but works by Chinese creators lost their claim on the market. *Xiao Erhei Jie Hun* [Xiao Erhei gets married] (1995a, b), illustrated in Chinese color brush-painting by Youzhi He, had a tiny first print run of 1,000 copies, not unusual for domestic new works of that decade. Meanwhile, according to Lin's (1997) estimation, Japanese manga occupied more than 90% of China's LHH market in 1994. Alerted by the sweeping preference of Chinese youth for imported *man hua* books and animated cartoon shows, the CCP's Propaganda Department and the national Administration of Press and Publication even launched a "5155 Project" in 1995 to sponsor native *man hua* publications and cartoon works. These Chinese works, however, were not successful (Lin 1997). Unlike the effective LHH campaign in the first half of the 1950s, the attempts of these two agencies to curtail rampant piracy of Japanese manga largely failed, leading to a considerable loss of control over what LHH titles were available to young readers (Jiang 1995a). An illegal market of pirated manga has remained so robust in China today that publishers can hardly profit from importing authorized editions (Liu 2009).

For both its content and style, Japanese manga quickly acquired a bad reputation among concerned adults in China. Senior LHH editor Weipu Jiang was the most active critic of the negative impact of Japanese manga on Chinese youth. His 1995 survey of a bookstand in his own Beijing neighborhood found violence and "seductive beauties" depicted on the covers of these foreign LHH works (Jiang 1995a, p. 2). In another article, he juxtaposed crudely drawn, nonsensical, and vulgar Japanese LHH with other pornographic publications apparently responsible for juvenile delinquency (Jiang 1995b). Echoing comic artist Junwu Hua's condemnation that Japanese manga's invasion of Chinese children's minds was equivalent to "the Incident of July 7"[7] in the comics realm, Jiang (2000, 2001) warned of the pernicious messages—ranging from capitalism to imperialism to militarism—that were embedded in Japanese LHH publications. Many teachers and parents frowned upon young readers' strong interest in manga, discounting such reading choice as less valuable than school textbooks, informational books, and classic literature.

Recently, the huge success of a domestic anime television show *Xiyangyang yu Huitailang* [Pleasant Goat and Big Big Wolf] (first aired in 2005), whose protagonists are now national household names, is beginning to give people hope about the revival of Chinese anime and related industries. The tie-in comic book series of the show sold more than one million copies within 3 months after hitting the market (Zan 2009). The first anime movie adaptation and its three sequels, shown in theaters from 2009 to 2012, were all box office hits.

10.7 Research on Lian Huan Hua and Literacy

History has provided ample footnotes to the power of this visually-based reading format, be it in literacy acquisition, information delivery, or political socialization. LHH offers us great potential for innovative approaches to literacy education and learning. In fact, its appeal to youth has lured Chinese publishers to market LHH of "educational" value to parents who have high hopes for the academic excellence of their only child. Since the 1990s there has been no shortage of informational LHH that intend to "spice up" the learning of various topics and subjects from ancient Chinese philosophy to history, English language, mathematics, and more. As a starting point of engaging in LHH research, teachers and librarians can certainly evaluate the quality of educational titles in terms of appeal, lucidity, accuracy, etc.; recommend notable ones to students; and even experiment with the format in classroom instruction to attend to diverse learning styles.

The more fruitful questions, however, lie in the vast number of popular native and imported LHH titles, which tend to be imaginative works and fantasy titles, often dismissed by adults as a distraction to formal learning. Much of the stereotypical devaluation of the popular LHH is not based on a comprehensive and in-depth understanding of publications in this format, which is a necessary step researchers must take towards a respectful and effective use of LHH in teaching and learning. Krashen's (2004) review of Western comic books and language development could generate many questions about parallel LHH works available in China. What is the amount of exposure to language, and at what reading level, is an average LHH book? How does LHH compare to text-heavy youth literature in developing students' reading comprehension and vocabulary?

---

[7] The Marco Polo Bridge Incident on July 7, 1937, marked the beginning of Imperial Japan's full-scale aggression against China.

For reluctant as well as average readers, is LHH reading conducive to expanded reading of books in general? Can a LHH collection in a library stimulate young people's use of other library materials? McCloud's (1993) study of Western and Japanese comic books suggests many facets, such as the elements of comics and the relationship between panels, which we can similarly examine in Chinese LHH works. The task may help us understand how native works differ from foreign titles and where they excel or fail as narrative art. Researchers can develop criteria for evaluating LHH for different age groups. Nodelman's (1988) scholarship on picture books offers another lens one could use to examine relationships between pictures and words in Chinese LHH. Content analysis and literary criticism of LHH stories can help us identify titles that are appropriate for curriculum goals. Pedagogical explorations can identify ways to allow students to demonstrate their learning outcomes via the format of sequential visuals. Last but not least, gender issues related to using LHH as curriculum material can be explored. Many Japanese manga imports depict sexualized female bodies, challenging Chinese teachers to develop media literacy curriculum informed by such gender messages in youth popular culture.

10.8 Summary

At the intersection of popular culture and youth literature, a publication format known as "linked images" gained popularity in China during much of the twentieth century, as long as it successfully adapted to the literacy status, entertainment needs, and financial capability of the populace. LHH thrived as cross-age reading material when the growing body of literature strictly defined as "youth literature" was inadequate in many respects. The subject matter of LHH was politicized following Imperial Japan's invasion, intensified with the Communist victory, and, after the Cultural Revolution, depoliticized to a great extent if still subjected to government censorship. From the 1980s, LHH publications are also increasingly age-distinct and aligned with youth literature. Although largely replaced by imported titles today, the format of visual storytelling continues to make up a significant part of emergent and young readers' literacy environment outside of school. However, educators have ignored the format or dismissed it as a mere distraction, or occasionally considered its content an evil influence on children's minds. A non-biased understanding of this unique sequential narrative art will help instructors explore effective means to employ the format in literacy teaching and formal learning.

Acknowledgments The author wishes to express heartfelt thanks to Professors Betsy Hearne and Christine Jenkins, faculty members of the University of Illinois Graduate School of Library and Information Science, for kindly reading early versions of this article and providing insightful feedback.

References

Aying. (1957). 中国连环图画史话 [A historical account of Chinese *lian huan tu hua*]. 北京: 中国古典艺术出版社.
Bai, R. (1950). 夺取旧小人书阵地 [Seizing the territory held by old LHH]. 文艺报, 2(4), 26.
Bian, C. (1982). 边春光同志在全国部分省、市、自治区连环画出版工作座谈会上的讲话 [Comrade Chunguang Bian's talk at the forum on the LHH publishing work of some provinces, cities, and autonomous regions]. 中国出版, 6, 5–10.
Blumenthal, E. P. (1976). *Models in Chinese moral education: Perspectives from children's books*. Doctoral dissertation, University of Michigan.
Chang, P. H. (1979). Children's literature and political socialization. In G. C. Chu & F. L. K. Hsu (Eds.), *Moving a mountain: Cultural change in China* (pp. 237–256). Honolulu: Published for the East–west Center by University Press of Hawaii.
Chen, X. (1996). The disappearance of truth: From realism to modernism in China. In H. Chung & M. Falchikov (Eds.), *In the party spirit: Socialist realism and literary practice in the Soviet Union, East Germany and China* (pp. 158–165). Atlanta: Rodopi.
Chi, K. (1987). 连环画《枫》的时代意义 [The historic significance of LHH work *Maple Leaves*]. In M. Lin, & S. Zhao (Eds.), 中国连环画艺术文 (pp. 905–910). 太原: 山西人民出版社. (Original work published 1979)
Duan, X. (2000). 贺友直的"伤心" [Youzhi He's "sadness"]. Retrieved from http://www.cartoonwin.com/personage/mjft/person.php?cat=x&own=heyz&name=x_01
Fang, H. (1999). 新中国少儿读物出版 50 年 [Fifty years of publishing for youth in the new China]. 出版科学, 4, 10–15.
Farquhar, M. (1999). *Children's literature in China: From Lu Xun to Mao Zedong*. Armonk: M. E. Sharpe.
Fei, S. (1987). 谈谈连环画的图文并茂 [On images and text of LHH]. In M. Lin, & S. Zhao (Eds.), 中国连环画艺术文集 (pp. 470–475). 太原: 山西人民出版社. (Original work published 1982)
Gu, B. (1999). 二十年代连环画精品值得收藏 [Choice LHH works from the 1920s are worth collecting]. In G. Wang, & M. Li (Eds.), 老连环画 (p. 8). 上海: 上海画报出版社.
He, G. (1947a, May 18). 连环图画在蜕变中(上) [*Lian huan tu hua* is in transmutation, part 1]. 大公报, p. 2.
He, G. (1947b, May 25). 连环图画在蜕变中(中) [*Lian huan tu hua* is in transmutation, part 2]. 大公报, p. 2.
He, G. (1947c, June 1). 连环图画在蜕变中(下) [*Lian huan tu hua* is in transmutation, part 3]. 大公报, p. 2.
Huang, R., Wang, Y., & Li, M. (1999). 老连环画历史概述 [An introduction to the history of old LHH]. In G. Wang, & M. Li (Eds.), 老连环画 (pp. 2–5). 上海: 上海画报出版社.
Hung, C. (1994). *War and popular culture: Resistance in modern China, 1937–1945*. Berkeley: University of California Press.
Hwang, J. C. (1978). Lien huan hua: Revolutionary serial pictures. In G. C. Chu (Ed.), *Popular media in China: Shaping new cultural patterns* (pp. 51–72). Honolulu: Published for the East–west Center by the University Press of Hawaii.
Jiang, W. (1986). 新连环画艺术的三十五年 [New LHH art of the past 35 years]. 连环画艺术论 (pp. 228–250). 沈阳市: 辽宁美术出版社.
Jiang, W. (1987). 连环画编辑工作大有可为. In M. Lin, & S. Zhao (Eds.), 中国连环画艺术文集 (pp. 549–553). 太原: 山西人民出版社. (Original work published 1981)
Jiang, W. (1995a). 保卫孩子,就是保卫未来——再谈国外连环画的翻印出版 [Protecting children is protecting future – revisiting LHH duplicating and publishing in foreign countries]. 出版参考, 18, 2.
Jiang, W. (1995b). 清除精神毒品 保护青少年 [Cleaning up spiritual drugs and protecting youth]. 群言, 6, 23–24.
Jiang, W. (2000). 面对世纪之交关于连环画、年画、宣传画等通俗美术的一些思考 [Some thoughts on popular fine arts such as LHH, New Year print, and propaganda pictures at the turn of the century]. 美术, 2, 73–77.

Jiang, W. (2001). 警惕军国主义的文化入侵 [Be alert to a militaristic aggression in culture]. 美术, 5, 54–55.

Jiang, W. (2002). 追忆周恩来同志对连环画事业的关怀 [In memory of Zhou Enlai for his care for LHH]. 美术之友, 2, 14–16.

Jie, Z. (2004). 褪色的记忆: 连环画 [A fading memory: LHH]. 太原市: 山西古籍出版社.

Krashen, S. D. (2004). *The power of reading: Insights from the research* (2nd ed.). Westport, Conn.: Libraries Unlimited.

Lin, Y. (1997). 中国连环画的昨天、今天和明天 [Chinese LHH in yesterday, today, and tomorrow]. 百科知识, 8, 42–44.

Liu, T. (2009, March 26). 中少社引进日本漫画遇到难题 [China Children's Press encounters challenge in importing Japanese manga]. 北京晨报, p. A13.

Lu, X. (1973). "连环图画"辩护 [A defense of *lian huan tu hua*]. In Memorial Committee of Mr. Xun Lu (Ed.), 鲁迅全集.第五卷 (pp. 39–44). 北京: 人民文学出版社. (Original work published 1932)

Mao, D. (1989). "连环图画小说" [Novels in *lian huan tu hua*]. In Q. Wang (Eds.), 中国现代儿童文学文论选 (pp. 650–653). 南宁市: 广西人民出版社. (Original work published 1932)

Mao, Z. (2004). 在延安文艺座谈会上的讲话 [*Talks at the Yen'an Forum on Literature and Art*]. Retrieved from http://news.xinhuanet.com/ziliao/2004-06/24/content_1545090.htm. (Original work published 1942)

McCloud, S. (1993). *Understanding comics: The invisible art*. New York: HarperPerennial.

Mo, W., & Shen, W. (2006). "Sanmao, the vagrant": Homeless children of yesterday and today. *Children's Literature in Education, 37*, 267–285.

Nebiolo, G. (1973). Introduction. In *The people's comic book* (trans: F. Frenaye, pp. vii–xvi). Garden City: Anchor Press.

Nodelman, P. (1988). *Words about pictures: The narrative art of children's picture books*. Athens: University of Georgia Press.

People's Republic of China: Educating the masses with picture-story books. (1974). *Interracial Books for Children, 5*(1), 7–10.

Pu, M. (1989). 导言 [Introduction]. In M. Pu (Ed.), 中国儿童文学大系.童话 [*Chinese children's literature series: Fairy tales*] (pp. 1–39). 太原: 希望出版社.

Qian, D. (1987). 让小人书发挥更大的作用. In M. Lin, & S. Zhao (Eds.), 中国连环画艺术文集 (pp. 290–295). 太原: 山西人民出版社. (Original work published 1982)

Qiu, Y., & Zhang, W. (2007). 三毛之父"从军"记 [Sanmao's father "joins the army"]. 上海: 上海科学技术文献出版社.

Ross, H. (2005). *China country study*. Retrieved from http://unesdoc.unesco.org/images/0014/001461/146108e.pdf

Shanghai lian huan hua gai zao yun dong shi liao/上海连环画改造运动史料 (1950–1952) [Historical materials on the LHH reform campaign in Shanghai (1950–1952)]. (1999). 档案与史学, 04, 18–27.

Shen, J. (1999). 我和连环画有缘 [My lucky tie with LHH]. In G. Wang, & M. Li (Eds.), 老连环画 (pp. 6–7). 上海: 上海画报出版社.

Shen, K. (2001). Lianhuanhua and manhua – picture books and comics in old Shanghai. In J. A. Lent (Ed.), *Illustrating Asia: Comics, humor magazines, and picture books* (pp. 100–120). Honolulu: University of Hawai'i Press.

Shi, C., & Hu, J. (2008). 中国连环画衰落的原因 [Reasons for the decline of Chinese LHH]. 浙江艺术职业学院学报, 1, 95–100.

Wang, P. (1987). 谈连环画的读者对象问题 [On the targeted readership of LHH]. In M. Lin, & S. Zhao (Eds.), 中国连环画艺术文集 (pp. 577–579). 太原: 山西人民出版社. (Original work published 1982)

Wang, H. (2003a). 血染红《枫》噙泪读 [In tears reading blood-stained red *Maple Leaves*]. In G. Wang, & M. Li (Eds.), 新中国连环画: 70 年代 (p. 11). 上海: 上海画报出版社.

Wang, Y. (2003b). 中国连环画目录汇编 [A bibliography of Chinese LHH]. 上海: 上海画报出版社.

Wang, G., & Li, M. (Eds.). (1999). 老连环画 [Old LHH]. 上海: 上海画报出版社.

Wu, B. (1987). 连环画出版综述 [Summary of LHH publication]. In M. Lin & S. Zhao (Eds.), 中国连环画艺术文集 (pp. 302–307). 太原: 山西人民出版社. (Original work published 1982)

Xu, G. (1951). 小人书《关连长》编者的检讨 [Self-criticism by the editor of LHH *Company Commander Guan*]. 文艺报, *10*(4), 36.

Xu, G. (1986). 三次恶性循环的教训 [Lessons from three vicious cycles]. 出版发行研究, *2*, 41–46.

Xu, G. (2001). 昨夜西风凋碧树 [Last night's west wind and a withered tree]. 北京: 北京十月文艺出版社.

Yi, D. (1987). 连环画出版工作为什么处于低潮 [Why publishing of LHH is declining]. 出版工作, *1*, 75–76.

Zan, J. (2009, March 12). Goats and wolves spring a surprise: A homegrown animated movie turns out to be a runaway hit. *Beijing Review, 52*. Retrieved from http://www.bjreview.com/print/txt/2009-03/07/content_184178.htm

Zhang, R., & Sun, Y. (Eds.). (1999). 争鸣小说百年精品系. *2* [One hundred years of best controversial novels series: Part 2]. 北京: 当代世界出版社.

Zhang, Y. (1987). 选题要严肃 [Selecting subject matter seriously]. In M. Lin & S. Zhao (Eds.), 中国连环画艺术文集 (pp. 585–586). 太原: 山西人民出版社. (Original work published 1982)

Zhao, J. (1987). 回忆鲁迅与连环图画 [A recollection of Xun Lu and *lian huan tu hua*]. In M. Lin, & S. Zhao (Eds.), 中国连环画艺术文集 (pp. 121–131). 太原: 山西人民出版社. (Original work published 1979)

Zhong yang. (2004). 中共中央关于处理反动的、淫秽的、荒诞的书刊图画问题和关于加强对私营文化事业和企业的管理和改造的指示 [Instructions by the Central Committee of the Chinese Communist Party on handling reactionary, obscene, and absurd books, periodicals, and pictures and on strengthening the management and reformation of private cultural entities and enterprises]. Retrieved from http://news.xinhuanet.com/ziliao/2004-12/29/content_2390374.htm (Original work published 1955)

Zhong, Y. (2004). 新中国传统连环画的兴与衰 [The boom and decline of traditional LHH in new China]. 图书馆建设, *1*, 107–108.

Major LHH titles examined:

Chen, Y., Liu, Y., & Li, B. (1981). 枫 [Maple leaves]. 北京: 人民美术出版社.

Hua, S., & Yan, H. (Illustrator). (1945). 狼牙山五壮士 [*Five heroes at the Langya Mountain*] (4th ed.). 上海: 群育出版社 (first published in 1945).

Huadong People's Publishing House. (1951). 婚姻法图解通俗本 [*The marriage law in illustration: A popularized edition*]. 上海: 华东人民出版社.

Huang, S. (1943). 战地恩仇记 [*Friends and foes in the battlefield*]. 联友出版社.

Liu, L., & Dai, Y. (1984). 烈火金钢 [*Steel meets fire*]. 石家庄: 河北美术出版社.

Liu, L., & Zhou, N. (1998). 烈火金钢 [*Steel meets fire*]. 深圳: 海天出版社.

Mo, P., Lü, M., & Ya, J. (1984). 铁佛寺: 木刻连环画 [*Iron Buddha Temple*]. 北京: 人民美术出版社 (first published in 1943).

Shang, M., & Wang, Q. (1944). 三兄弟踊跃从军 [*Three brothers eagerly join the army*]. 重庆: 教育编译馆.

Shang, M., & Wang, Q. (1944). 荣誉军人 [*The disabled veteran*]. 重庆: 教育编译馆.

Political Propaganda Team of Suichuan County Revolution Commission. (1971). 沙子岭机场 [*Shaziling Airport*]. 南昌: 江西人民出版社.

Zhang, L. (1949). 三毛从军记 [*Saomao joins the army*] (上册) (2nd ed.). 香港: 四方书局.

Zhang, L. (2005). 三毛在1935年 [*Sanmao in the year 1935*]. 南昌: 二十一世纪出版社.

Zhang, L. (2006). 三毛流浪记全集 [*A complete story of Sanmao the vagrant*] (2nd ed.). 上海: 少年儿童出版社.

Chapter 11
Information and Communication Technologies for Literacy Education in China

Xun Ge, Jiening Ruan, and Xiaoshuai Lu

11.1 Introduction

The rapid development of information and communication technologies (ICTs) has initiated a multitude of changes in schooling around the world. In particular, the impact of ICTs on literacy teaching and learning is immense due to the close connection between literacy and technology (Bruce 2003; Valmont 2003). Effective integration of technologies helps students become competent information technology users, information seekers, analyzers, evaluators, problem solvers, decision makers, creative and effective users of productivity tools, communicators, collaborators, publishers, producers, as well as informed, responsible, and contributing citizens (ISTE 2002).

In China the issue of technology integration to support student learning has attracted attention from the central government in recent years. Several mandates have been issued to address technology in education. Although the degree of integration varies from school to school and from teacher to teacher, various technologies have been used in many classrooms across the nation. In this paper, we first briefly review the history of technology use in literacy education in China. Next, we provide a synthesis of the current state of ICT use in China's literacy education based on an extensive literature review and critical analysis of academic journals and web resources related to ICTs. Finally, we conclude our paper with a discussion of the implication of ICT integration for Chinese literacy students and teachers and make recommendations for literacy researchers studying effective integration of ICT in Chinese literacy education.

X. Ge (✉)
Educational Psychology, University of Oklahoma, Norman, OK, USA
e-mail: xge@ou.edu

J. Ruan
Reading/Literacy Education, University of Oklahoma, Norman, OK, USA

X. Lu
Information and Communication Technology, China University of Petroleum-Beijing, Dongying, Shandong, China

11.2 Historical Review of ICT Integration in Literacy Education in China

China had a late start in its effort to integrate technology into education due to its slow economic development and lack of resources in most of the twentieth century. Thus, technology integration in education is a rather recent phenomenon in China (Liu and Zhang 2006). Before the 1990s, educational technologies were rarely used and could only be observed in highly selective university settings. Common technologies for language and literacy teaching and learning, if schools could afford them, included TV programs, audio cassette tapes, radios, and overhead projectors. Computers were luxury items beyond the reach of most schools. In a very limited number of well-resourced city schools where computers were available, they were reserved for technology classes in labs where students were taught basic computer literacy skills as an isolated subject. The concept of integrating technologies into various subject areas was nonexistent.

Since the late 1990s, the Chinese government has recognized the importance of information technologies to the future development of the country and started to form an active agenda to promote ICTs in education. Information technology education became one of the major national educational priorities. In 2000, the Chinese Ministry of Education (MOE) issued a policy document entitled *Information Technology Curriculum Guide for Primary and Secondary Schools*. This ground-breaking document stipulated that primary and secondary schools should offer information technology courses. Most recently, the Chinese government published a strategic document, *Outline for National Mid- and Long-Term Education Reform and Development Plan* (MOE, 2010), that sets the direction for education for the upcoming decade (2010–2020). ICT in education is one of the key elements of the document.

The Chinese government put into motion an extensive curriculum reform in 2001. New curriculum standards were set for various subject areas, and content related to ICTs was added to the curriculum guides for each subject area. In particular, the new curriculum standards for Yuwen (Chinese language and literacy education) have for the first time included items specifically addressing ICTs for Chinese literacy teaching and learning (MOE 2001b, 2003). The curriculum guide for grades 1–9 (compulsory education) specifically highlights the importance of equipping future citizens with the knowledge and skills to use modern technologies to collect and process information (MOE 2001a). Detailed objectives include using computer programs for word recognition and typing Chinese characters (3rd–4th grades) and for collecting information and using libraries, the Internet, and other information channels for inquiry-based learning (5th–6th, 7th–9th grades). The high school Chinese literacy curriculum guide also includes objectives that require students to develop competence in locating and processing information through various media channels and in using computers for word processing, editing, interface design, developing personal websites, and making presentations. Both curriculum guides also make recommendations for teachers to utilize rich curriculum resources available on the Internet and to incorporate ICTs into the teaching of Chinese.

11.3 Current State of ICT Integration in Literacy Education in China

Much progress has been made at the school and classroom level where Chinese literacy teachers actively integrate ICT to support teaching and learning. This section is a comprehensive review of the current state of ICT integration in literacy education in China, including the types of ICTs, various ICT applications and resources, as well as ICT-supported pedagogy in Chinese literacy education. We searched, reviewed, analyzed, categorized, and synthesized various periodical articles (journals and magazines) and website resources on the uses of ICTs over the past 10 years in literacy education in China. Our goals were to acquire a better understanding of the strategies, resources, and tools currently used for literacy education in China, to inform Chinese educators of available ICT tools and resources that can be used to improve Chinese learning and instruction, and to suggest to Chinese educators the most effective strategies for the use of ICTs in teaching literacy. At the same time, we were interested in identifying gaps in the existing literature on ICT integration in literacy education in China.

11.3.1 Data Sources

Our primary data source was the database *China Academic Journals* (中国知网) (2000–2010). We also reviewed popular education websites frequently used by educators in China. We chose these two data sources because they extensively capture and represent the current status of and trends in the development of ICTs in literacy education in China. We selected eight major journals at the national level to review: *China Educational Technology*/中国电化教育 (2000–2010), *E-education Research*/电化教育研究 (2000–2010), *Modern Educational Technology*/现代教育科学 (2004–2010), *Distance Education in China*/中国远程教育 (2001–2008), *China Information Technology Education*/中国信息技术教育 (2003–2010), *Modern Education Science (Middle School Teachers)* /现代教育科学 (中学教师) (2008–2009), *Modern Education Science (Primary School Teachers)* /现代教育科学 (小学教师) (2007–2010), and *Primary and Middle School Educational Technology*/中小学电教 (2007–2010). In addition, we reviewed some regional magazines, such as *Jilin Education*/吉林教育, *Monthly Journal for Principals*/校长月刊, and *Journal of Subject Education*/学科教育. From a myriad of journal and magazine articles, we selected, examined, and analyzed a large number of articles related to ICT use in K-12 literacy education, including Chinese reading, writing, literature, and character recognition. Altogether, we examined over 600 articles.

11.3.2 Analysis of Data

We went through a rigorous process of searching, selecting, classifying, coding, analyzing, and interpreting. First, we created research logs containing abstracts and additional information about the selected articles (e.g., key words, author, title, year, etc.). Then we went through the selected abstracts and articles to obtain preliminary information and to categorize the articles. As part of the coding process we assigned labels, highlighted key words, and wrote reflective notes as we coded the abstracts and articles.

Following the coding procedure, we created a database using a spreadsheet to help us organize the information we had coded. We created different sheets for different categories, classifying articles in two ways: by functions or purposes (e.g., reading, writing, literature, types of technology, technology integration, resources, tools, etc.) and by codes/keywords (e.g., motivation, interest, self-regulation, metacognition, self-control, interest, wiki, integration, etc.). We set up each sheet for a designated function, such as reading and writing. For each of the article entries, we entered the keywords, codes/labels, functions, author names, titles, journal titles, and dates. Subsequently, we identified major themes regarding ICT integration in Chinese literacy education. In addition, we explored online resources dedicated to teaching with ICTs. We identified and annotated a number of websites that were intended to assist teachers to integrate ICTs into their classroom instruction, including courseware, lesson plans, discussion forums, and resources for K-12 teaching.

11.3.3 Findings

Through our analysis we identified a number of themes that reflect the current state, trends, and impact of ICT integration in Chinese literacy education, including types, functions, and uses of ICT tools and resources; the role of ICT in literacy education in China; and current trends in ICT integration in literacy education in China. According to the articles we reviewed, a variety of ICTs have been widely used in various instructional contexts to teach reading, writing, and literature. Generally, these tools can be categorized into (a) standalone multimedia programs or courseware, (b) character encoding and input systems, (c) communication and collaboration tools, (d) mobile technology, (e) corpora, and (f) instructional delivery devices (e.g., LCD projectors and whiteboards). Below we focus on the first five types of technologies.

11.3.3.1 Multimedia Programs and Courseware

Standalone courseware refers to multimedia programs integrated with texts, graphics, audio, and animations, created with popular presentation tools—Microsoft PowerPoint or interactive web development software, such as Adobe

Flash. The multimedia-based courseware is often used to stimulate students' interest in language learning, to enhance reading comprehension, and to support interpretation of literature. Some of the exemplary uses of multimedia programs include displaying the procedures for writing Chinese characters, illustrating literary concepts, creating a simulated environment by representing real-world situations or problems, and evoking students' emotional responses by representing the environment or culture depicted in stories, prose, or poems (Li 2009; Xu 2010; Zhong 2008).

11.3.3.2 Chinese Character Encoding and Inputting Systems

Character encoding and input systems are essential communication tools in this digital age because they are required for information retrieval, word processing, and composing emails. Therefore, computer literacy skills related to inputting relevant information in a specific written language form have become basic literacy skills (Liu and Zhang 2006). While Chinese computer inputting is taught in schools as a basic communication skill, character encoding and input systems also have been used as an instructional method to teach young learners pinyin and the phonetic input method, to assist learners in the recognition of Chinese characters, and to facilitate learners in beginning to write stories at an early stage before they can write many characters. Research shows that with a combined method of teaching pinyin and character recognition using a computer input system, students significantly shorten the time needed to develop a good command of pinyin while mastering more characters, compared with the conventional teaching method without a computer input system (Gui 2009; Liu and Zhang 2006; Xing 2008).

It is important to note that many methods have been devised for inputting Chinese characters on computers. In general, three major inputting systems are in use: phonetic- or pinyin-based, structure-based, and hybrid (combined phonetic- and structure-based) methods. Among the three major types of input methods, the phonetic-based methods are most popular among school children because these methods are easy to use and do not require much training.

The phonetic-based input methods utilize standard pinyin. In addition, these methods are subcategorized into Quanpin (全拼/full spelling), Shuangpin (双拼/double spelling), and Jianpin (简拼/simple spelling). Quanpin involves inputting the full string of pinyin letters that represent a Chinese character when typing the character, for example typing "zhang" for 张. This method can be used by anyone who has knowledge of pinyin, which includes first graders. Shuangpin simplifies the input process by using only two predetermined letter keys to represent the whole string of pinyin, for example "vh" for zhang/张 (v for zh and h for ang). Users of Shuangpin need to study the predetermined rules that specify which letter key represents which letter or letter strings before they can use this method efficiently. Jianpin allows users to input just the first letter in the pinyin string to come up with the corresponding character. This method produces a list of homophones, so users have to decide which character is the exact one they want. Current popular phonetic-based input methods include Sougou Pinyin (搜狗拼音), Google Pinyin (谷歌拼音), QQ Pinyin (QQ 拼音), and Microsoft Pinyin (微软拼音).

Structure-based input methods assign specific keys to represent different structure components or strokes of Chinese characters. Compared with phonetic-based methods, they are more difficult to master, but one can input a character without knowing its pronunciation. Some well-known structure-based input methods include the Wubi method (五笔字型输入法) and the Zheng Ma method (郑码输入法).

Hybrid input methods combine the phonetic approach with the structure-based approach. These methods draw on learners' knowledge of both pinyin and character formation. One of the most common hybrid input methods used in China is the Renzhi Ma method (认知码). Using this method, the structure of the character, such as 树/shu/, can be divided into three roots: 木/mu/, 又/you/, and 寸/cun/, all of which are characters themselves (i.e., simple characters in a grammatical sense). Based on the pinyin of these three roots, 树/shu/ is encoded as "myc," the initials of the syllables of the three roots. Therefore, by typing the three parts, m, y and c, the character 树/shu/ is inputted into the computer (Liu and Zhang 2006). This method helps students decode and encode Chinese characters and understand their meanings at a deeper level, which in turn helps them retain the information in their long-term memory.

Additionally, voice recognition systems are used to improve the writing skills of students with writing disabilities (Hu 2007). For those students with writing difficulties, voice recognition software allows them to tell stories verbally and concentrate on the content. Further information on input systems can be found at http://seba.studentenweb.org/thesis/im.php.

11.3.3.3 Communication and Collaboration Tools

Communication tools include email, instant messaging (e.g., MSN), chat rooms, and software applications that allow users to make simultaneous voice calls over the internet (e.g., Skype). E-mail allows students to exchange information and supports their development of writing skills, whereas synchronous communication tools, including instant messaging and chat rooms such as MSN and Skype, can be used to support collaborative reading and writing tasks.

In addition, emerging online collaborative applications, such as bulletin boards and wikis, have provided educators with additional tools to guide students in collaborative learning activities. For instance, several articles discussed wikis as an effective collaborative software application to support collaborative writing (e.g., Jiang and Xue 2006; Lu 2009; Ye and Zhou 2007). The teacher can use collaborative technologies to guide writing on an interesting topic and provide prompt feedback. Students can make revisions based on the teacher's feedback and ask further questions or seek clarification in a timely manner (Xia and Sun 2010).

Learning management systems, such as Blackboard and Moodle, are specifically designed to provide a platform for interactive and collaborative learning. These systems are now used to create comprehensive courses to teach reading, writing, and literature. Yu and Xu (2009) illustrated that utilizing the collaborative platform and interactive features afforded by Moodle not only allowed students to publish their work, but also engaged them in social interaction and peer review processes, including sharing information and resources and providing comments and feedback to each other.

Some popular and emerging social network tools have quickly found their way into Chinese literacy education, for instance QQ and Qzone developed by Tacent Inc. QQ combines all the common communication tools into a single system. It consists of a communication space, instant message, BBS for information sharing and group discussions, chat rooms for one-to-one or group chatting, email for communication, an album for sharing pictures, and a dropbox for uploading, downloading, storing, and sharing files. With its popularity and user-friendly features, QQ has quickly gained the attention of many educators. Some educators have taken advantage of the various features of QQ to support Chinese literacy education, for instance, to carry out discussions on a given topic, brainstorm ideas for a composition, or conduct a collaborative writing task. Some educators use Qzone, another product created by Tacent, to encourage students to use the blog function to write journals. Qzone gives students the freedom to write what they want to write without having to worry about being criticized by teachers or laughed at by peers. Students can create their "zone" according to their interest and needs. In this sense, Qzone offers a vehicle for self-expression and creativity and helps promote self-image and self-confidence, especially for those students who are introverted or emotionally troubled (Li 2010).

11.3.3.4 Mobile Technology

China has witnessed the rapid development and widespread use of mobile technology, such as mobile phones, digital PDAs, and Pocket PCs. Mobile technology is characterized by being small, light, easy to carry, and convenient to communicate through voice or text messages. With a wireless internet connection, users can search for resources and share information conveniently. These technological affordances have caught the attention of Chinese educators. Ji and Bai (2009) explored how this new technology could be integrated into teaching language and literature. Given its affordances, mobile technology allows learners to receive instruction anytime and anywhere. They illustrated the various ways a teacher used mobile technology in a junior middle school Chinese class: to provide materials for previewing a lesson, to deliver pictures or graphics to help students establish mental representations of a text and to evoke their emotional responses, to provide instant feedback to students' reading and writing tasks, and to provide online resources to help students complete a writing task or after school exercises. Mobile technology also enables students to study an object closely. For example, when students study a particular breed of birds and its characteristics, they can search for information about those birds, listen to their twittering through an MP3 file, and watch a video clip of their behaviors and habitats delivered by the mobile devices. Mobile technology is used to help students develop observation abilities and descriptive writing skills.

11.3.3.5 Learner Corpora

Corpora is a term that originated in the field of applied linguistics. It refers to a large-scale database that automatically collects and processes a corpus of natural language and analyzes rules, patterns, syntax, semantics, and so on (Wei et al. 2008). The purpose of corpora is to automatically analyze, index, and store natural language in a computer system, so users can easily retrieve information from a large database by various searching techniques. Chinese educators have been using corpora to serve instructional purposes. Different kinds of learner corpora have been built, such as a reading corpus for elementary school students, an ancient Chinese corpus, a famous writers' corpus, (e.g., Wei 2008; Wei et al. 2008). These corpora have become rich resources for both students and teachers. Students can refer to exemplary writings and engage in guided language tasks, such as examining a specific language pattern in a language context and exploring various language devices employed by a particular writer. Teachers can draw resources from the corpora to help them prepare their Chinese lesson plans and integrate them in their instruction (Wei 2008; Wei et al. 2008).

11.3.3.6 Online Resources for Teachers

In addition to ICTs, there are numerous teaching websites and networks that provide a wealth of teaching resources, forums, and tools for Chinese language teachers to share lesson plans, instructional strategies, and teaching experiences aimed at improving the quality of Chinese literacy instruction. We have identified several major web resources specifically related to Chinese literacy and literature, including

- Primary School Chinese Teaching Resources (小学语文教学资源网) http://xiaoxue.ruiwen.com/
- Middle School Chinese Teaching Resources (中学语文教学资源网) http://www.ruiwen.com
- Chinese Language and Literature Network (中学语文网中网) http://www.ykyz.net/yuwen
- Chinese Language Network (中华语文网) http://www.zhyww.cn

These web resources provide thousands of instructional courseware or multimedia programs, video clips, articles, and lesson plans on teaching Chinese, as well as quizzes and tests. In addition, these sites offer support centers, various forums or channels on different topics and content areas, and many other links to additional resources.

The Docin Network (豆丁网 http://www.docin.com/) claims it has the largest collection of Chinese articles on various topics, including PowerPoint files, Courseware, and many other formats of files (e.g., doc, xls, ppt, txt, pdf, jpg, rtf, mpp, vsd, pps, pot, wps). The Docin Network offers resources ranging from fiction, art, fashion, psychology, physical education, and general education to science and technology, engineering, and computer science. A noticeable feature of this site is teachers can freely share lesson plans by uploading and downloading materials. Since the Docin Network has a wide coverage of topics, it is fairly easy to find materials related to literacy education. For example, when typing "multimedia" (in Chinese), we found articles like "Smart Uses of Multimedia Programs in Elementary School Chinese Classes" ("多媒体技术在小学语文课堂的妙用"), and "Principles and Methods of Using Information and Communication Technology in Elementary School Chinese Teaching" ("小学语文教学使用信息技术的原则和方法"). Teachers also have the option of selecting resources by file type, such as doc, pdf, or ppt. Docin fully illustrates the notion of communities of practice that build, share, and use databases and knowledge.

11.4 Roles of ICTs in Chinese Literacy Education

The literature reveals that ICTs play important roles in supporting Chinese literacy education in China in terms of cultivating students' motivation, interest, and affective development, promoting skills development, and supporting self-regulated, independent literacy learning.

11.4.1 Motivation, Interest, and Affective Development

A large number of articles discuss how to use ICTs to motivate students' interest in learning language, reading, writing, and literature. For example, Zhong (2008) described how a teacher used multimedia programs to enhance teaching Chinese characters. When teaching the concept *water* to young learners, the teacher played a video clip with music in the background, showing a winding stream, the magnificent Yangtze River, the vast ocean, and the peaceful West Lake. This video clip immediately grabbed the attention of the elementary school students. While they enjoyed the beautiful scenery, the students were completely immersed in the simulated natural environment. It evoked the students' feelings and understandings about water and the relationship between water and their day-to-day life. At this point, the teacher paused the video clip and began to explain the concept of *water* and the formation and characteristics of the character *water* (水). The multimedia program created a visual effect for the learners and presented a vivid image in their minds to help them retain the information in their long term memory. The students not only learned how to recognize and read the character *water*, but they also understood the deep connotations associated with the concept *water*. Therefore, ICTs make learning Chinese fun and interesting (Yang 2007).

Multimedia affordances are used not only to motivate students' interest in studying literacy, but also to support their affective and cognitive development. Emotions and cognition go hand in hand in reading comprehension and literature appreciation. A large number of articles examined how ICTs can be used to provoke senses, feelings, and the imagination, and to present simulated environments depicted by texts to help students experience and understand literature. For example, Xu (2010) demonstrated how she used multimedia programs to stimulate learners' imaginations and evoke their feelings when she taught reading comprehension on a lesson titled "Chinese International Rescue Team is Terrific!" This text described how Chinese rescue workers in a foreign country worked hard to rescue people from a natural disaster. The vivid pictures moved the students to tears as their teacher read aloud the text. The use of pictures created an atmosphere in which silence speaks more than words.

11.4.2 Skills Development

ICTs have been used to support the teaching of Chinese characters. At the elementary level multimedia programs have been used to teach character recognition and writing. Animations have been designed and used to explain the formation of Chinese characters from historical and etymological perspectives. For example, the image of *water* (水/shui/) represented by streams, rivers, lakes, and oceans, can be designed to be gradually transformed into the Chinese character for water through animation created with authoring software, such as Adobe Flash (Zhong 2008). The animation can be followed by demonstrating the process of character writing, showing how the strokes of *water* (水/shui/) are written and explaining the stroke writing sequence of that character (Bian and Wang 2005).

Chinese input systems, an increasingly important type of ICT for learning Chinese, enable young students to recognize characters and to develop into independent writers more effectively and efficiently. With the knowledge of pinyin and the help of an input system, young children can compose stories on computers even when they do not know how to actually write many of the characters they want to use in their stories (Liu and Zhang 2006). According to Gui (2009), it is much easier to recognize Chinese characters than to write them. If students know a character but cannot write it, they can type pinyin for that character and select a suitable character from among a list of characters produced by the typing output. Chinese input systems help to increase the number of characters students can recognize and memorize within a limited period of time, compared with the traditional teaching method that does not involve the use of a Chinese input system. Liu and Zhang

(2006) noted that normally many Chinese children cannot write much when they first start their formal schooling. However, with the help of a computer and the Shuangpin (double spelling) input method, these young learners are able to write what they want to say using the computer, and they learn to write essays within a year. In addition, some students who were already trained to recognize about 1,000 characters before their formal schooling can write stories on computers after a few weeks' training (Zhou 1999).

A great number of articles also share ideas on how technology can be used to develop students' knowledge and skills important to learning a language and understanding literature, including making observations, thinking critically, using imagination, and expressing creativity. For example, Li (2009), who was also a teacher, found that many of her students were unable to make careful observations of people, things, or scenes in real life or to form connections between things they observed in their own life experiences, so she took advantage of multimedia technology to develop students' observation skills. In teaching young children to write an essay on "A Small Lovely Animal," she first demonstrated how to describe a white rabbit by using a multimedia program. The program showed the rabbit in an instructionally logical order, first showing the entire white rabbit and then gradually moving to different parts of the rabbit, zooming in and out from different angles and perspectives (Li 2009). Students could choose to pause at a specific point in the program or to replay the program. With the help of the multimedia program, she engaged the students in the writing task of describing the small white rabbit clearly and vividly, and in a logical and sequential order.

At a more advanced level, ICTs have been used to teach abstract concepts, especially when students do not have experience with the subject being studied. Multimedia programs have often been used to address difficult concepts and to convey specific moods depicted by poems and prose, especially ancient poems characterized by concise and vivid language and the use of images, similes, metaphors, and other literary devices (Zheng et al. 2008). A famous ancient poem about Mt. Lu vividly presents a picture of the majestic mountains through the lines, "hen kan cheng ling ce cheng feng, yuanchu gaodi ge bu tong" ("横看成岭侧成峰, 远近高低各不同"). These lines mean "When the mountains are seen from one side, they are mountain ranges, and when seen from the other side, they are peaks; they show different heights when they are viewed from different distances." A teacher used pictures to help her students visualize the mountains and the poetic imagery. By viewing pictures of Mt. Lu taken from different perspectives, students closely examined the shapes of the mountains and pondered on the poetic words used by the poet. As another example, when teaching a lesson on the poem "Waterfalls," a teacher used a multimedia program to present to her students a simulated environment depicting the scene of a roaring waterfall rushing down 10,000-foot high mountains and layers upon layers of waves surging onto the shore while the wind blows over a pine forest. This simulated environment stimulated her students' imagination about waterfalls, evoked their emotional responses, and allowed them to gain a better understanding of the rhetorical devices used in the poem.

11.4.3 Self-regulated Learning

Rich web resources allow teachers to create open-ended learning environments that encourage inquiry, problem solving, and self-regulated learning activities. Wang (2006) illustrated the design of an open learning environment using web resources to promote self-regulated learning. During instruction of the lesson "Taiwan Butterfly Valley," students would first read the text to acquire a preliminary understanding of the fascinating butterflies. Then the teacher would prompt the students with questions, such as "In what ways do you find Butterfly Valley fascinating?" The students would be asked to search for, underline, and read the sentences describing the magnificent views of the butterflies. Next, they would be further prompted to search for relevant information from web resources, including articles, pictures, and animation to help them further experience the views described in the texts. Wu (2002) discussed how web resources could be integrated with texts to foster reading comprehension. In order to engage students in self-monitoring and self-regulated learning processes, Wu suggested providing students with question prompts to guide them in the inquiry process of searching, selecting, classifying, and reorganizing relevant information in order to generate solutions to problems. For instance, when teaching the lesson "We Only Have One Earth" related to environmental protection, the following question prompts could be provided: "Why should we pay attention to environmental protection? How do we deal with emissions and waste in the chemical industry? In agriculture, which chemical fertilizers and pesticides will cause pollution to soil and water?" Students can use the question prompts as a guide while browsing websites and resources to gain relevant information and to formulate answers to the questions. After the web searching activities, students are asked to discuss the issues with their group members and to generate reports on environmental protection.

11.5 Trends in ICT Integration in Literacy Education in China

In order to understand the trends in ICT integration in literacy education in China, we grouped the selected articles into two periods: 2000–2005 and 2006–2010, and we performed a general analysis of those articles. Comparing the 2000–2005 period with the 2006–2010 period, we observed that there was a significant increase in the number of articles on ICTs in Chinese literacy in recent years, with 16% of the articles published in 2000–2005 compared with 84% published in 2006–2010.

We also found that there were more articles discussing the teaching of reading (116 articles, 48%) and writing (96 articles, 40%) than the teaching of literature (28 articles, 12%). Within the reading instruction category, 13% of the articles were on teaching character recognition. Regarding teaching literature, more articles focused on teaching ancient poems than on contemporary literature. This could be due to the fact that ancient poems are difficult to decode and understand because archaic

Chinese was more succinct, comprehensive, and profound than modern Chinese. More articles were published on the use of ICTs to motivate students, stimulate their interest, develop cognitive and metacognitive skills, and evoke their emotions, imagination, and creativity than on how to teach difficult concepts and literary devices. We expect that articles in the latter categories will increase in the next 5–10 years as teachers continue to explore pedagogical uses of ICTs and deepen their understanding of the roles of ICTs in literacy education. Furthermore, we have also noticed an increase in the number of articles discussing the changing role of teachers over the past 10 years.

11.6 Discussion and Implications

According to the Ministry of Education's *Guidelines for Curriculum Reform of Basic Education* (2001a) educators should fully take advantage of ICTs and promote technology integration in curriculum. Our literature review shows that ICTs play important roles in supporting motivation, cognition, metacognition, and skill development (e.g., imagination, self-expression, creativity) and in promoting information sharing, idea exchange, and collaborative learning in students' reading and writing. Our findings indicate numerous opportunities and possibilities for ICTs to improve the teaching and learning of Chinese literacy.

The integration of ICTs into Chinese literacy teaching not only shows the impact of technology on learning and instruction in China, but more importantly, also reflects new perspectives on learning and instruction. We argue that ICTs promote Chinese teachers' reconsideration of their role in literacy education. Many articles indicate that the role of teachers in literacy classes should change from lecturing to supporting, from teacher-centered instruction to student-centered learning, from the paradigm "The teacher asked me to learn" to the paradigm "I want to learn" (Lin and Ouyang 2007; Zhang 2003). Wen (2006) contended that students should take ownership of their own learning and actively construct and build knowledge while teachers should be mentors, guides, and facilitators.

According to our observations and analysis, the role of ICTs in literacy education has gone beyond being a tool to support the learning and teaching of Chinese literacy. ICTs have caused a transformation in teachers' beliefs about learning and instruction and motivated teachers to break away from the traditional instructional approach and seek innovative teaching approaches to guide learners in self-directed and self-regulated learning. Some of the new pedagogical concepts that have been increasingly discussed in recent literature include development of metacognition (e.g., Ding et al. 2009), self-regulated and self-monitored reading and writing activities (e.g., Wang 2006), knowledge acquisition and transfer of skills (e.g., Sun 2008), integration of Chinese literacy and other subjects, and interactive and collaborative learning (e.g., Hu and Bei 2008). We are inclined to say that the development of ICTs have become one of the determining factors promoting a paradigm shift in learning and instruction in China's literacy classrooms. This paradigm shift meets the needs of the society and is consistent with fundamental changes in instructional supersystems as China rapidly moves away from an agricultural and industrial society into a digital/information society, in which employees are required to be able to solve problems, work in teams, communicate, take initiative, and bring diverse perspectives to their work (Reigeluth 1999).

While there is no lack of articles on a variety of topics on the use of ICTs in literacy education in China, our literature review revealed some gaps in research on ICT integration in literacy education. The majority of articles were short write-ups, one to six pages long, of experience sharing or issue discussions. Few articles reported data-based empirical studies. Although it is exciting to see the rapid infusion of ICTs into Chinese literacy education and the rising number of articles covering a wide range of topics related to literacy education, most of the articles were piecemeal descriptions of the uses of isolated tools: using ICTs to design a specific lesson or learning environment, integrating ICTs with specific instructional strategies, or discussing the use and benefits of a particular learning management system. There is a lack of research on systemic change and ICT infusion on a large scale in China's literacy education reform. To bring about systemic changes in Chinese literacy education, researchers, learning scientists, educational psychologists, and teachers must work together to promote empirical research grounded in learning theories and instructional design principles. In addition, it is critical that educational researchers studying Chinese literacy teaching and learning receive training in research methodologies, so they will be able to design and conduct empirical research or design-based research to produce greater insight into how to further improve literacy education in China.

In conclusion, we would like to make a number of recommendations for Chinese literacy educators based on the critical analysis and discussion of the literature on Chinese literacy in China. First, while it is important to use ICTs to teach basic literacy skills, it is even more important for educators to focus on developing students' higher-order thinking skills, such as reasoning, information searching, selecting and evaluating, self-monitoring and self-regulation, inquiry, collaborative learning, and problem solving. Second, ICTs should be used to motivate students and engage them in meaningful learning situations that will encourage them to apply their literacy skills in their day-to-day life to solve real-world problems. Third, ICT training should be an essential component of teacher professional development programs. Not only should teachers learn how to use ICT tools, but most importantly they also should understand the constructivist epistemological paradigm of learning and instruction. Professional development programs should emphasize the transformative power and pedagogical value of ICTs by integrating specific instructional approaches, models, and best practices with the use of ICTs. Furthermore, professional development programs should encourage Chinese literacy educators to be involved in classroom-based design research and should help them develop design research skills for the purpose of improving literacy education in their specific instructional settings.

Acknowledgment This research was supported by a Faculty Development Research Grant sponsored by the Institute for US-China Issues, University of Oklahoma, awarded to Xun Ge and Jiening Ruan.

References

Bian, C., & Wang, Q. (2005). 制作汉字笔画演示课件的几种方法 [A number of ways of creating courseware for displaying Chinese characters strokes]. 中小学电教 (上半月), 12, 60–61.
Bruce, B. C. (Ed.). (2003). *Literacy in the information age: Inquiries into meaning making with new technologies*. Newark: International Reading Association.
Chinese Ministry of Education. (MOE). (2000). 教育部关于印发《中小学信息技术课程指导纲要(试行)》的通知 [*The announcement on the publication and distribution of the information technology curriculum guide for primary and secondary schools (trial version)*]. Retrieved from http://emic.moe.edu.cn/edoas2/website18/level3.jsp?id=1217120151246543
Chinese Ministry of Education. (MOE). (2001a). 基础教育课程改革纲要 [*Guidelines for curriculum reform of basic education*]. Beijing: Ministry of Education.
Chinese Ministry of Education. (MOE). (2001b). 全日制义务教育语文课程标准(实验稿) [*Yuwen curriculum standards for full-day compulsory education (trial version)*]. Beijing: Ministry of Education.
Chinese Ministry of Education. (MOE). (2003). 全日制普通高中语文课程标准 [*Full-day common high school Yuwen curriculum standards*]. Beijing: Ministry of Education.
Chinese Ministry of Education. (MOE). (2010). 国家中长期教育改革和发展纲要 [*Outline for national mid- and long-term education reform and development plan*]. Beijing: Ministry of Education.
Ding, G., Zeng, Z. Yang, S., & Zhang, X. (2009). 信息技术课堂教学中的学生元认知能力培养 [*Developing metacognitive skills in a class using information communication and technologies*]. 中国电化教育, 10, 83–85.
Gui, X. (2009). 利用"汉文华"输入系统优化识字教学 [Improve teaching character recognition by using the Chinese input system "Han Wenhua"]. 中小学电教 (上半月), 9, 35–36.
Hu, L. (2007). 语音识别支持写作困难学生的个案研究 [A case study of using the sound recognition system to support students with writing difficulty]. 中国电化教育, 3, 104–108.
Hu, S., & Bei, J. (2008). 基于网络环境的小学语文"互动式"教学研究 [Research on interactive learning in a web-based Chinese class of primary school level]. 中国电化教育, 6, 83–86.
International Society for Technology in Education (ISTE). (2002). *National educational technology standards for teachers: Preparing teachers to use technology*. Eugene: ISTE.
Ji, E., & Bai, L. (2009). 移动学习在初中语文教学中的应用 [Applying mobile technology in a middle school Chinese class]. 中小学电教 (下半月), 9, 28–30.
Jiang, L., & Xue, H. (2006). Wiki在作文教学中的应用初探 [Exploring the use of wiki to teach writing]. 中国电化教育, 1, 46–49.
Li, Q. (2010). 学生QQ空间给写作教学的启示 [The implications of QQ zone to support the teaching of writing]. 现代语文 (教学研究版), 1, 134–135.
Li, X. (2009). 小学生的写作能力培养与多媒体辅助教学 [Multimedia instruction for developing primary school students' writing ability]. 现代教育科学 (小学教师), 3, 108.
Lin, Y., & Ouyang, W. (2007). 网络环境下低年级学生语文自学能力的培养 [Developing self-study ability among students of the lower primary school level in a web-based learning environment]. 中小学电教 (上半月), Z2, 62–65.
Liu, Y., & Zhang, D. (2006). ICT and Chinese literacy education: Recent developments. In M. C. McKenna, L. D. Labbo, R. D. Kieffer, & D. Reinking (Eds.), *International handbook of literacy and technology* (Vol. 2, pp. 193–210). Mahwah: Erlbaum.

Lu, F. (2009). 基于Wiki的语文作文教学探讨 [Exploring instructional methods for teaching writing using wiki]. 中小学电教 (上半月), 3, 37–39.

Reigeluth, C. M. (1999). The elaboration theory: Guidance for scope and sequence decisions. In C. M. Reigeluth (Ed.), *Instructional-design theories and models: A new paradigm of instructional theory* (Vol. 2, pp. 425–453). Hillsdale: Erlbaum.

Sun, Z. (2008). 网络环境下扩展阅读对小学生阅读保持与迁移能力的影响研究 [Investigating the effect of extensive reading on primary students' knowledge retention and transfer in a web-based learning environment]. 中国电化教育, 11, 72–75.

Valmont, W. J. (2003). *Technology for literacy teaching and learning.* Boston: Houghton Mifflin.

Wang, H. (2006). 网络环境下的小学语文课堂教学-《台湾的蝴蝶谷》教学设计 [Instructional design of a Chinese lesson on "Taiwan's Butterfly Valley" at the primary school level in a web-based learning environment]. 中国电化教育, 1, 65–67.

Wei, S. (2008). 语料库支持下的小学语文阅读环境创设研究 [Research on the design of a learning environment using corpora to support primary school students' reading comprehension]. 中国电化教育, 1, 45–51.

Wei, S., Zhao, P., Yang, X., & Chen, L. (2008). 大型中国小学生作文语料库的生成 [Creating a large-scale corpus of essays for China's primary school students]. 现代教育技术, 18(12), 31, 45–48.

Wen, M. (2006). 网络文化背景下的语文教师角色定位 [Defining Chinese teachers' role in the context of the internet culture]. 中国电化教育, 12, 53–55.

Wu, J. (2002). 创设丰富的"智力背景"提高学生的认知能力-浅谈网络在阅读中的应用 [Improving students' cognitive ability by creating a rich "intellectual background" – Application of the Web to enhance reading]. 中小学电教 (上半月), 6, 53–54.

Xia, M., & Sun, A. (2010). 借助信息技术培养学生语文能力 [Using information and communication technology to develop students' literacy]. 中国信息技术教育, 10, 48.

Xing, X. (2008). 论汉字输入如何有效促进识字教学 [How Chinese input systems effectively promote teaching character recognition]. 电化教育研究, 7, 28–30.

Xu, X. (2010). 信息技术在语文教学中"扶"的作用 [Using information and communication technology to scaffold Chinese teaching]. 现代教育科学 (小学教师), 1, 72.

Yang, J. (2007). 在语文课改中恰当引入信息技术 [Introduce information and communication technology to Chinese classes as an innovative teaching approach]. 校长月刊, 12, 13.

Ye, X., & Zhou, S. (2007). 基于Wiki的写作教学实验研究 [An experimental study of teaching writing using wiki]. 中国电化教育, 1, 80–82.

Yu, H., & Xu, A. (2009). 依托Moodle平台的"多元化快乐作文"校本课程 [The design of a course "Multiple and Happy Compositions" built in Moodle]. 中国信息技术教育, 23, 70–73.

Zhang, G. (2003). 实现教师角色转变,把语文课改实验推向深入 [Promote the change of teachers' roles and carry out research in Chinese teaching]. 学科教育, 4, 6–9.

Zheng, L., Ding, W., & Wu, X. (2008). 利用信息技术,有效突破语文教学的重、难点 [Breaking through difficult and key points in teaching Chinese by using information communication and technologies]. 中国信息技术教育, 4, 59–60.

Zhong, Y. (2008). 运用电教方法,激发识字兴趣 [Motivate students' interest in character recognition using educational technology]. 中小学电教 (上半月), 5, 56–57.

Zhou, Q. (1999). 多媒体技术与识字教学 [Multimedia technology and teaching character recognition]. 课程教材教法, 19(11), 16–21.

Chapter 12
Family Literacy in China

Cynthia B. Leung and Yongmei Li

12.1 Introduction

Children develop language and literacy skills gradually through meaning making within the context of school, home, and community (Chow and McBride-Chang 2003; Clay 1991; Halliday 1975; Perez 1998). Although we often assume the responsibility for teaching literacy skills falls on classroom teachers, family background and home environment, including socioeconomic status, parent–child literacy-related activities, a literacy-rich environment, and parental education and occupation, play a significant role in children's literacy development (e.g., Frijters et al. 2000; Heath 1983; Snow 1991; Taylor 1983; Taylor and Dorsey-Gaines 1988; Teale 1978). Parent support is also associated with literacy achievement in schoolage children, and home literacy practices may be as important as formal reading instruction in promoting literacy skills (Hewison and Tizard 1980; Snow et al. 1991).

Most research studies on family literacy have focused on young children learning English or other alphabetic languages. Few studies have been conducted on family literacy among children learning Chinese. Furthermore, cross-cultural studies have shown Chinese parents hold different beliefs about their children's literacy learning at home compared to their Western counterparts (Stevenson and Lee 1996). For example, Chinese parents pay more attention to their children's academic achievement (e.g., Ho 1994; Stevenson and Lee 1996; Tseng and Wu 1985). Moreover, the orthographic nature of Chinese characters may make parents' teaching of reading and writing more valuable for children learning Chinese than for children learning English and other alphabetic languages with letter-sound correspondence (Li et al. 2008). Yet the review of literature suggests Chinese parents may not fully

---

C.B. Leung (✉)
Literacy Education, University of South Florida St. Petersburg, FL, USA
e-mail: cleung@mail.usf.edu

Y. Li
Academic Affairs, Shaw University, Raleigh, NC, USA

understand the extent of the impact the home literacy environment and practices can have on their children's reading and writing development.

The most recent Chinese language and literacy curriculum standards for grades 1–9, *Yuwen Curriculum Standards for Full-Day Compulsory Education* (Chinese Ministry of Education 2011), set high standards for reading and writing Chinese. Extensive after school reading was mandated by the standards document. Children in first and second grade are expected to read 50,000 Chinese characters per year in after school reading, children in third and fourth grade should read 400,000 characters, and fifth and sixth graders no fewer than 1,000,000 Chinese characters per year in after school reading. The standards call for a more communicative approach to teaching writing than in the past. Students are expected to experiment with language they encounter in everyday life, to write letters, and to enjoy communicating with writing. Parent involvement with their children in home literacy practices can help children meet the new standards. Many parents are eager to learn how to help their children become successful readers and writers. Yet they may not know the best strategies to help their children in their literacy development.

This chapter reviews research studies on family literacy practices among families in China. While few studies to date have been carried out on family literacy in China, the findings can shed light on ways parents can assist their children in learning the complex Chinese writing system. Given the new Chinese language and literacy standards, a chapter on family literacy in China is timely and shows the importance of carrying out further studies on the most effective home literacy practices and strategies to help children master literacy skills while at the same time develop an appreciation for the Chinese language.

Family literacy research carried out in different cultures has identified aspects of the home environment that influence children's reading development: (a) types of literacy activities and quality of interpersonal interactions of family members centering around literacy events, (b) the home literacy environment, including types and number of print materials available in the home, (c) motivation provided by parents and other family members for children to practice literacy skills and engage in out-of-school and in-school reading and literacy activities, and (d) parent characteristics, such as socioeconomic status and education level (Leichter 1984; Shu et al. 2002a; Snow et al. 1998). In this chapter, we review studies of research on these aspects of the home environment of Chinese families conducive to Chinese literacy development. This review can be a starting place for future researchers, parents, teachers, and policy makers who plan to further explore ways the literacy learning of Chinese youth can be enhanced through out-of-school family and community literacy-related activities. We also make recommendations for future research in this area.

12.2 Parent–Child Shared and Dialogic Reading

Parent–child reading provides an ideal context for children to interact with their parents orally while reading the same book. During the process, children learn concepts of print, letters/characters, vocabulary, and comprehension strategies in reading (Chow and McBride-Chang 2003). Joint picture book reading by an adult and child is one of the most frequently recommended practices for English-speaking preschool children to build vocabulary and emergent literacy competencies (Snow et al. 1998). This recommendation is supported by a number of research studies that have shown preschool children learn words incidentally, without direct instruction, from listening to books read aloud by parents and child care providers (e.g. Hargrave and Sénéchal 2000; Leung 2008; Sénéchal and Cornell 1993; Whitehurst et al. 1988). Parents' specific behaviors and practices while reading, such as asking questions at different levels (e.g., factual, inference) and providing positive feedback, lead to enhanced oral language development (Flood 1977; Ninio and Bruner 1978; Roser and Martinez 1985). When children are provided ample opportunities to experiment with language and make meaning of texts, they show greater language gains than when they are simply read to by their parents (Whitehurst et al. 1988).

The effects of reading aloud books to young children have been studied extensively by literacy researchers in English-speaking countries. Meta-analyses have been conducted on the findings from numerous studies in this area. For example, Marulis and Neuman (2010) carried out a meta-analysis of vocabulary learning of young children from various interventions, including modifications to ways books were read aloud to children. In the United States, the National Early Literacy Panel (NELP) was convened in 2002 to summarize empirical evidence on children's early literacy development and home and family influences. Studies included effects of reading aloud picture books to children on their development of various early literacy skills, such as oral vocabulary development and phonemic awareness. Their report, *Developing Literacy: Report of the National Early Literacy Panel* (NELP 2008), provides a model and examples for future studies of home and family literacy influences on Chinese reading and writing development and early literacy skills of young children in China. Such research with Chinese children from different regions of the country and from different socioeconomic groups is in its infancy.

Several studies of family literacy activities have included Chinese families, as well as families of other cultural backgrounds, engaged in family literacy events. These international comparative studies offer information on family shared reading activities in China. Wang, Bernas, and Eberhard (2002) examined mothers' oral support for early literacy development during interactive reading sessions. Included in their study of Chinese and American Indian mother-child dyads were mothers of twenty 4-year-old Chinese children in an industrial area of Nanjing, China, where residents worked at a factory that manufactured vehicles. Wang and colleagues observed and videotaped the manner in which mothers interacted with their children in literacy-related activities over a period of 4 weeks, for a total of 345 h of video-recorded data. They found three types of maternal literacy support: explicit and implicit support, contextual and text-explicit support, and elaboration. Chinese mothers in the study tended to emphasize print-based literacy activities, as in the example of an explicit support that follows.

When opening a letter, a Chinese mother asked her child whether she knew the character *receiving* (shou) on the letter cover. After getting no answer from the child, the mother told the child that the character meant "Shou" (receiving). Then she traced her right index finger in the air as if she was writing it. (p. 15)

Chinese mothers also used event-specific support. For example, when a child saw a girl in the shared reading book holding a piece of sugar-coated preserved fruit, he related the reading to his own experience, telling his mother his father had bought him some a long time ago. Then the mother asked him some follow-up questions focused on the topic of fruit candy, such as "Was yours sugar-coated? Can you point out the Chinese characters for sugar-coated hawthorn fruit in the book?" In another situation, a mother used elaborative support when her child saw a rabbit in the picture of a book and said, "It's a rabbit." His mother asked him to elaborate on the statement saying, "Can you show me the word *rabbit* in the book? How many strokes does the word rabbit have?" By asking follow-up questions, the mother helped her child deepen his understanding of the reading and relate the text to his life experiences. (Examples are all from page 15.)

Whitehurst and colleagues (e.g., Whitehurst et al. 1988) developed a style of storybook reading they called dialogic reading. This method of adult-child shared reading was the focus of several intervention studies where parents and/or child care providers were asked to read aloud to preschool children in a dialogic style. The adult first read aloud to the child and asked *wh-* questions, praised and encouraged the child to verbally respond, repeated what the child said, and made corrections. Books were never read verbatim to the child. As the child became more verbal during the read-alouds, the adult encouraged the child to take over more and more of the responsibility of telling the story, so that eventually the child was providing most of the verbal text of the storybook. A number of studies (Arnold et al. 1994; Hargrave and Sénéchal 2000; Valdez-Menchaca and Whitehurst 1992; Whitehurst et al. 1994) showed dialogic reading could be carried out successfully in home and preschool settings and resulted in higher scores on standardized vocabulary assessments of young children in the United States, Mexico, and Canada.

Chow and McBride-Chang (2003) investigated the effectiveness of dialogic reading as a parent–child reading technique intended to facilitate children's learning of Chinese language and literacy skills. Although the subjects of their study were Hong Kong children and their parents, and not mainland Chinese families, their methodology and findings can potentially be applied to future research with different Chinese populations. Eighty-six third year kindergarten children, 4.8–5.9 years old, and their parents participated in the study. Children in the intervention group were given eight books each with guidelines for parents to dialogically read with their children. Hints for prompt questions and recall prompts were provided to parents, along with pictures related to story questions, a dialogic reading guideline, and a calendar checklist to remind parents when to read. One book was given to the families each week. Parents read the book twice a week for 15 min each time with their children. Two other groups of children and parents were compared to the dialogic reading group: a group that received all eight books and read them together in their typical way but following the same schedule as the dialogic reading group, and a control group that followed their usual home literacy activities during the treatment period, then received the books after the other two groups completed their readings and assessments.

Results showed the dialogic reading intervention had significant gains in the kindergarten children's Chinese literacy skills, particularly in character identification, visual and auditory discrimination, and receptive vocabulary (words understood when you hear them spoken but you do not necessarily use them when speaking) compared to the control group and typical reading group. Chinese skills were measured by the *Preschool and Primary Chinese Literacy Scale* (PPCLS, Li 1999), and receptive vocabulary was measured by the *Peabody Picture Vocabulary Test III* (*PPVT-III*, Dunn and Dunn 1997, translated into Cantonese for this study). The typical reading group had significant gains in their receptive vocabulary from the 8-week intervention compared to the control group, but not in their Chinese literacy skills. The findings suggest parent–child dialogic reading can lead to skill development in reading Chinese and in receptive vocabulary development. Typical reading styles that do not involve interaction and discussion between parent and child may result in vocabulary growth but not development of Chinese reading skills.

Dialogic reading also has the potential to increase young Chinese children's interest in reading. Parent responses on a follow-up questionnaire given to parents in the dialogic reading group indicated the majority of parents thought their children's interest in reading Chinese increased over the 8-week period of the intervention: 75.9% thought reading interest had increased, 20.7% thought interest remained the same, and 3.4% thought interest decreased.

12.3 Role of Parent Characteristics and Home Literacy Environment

A few studies of home literacy in Chinese families have explored the relationship of parent characteristics, the home literacy environment, and parent–child out-of-school and home literacy activities on children's Chinese literacy development (e.g. Meng et al. 2002; Shu et al. 2002a, b; Wang and Hu 2007). These studies collected data about family literacy through parent questionnaires, and children's literacy skills were accessed through standardized tests or researcher-created tests focused on particular literacy skills. Overall, findings from the studies indicate the following factors may be positively related to children's learning to read and write Chinese: number and type of books owned by the family, parents' reading attitude, parents' reading habits and time spent reading daily at home, frequency of taking children to libraries and bookstores, parental educational level, parent–child reading activities, child's age when parents began home instruction in Chinese character reading and writing, and children's out-of-school independent reading activities.

Shu et al. (2002b) examined family-related factors in relation to children's Chinese reading achievement among 574 first- and fourth-grade children in the West-district of Beijing. Half the children were from working class families and half from middle class families. Family-related factors were assessed by parent questionnaires and included four areas: amount of reading material in the home for both adults and children, such as magazines, newspapers, books, dictionaries, and encyclopedias; interactions and literacy activities between children and parents, such as parents' time spent reading daily, frequency of parents' taking their children to bookstores and libraries, age of the child when parents started to read to their children and teach reading Chinese characters; child's independent activities related to literacy, such as frequency of child's independent reading at home, duration of watching TV daily; and parents' educational level. Chinese reading achievement was represented by three components for first graders (Chinese alphabet reading, simple sentence reading, and vocabulary test) and five components for fourth graders (paragraph reading, sentence reading comprehension, cloze test, sentence correction, and vocabulary test).

Correlations among the four areas of the home literacy environment significantly related to children's Chinese literacy development, but children's independent literacy-related activities outside of school were not significantly related to reading proficiency for first graders. All the areas, however, were interrelated to each other for children in both grades. The first graders were not yet proficient readers, so time spent working independently out of school may not have influenced their literacy learning to the extent it did for fourth graders. Path analysis for the first graders found parent–child literacy activities directly contributed to children's beginning reading knowledge. Parent's education level and literacy resources in the home contributed to parent–child literacy activities. For fourth graders, both parent–child literacy activities and children's independent after-school literacy activities contributed directly to Chinese language achievement, and literacy resources in the home contributed directly to parent–child literacy activities. This study shows the importance of parent involvement in their children's literacy development and the importance of children's independent reading and writing practice to develop proficiency in Chinese written language.

Shu et al. (2002a) computed correlations between individual items on the parent questionnaire and children's reading scores. For first and fourth graders, the number of adult reading materials in the home related strongly to children's reading development. Visits to bookstores and libraries related highly to parent–child literacy activities, and the age parents began reading to children and teaching them Chinese characters related strongly to children's reading proficiency. However, availability of children's magazines and newspapers at home related strongly to fourth graders' reading proficiency, and not first graders, most likely because the older children were reading at a more advanced level, so they could take advantage of the age-appropriate reading material in the home. The age at which parents began character instruction was found to be important for children from less educated, as well as more educated, families and may be an important consideration for parents who want to enhance their children's learning of the Chinese written language.

In another study, Meng, Zhou, and Kong (2002) investigated the relationship between factors pertinent to Chinese reading and writing (literary understanding of print, basic cognitive ability, handwriting, family reading background, motion ability, oral language ability, read-aloud, dictation, and writing ability) and Chinese reading and writing achievement among 2,187 children in first, third, and fifth grades in Beijing. Basic cognitive ability (e.g., ability to distinguish the tones of Chinese characters, whether reversing Chinese character writing or number writing, ability to use the Chinese alphabet, etc.), family reading background (e.g., my father seldom reads, my mother seldom reads, at least one person among my parents and relatives is not good at Chinese, at least one person among other family members, such as parents, grandparents, uncle, aunt, and cousins, has difficulty in Chinese oral language, reading or writing, etc.), motion ability, and oral language ability were significantly and positively related to children's literacy achievement. Meng, Liu, Zhou, and Meng (2003) found similar positive relationships between family reading background and children's Chinese oral language ability, as well as character recognition.

Wang and Hu (2007) examined family reading in Chinese in relation to Chinese reading achievement among 114 third-grade students in Shanghai. The results showed the number of books owned by the family, reading activities at home, parents' attitude toward reading, parents' reading habits, and the amount of independent reading by children were strong indicators of children's Chinese reading achievement. These studies provide a strong foundation for future studies on the effects of the home literacy environment on children's Chinese literacy development. All these studies took place in large cities, Beijing and Shanghai. Future studies can explore family literacy practices and home literacy environments of families living in different geographical regions of China and families of different socioeconomic backgrounds.

Li and Rao (2000) and Li, Corrie, and Wong (2008) compared home literacy practices of families in Beijing and Hong Kong with children's Chinese literacy development. Their findings for the Beijing sample were similar to findings from the other studies reported here. Hong Kong parents, however, started teaching their children to read and write Chinese characters at home at a younger age than the Beijing parents, which resulted in the Hong Kong children having a greater mastery of written Chinese by 8 years of age. The Hong Kong children began the formal study of Chinese characters in preschool, at 2 years 8 months, and their parents supported their learning of characters through home instruction. The Beijing parents, middle class from the Western District, provided children with more informal literacy activities in the home and did not teach characters until the children began formal literacy instruction in school. The researchers concluded early instruction in Chinese characters is important to children's subsequent mastery of the Chinese written language. Other findings about the Beijing parents' home literacy practices were the majority of homes had more than 30 books, the majority of children witnessed their parents reading every day, and parents paid more attention to moral education than the entertainment value of books read to children.

12.4 Home Motivational Climate for Chinese Literacy Development

Zhou and Salili (2008) explored the relationship between intrinsic motivation and home literacy of 177 preschoolers (ages 3.75–6.58) in Beijing. Persistence and voluntary engagement in reading-related activities were used as indicators of intrinsic motivation, which was measured by parent ratings on five items: voluntary reading at home, persistence in reading a whole story, paying attention when others read to the child, concentration on reading in a noisy environment, and liking to go to bookshops. The home literacy environment was measured by six indicators: number of children's books at home, how often new books were bought, how often storybooks were read to the child, how long the child was taught characters at home, how often the child freely selected books, and how often the child saw a parent model reading. Bivariate correlations showed all six indicators were positively related to intrinsic motivation in reading. After controlling for age of children, father's educational level was the most significant predictor of children's reading motivation, and three home literacy components—parental model of reading behavior, number of books in the home, and years of character teaching by parents—also predicted children's intrinsic motivation to read Chinese. Parent modeling of reading Chinese was the strongest predictor of children's intrinsic motivation.

However, unlike what is typical for children in Western societies, Chinese children's freedom to choose their own books for reading did not lead to intrinsic motivation to read Chinese. This phenomenon is supported by Iyengar and Lepper's (1999) study that found American children were more intrinsically motivated to read when they chose their own books, while Asian American children were more motivated to read when a trusted authority figure, such as a parent, selected books for them. This may be a culturally-specific response to choice.

Wang and Coddington (2010) explored the relationship between beginning Chinese readers' motivation to read and their proficiency in reading through a study of 102 first graders, ages 7 years 6 months to 7 years 10 months, from a southern suburb of Beijing. Parent background varied from working class with elementary to middle school education to middle class with college education. Motivation was measured by Chapman and Tunmer's (1995, 1999) Reading Self-Concept Scale, adapted and translated into Chinese. The scale measured children's perceptions of reading difficulty, perceptions of reading competence, and attitudes toward reading. Parents completed a survey about their attitudes toward external feedback, encouragement for challenging reading, reading materials made available in their homes, and the value they associated with different reading tasks. The Test of Basic Reading Skills (TBRS), a district level test of Chinese reading skills for first graders, was used to measure the children's reading proficiency. Correlations between parents' beliefs and students' motivation were statistically significant. Children's reading achievement was positively related to their total motivation scores and parent's encouragement, support, value of reading tasks, and attitude towards reading, while reading achievement was negatively related to children's perceptions of reading difficulty.

An important finding from this study is Chinese children's perceptions of reading competence predict their reading performance. This is especially significant when the children are beginning readers. Another major finding is Chinese parents' attitudes towards reading predict their children's reading performance, and their attitudes, support, encouragement, and values relate to their children's sense of competence and motivation to read. This supports other findings that parents play a key role in their children's Chinese literacy development.

12.5 Implications for Chinese Literacy Practices and Policies

Findings from the limited amount of research conducted on family literacy in China provide several implications for Chinese literacy practices and policies. First, since oral language support from parents promotes children's Chinese literacy development, parents need to be encouraged to use oral language to support their children's Chinese reading at home. It is important to note that during the reading process, parents should actively engage their children in reading in an explicit and elaborative way, or a dialogic reading style, rather than just reading books aloud with no child–parent interaction. Parents can raise questions, initiate discussions, provide positive feedback, ask follow-up questions, encourage their children to elaborate on questions, and so on. Through interactive oral support, children learn to recognize Chinese characters, expand their vocabulary, and deepen their understanding of the text. In addition, parents can adopt some methods for teaching reading from their children's school teachers. For example, they can teach their children to do read-aloud activities, read intensively, skim and scan, and go back and reread. They need to provide a good model for their children to follow to be good readers and to enjoy reading. Early instruction in Chinese characters may also help children become more proficient in Chinese written language.

Second, since home literacy factors investigated in the studies reviewed here resulted in children's greater reading proficiency, parents can help their children develop Chinese reading skills by buying their children books, children's magazines, and newspapers; creating a literacy-rich environment; modeling good reading behaviors and positive reading attitudes; taking their children to libraries and bookstores frequently; setting a definite time to read with their children; and encouraging their children to read independently.

Third, parents need to know the importance of Chinese reading and writing for their children and should try to motivate them to read more outside of school. Since many parents do not know how to help their children read and write at home, they need to learn strategies to help their children improve reading, and they can spend more time reading to and with their children. One way for them to learn the strategies is for schools or communities to offer free tutoring sessions or workshops to teach parents these instructional skills.

12.6 Summary

In summary, home literacy related to the Chinese written language is an important topic for researchers, educators, and parents to explore. Family literacy is significantly related to children's literacy development. Specifically, research suggests the following factors are important: parents' oral language support, availability of home literacy resources, frequency of taking children to libraries and bookstores, parents' reading attitude and reading habit, and home literacy-related activities. Since few studies have been carried out on home literacy practices among Chinese families, more research is needed on the influence of home literacy practices on children's learning to read and write the complex Chinese written language. All of these studies involve families in urban communities. Further studies can explore family literacy in rural settings, in different regions of the country, and among minority groups in China. Further questions can be asked such as: What is the relationship between the age when parents begin teaching their children to read and write and children's subsequent literacy development? What are the best practices that parents can use at home to promote their children's Chinese literacy development? To what extent do parents influence their children's motivation to read and their reading and writing proficiency? What can be done to increase access to free books for children from lower socioeconomic families and communities? How can parents in rural areas or from minority groups best support their children's development of academic literacy?

References

Arnold, D. S., Lonigan, C. J., Whitehurst, G. J., & Epstein, J. N. (1994). Accelerating language development through picture-book reading: Replication and extension to a videotape training format. *Journal of Educational Psychology, 86*, 235–243.

Chapman, J. W., & Tunmer, W. E. (1995). Development of young children's reading self-concepts: An examination of emerging subcomponents and their relationship with reading achievement. *Journal of Educational Psychology, 87*, 154–167.

Chapman, J. W., & Tunmer, W. E. (1999). Reading self-concept scale. In R. Burden (Ed.), *Children's self-perceptions* (pp. 29–34). Windsor: NFER-Nelson.

Chinese Ministry of Education. (2011). 全日制义务教育语文课程 [*Yuwen curriculum standards for full-day compulsory education*]. Beijing: Beijing Normal University Publishing House.

Chow, B. W., & McBride-Chang, C. (2003). Promoting language and literacy development through parent–child reading in Hong Kong preschoolers. *Early Education and Development, 14*, 233–248. doi:0.1207/s15566935eed1402_6.

Clay, M. M. (1991). *Becoming literate: The construction of inner control*. Portsmouth: Heinemann.

Dunn, L. M., & Dunn, L. M. (1997). *Examiner's manual for the PPVT-III: Peabody picture vocabulary test* (3rd ed.). Circle Pines: American Guidance Service.

Flood, J. E. (1977). Parental styles in reading episodes with young children. *The Reading Teacher, 30*, 864–867.

Frijters, J. C., Barron, R. W., & Brunello, M. (2000). Direct and mediated influences of home literacy and literacy interest on preschoolers' oral vocabulary and early written language skill. *Journal of Educational Psychology, 92*, 466–477. doi:10.1037//0022-0663.92.3.466.
Halliday, M. A. K. (1975). The functional basis of language. *Language, 34*, 54–73.
Hargrave, A. C., & Sénéchal, M. (2000). A book reading intervention with preschool children who have limited vocabularies: The benefits of regular reading and dialogic reading. *Early Childhood Research Quarterly, 15*, 75–90.
Heath, S. B. (1983). *Ways with words: Language, life, and work in communities and classrooms.* Cambridge: Cambridge University Press.
Hewison, J., & Tizard, J. (1980). Parental involvement and reading attainment. *British Journal of Educational Psychology, 50*, 209–215.
Ho, D. Y. F. (1994). Cognitive socialization in Confucian heritage cultures. In P. M. Greenfield & R. R. Cocking (Eds.), *Cross-cultural roots of minority child development* (pp. 285–313). Hillsdale: Erlbaum.
Iyengar, S. S., & Lepper, M. R. (1999). Rethinking the value of choice: A cultural perspective on intrinsic motivation. *Journal of Personality and Social Psychology, 76*, 349–366.
Leichter, H. J. (1984). Families as an environment for literacy. In H. Goelman, A. A. Oberg, & F. Smith (Eds.), *Awakening to literacy* (pp. 38–50). Portsmouth: Heinemann.
Leung, C. B. (2008). Preschoolers' acquisition of scientific vocabulary through repeated read-aloud events, retellings, and hands-on science activities. *Reading Psychology: An International Quarterly, 29*, 165–193. doi:10.1080/02702710801964090.
Li, H. (1999, April). *Development and validation of the Preschool and Primary Chinese Literacy Scale.* Poster presented at the Society for Research in Child Development Conference, Albuquerque, NM.
Li, H., & Rao, N. (2000). Parental influences on Chinese literacy development: A comparison of preschoolers in Beijing, Hong Kong, and Singapore. *International Journal of Behavioral Development, 24*, 82–90. doi:10.1080/016502500383502.
Li, H., Corrie, L. F., & Wong, B. K. M. (2008). Early teaching of Chinese literacy skills and later literacy outcomes. *Early Childhood Development and Care, 178*, 441–459. doi:10.1080/03004430600789365.
Marulis, L. M., & Newman, S. B. (2010). The effects of vocabulary intervention on young children's word learning: A meta-analysis. *Review of Educational Research, 80*, 300–335. doi:10.3102/0034654310377087.
Meng, X., Zhou, X., & Kong, R. (2002). 中文读写能力及其相关因素研究 [A study of reading and writing ability and related factors]. 心理科学, 25, 544–547, 572.
Meng, X., Liu, H., Zhou, X., & Meng, Q. (2003). 中文阅读能力及其相关因素的结构模型 [Structure model of Chinese reading abilities and its correlates]. 心理发展与教育, 1, 37–43.
National Early Literacy Panel. (2008). *Developing early literacy: Report of the Early Literacy Panel.* National Institute for Literacy. Jessup: Ed Pubs. Retrieved from http://lincs.ed.gov/publications/pdf/NELPReport09.pdf
Ninio, A., & Bruner, J. (1978). The achievement and antecedents of labeling. *Journal of Child Language, 5*, 1–15.
Perez, B. (1998). Literacy, diversity, and programmatic responses. In B. Perez (Ed.), *Sociocultural contexts of language and literacy* (pp. 3–20). Mahwah: Erlbaum.
Roser, N., & Martinez, M. (1985). Roles adults play in preschoolers' response to literature. *Language Arts, 62*, 485–490.
Sénéchal, M., & Cornell, E. H. (1993). Vocabulary acquisition through shared reading experiences. *Reading Research Quarterly, 28*, 360–374.
Shu, H., Li, W., Anderson, R., Ku, Y.-M., & Yue, X. (2002a). The role of home-literacy environment in learning to read Chinese. In W. Li, J. S. Gaffney, & J. L. Packard (Eds.), *Chinese children's reading acquisition: Theoretical and pedagogical issues* (pp. 207–224). Boston: Kluwer.

Shu, H., Li, W., Gu, Y., Anderson, R., Wu, X., Zhang, H., & Xuan Y. (2002b). 家庭文化背景儿童阅读发展中的作用 [Role of family cultural background in children's reading development]. 心理科学, 25(2), 136–139.

Snow, C. E. (1991). The theoretical basis for relationships between language and literacy development. *Journal of Research in Childhood Education, 6*(1), 5–10.

Snow, C., Barnes, W., Chandler, J., Goodman, I., & Hemphill, L. (1991). *Unfulfilled expectations: Home and school influences on literacy*. Cambridge, MA: Harvard University Press.

Snow, C. E., Burns, M. S., & Griffin, P. (Eds.). (1998). *Preventing reading difficulties in young children*. Washington, DC: National Academy Press.

Stevenson, H. W., & Lee, S. Y. (1996). The academic achievement of Chinese students. In M. H. Bond (Ed.), *The handbook of Chinese psychology* (pp. 124–142). Hong Kong: Oxford University Press.

Taylor, D. (1983). *Family literacy*. Exeter: Heinemann.

Taylor, D., & Dorsey-Gaines, C. (1988). *Growing up literate*. Portsmouth: Heinemann.

Teale, W. (1978). Positive environments for learning to read: What studies of early readers tell us. *Language Arts, 55*, 922–932.

Tseng, W., & Wu, D. (1985). *Chinese culture and mental health*. New York: Academic Press.

Valdez-Menchaca, M. C., & Whitehurst, G. J. (1992). Accelerating language development through picture book reading: A systematic extension to Mexican day-care. *Developmental Psychology, 28*, 1106–1114.

Wang, Q., & Coddington, C. S. (2010). *Exploring the relationship of parental beliefs, motivation for reading and reading achievement in Chinese first graders*. Paper presented at the National Reading Conference/Literacy Research Association 60th Annual Meeting, Fort Worth, TX.

Wang, X., & Hu, Y. (2007). 小学生家庭阅读情况的调查研究 [A survey of elementary students' reading at home]. 内蒙古师范大学学报 (教育科学版), 20(6), 84–87.

Wang, X.-L., Bernas, R., & Eberhard, P. (2002). Variations of maternal support to children's early literacy development in Chinese and American Indian families: Implications for early childhood educators. *International Journal of Early Childhood, 34*(1), 9–23. doi:10.1007/BF03177319.

Whitehurst, G. J., Falco, F. L., Lonigan, C., Fischel, J. E., DeBarsyshe, B. D., Valdez-Menchaca, M. C., & Caulfield, M. (1988). Accelerating language development through picture-book reading. *Developmental Psychology, 24*, 552–558.

Whitehurst, G. J., Arnold, D. S., Epstein, J. N., Angell, A. L., Smith, M., & Fischel, J. E. (1994). A picture book reading intervention in day care and home for children from low-income families. *Developmental Psychology, 30*, 679–689.

Zhou, H., & Salili, F. (2008). Intrinsic reading motivation of Chinese preschoolers and its relationship with home literacy. *International Journal of Psychology, 43*, 912–916. doi:10.1080/00207590701838147.

Index

A
The ABCs of Chinese Font, 88
Access to books, 103, 137, 138
Adaptations and performances of Chinese children's literature, 108
Aesop's Fables, 108
Aesthetic appreciation, 132, 151
Affective development, 191–192
Affective factors in learning, 154
Agdronjan, A., 42
Alphabetizing Chinese writing, 11
Alternative formats of schooling, 59
American Flying Tigers, 170
The Analects, 61, 82, 83, 85, 142
Ancient China, 1, 2, 11, 12, 15, 19–32, 61, 84, 87, 170
Ancient Chinese historians, 26
Ancient Chinese literacy, 7–11, 14
Ancient Chinese literacy education, 7–11
Ancient Chinese texts, 51
Andersen, H.C., 120
Anne of Green Gables, 114, 120
"A noble action," 41, 44
Anti-Rightist Campaign, 62, 70, 115
Application, 25, 149, 150, 188
Archaic Chinese, 1, 3, 8, 36
Assessment and evaluation, 134, 135, 146, 150
Attitudes towards reading, 207

B
Bacteria and Bacterial Warfare, 113
Balance, 68, 81, 88, 137–139, 154
Beijing, viii, 2, 28–29, 49–51, 53, 54, 58, 65, 69–71, 90–93, 96, 97, 103, 109, 112, 116, 118, 123, 161, 176, 204–206
Big Character Posters, 50, 51, 53–54, 56, 59

Block printing, 11, 15, 21, 23
Block printing technique, 10
Bloom's taxonomy, 131
Boda, C., 50, 52
The Book of Changes, 82, 142
The Book of History, 82, 83
Book rental, 160
The *Book of Rites*, 82, 83, 142
The *Book of Songs*, 82, 142
Books and reading, 100, 207
Bookstalls, 160, 162, 163
Bookstores, 27, 29, 40, 92, 113, 117–118, 120, 163, 203, 204, 207, 208
The Book of Stories, 87
Bourgeoisie, 50, 51, 53, 168
"The boy traitor," 41, 43
Bronfenbrenner, 97
Bruner, J., vii, 97, 131, 201
Brush pens, 8, 9, 23–24
Buck, P.S., 168
Buddhism, 9, 22
Bulletin boards, 54, 188

C
Calligraphers, 22–23
Calligraphy, 22–24, 53, 54, 59, 133
Cao character style, 21
Capitalists, 58, 117, 162
Censorship, 111, 116, 122, 170, 173, 178
Chairman Mao quotations, 52–54
Challenges, x, 51, 64, 67, 96, 98, 103, 110, 119, 129, 133, 134, 136–138, 142, 147–149, 153–155, 170
Character books, 8, 21, 98
Character encoding and input systems, 186–188

Index

Characteristics of Chinese characters, 19–20, 29
Characteristics of Chinese orthography, 14
Character recognition, viii, 84, 85, 88, 131–133, 185, 187, 192, 194, 205
Character-rich environment, 98
Character segmentation, 24
Character texts, 8–10, 12–15, 87
Character writing, 12–14, 19, 21–24, 31, 59, 85, 132, 133, 205
Charlotte's Web, 120
Chat rooms, 188, 189
Chekhov, A., 41
Chen, G., 160
Chen, H. (father of Chinese preschool education), 90
The Child Paper, 108, 109
Children's books (and magazine), 92, 111, 116, 204, 207
Children's literature, 107, 109
  as an educational tool, 169
  in education, 35–46
Children's magazines, 92, 111, 116, 119, 204
Children's picture books, 99
China, 20th century, 81, 89, 93, 97, 101–103, 108, 157, 158, 160, 164, 173, 178, 184
Chinese calligraphy, 22–24, 53, 54, 133
Chinese characters, ix, 1, 3–9, 13, 14, 19–20, 22–25, 27–30, 84, 86, 88, 93, 95, 100, 101, 123, 130, 133, 142, 174, 184, 187–188, 192, 199, 200, 202, 204, 205, 207
  dictionaries, 9
  encoding and inputting systems, 187–188
  identification, 15, 22
  learning, 9–14, 97
  reading, 204
  riddles, 24
  writing, 23, 205
Chinese children's literature, 110
Chinese Communist Party (CCP), 49, 50, 52–54, 57, 62, 63, 68–74, 78, 113, 114, 116, 117, 161, 162, 164, 167, 168, 170, 171, 176
Chinese Communist Party ideologies, 143
Chinese culture, ix, vii, 20, 24, 25, 28, 30–32, 36, 51, 90, 101–103, 109, 133, 134, 136, 137, 150
Chinese dialects, 2
Chinese dynasties, 2, 9–12, 21, 22, 26, 28, 37, 86
Chinese education, 23–24, 37, 61, 89, 90, 119, 129, 135, 136, 143, 147, 154, 200

Chinese history, 2, 14, 25, 59, 110, 121, 172
Chinese history writing, 25
Chinese Idiom Stories, 172
Chinese Imperial examinations, 82, 83, 91, 102
Chinese language, x, ix, viii, 2, 20, 27, 28, 35, 51–57, 61–78, 91, 95, 107, 112, 123, 129–139, 141–155, 164, 184, 190, 200, 202, 204
  courseware, 186–187, 190–191
  and literacy (Yuwen), 35, 53, 55
  and literacy education, vii, viii, x, xi, 1–15, 49, 183, 189, 191–194, 196
  and literacy education (Yuwen), 138
  system, 7
  teaching, 63–67, 73–77, 144
Chinese literacy
  development, 200, 203, 204, 207
  history, 4
  textbooks, 55–56
Chinese literary history, 36, 142
Chinese literature, 37–39, 45, 64, 142, 144
Chinese Ministry of Education (MOE), 2, 130, 133, 141, 148, 149, 151, 184
Chinese Nationalist Party, 143
Chinese New Year couplets on door frame, 23, 24
Chinese opera stories, 108, 158, 160
Chinese orthography, 11–14
Chinese pedagogy, 93
Chinese People's Political Consultative Conference (CPPCC), 49
Chinese phonology, 22
Chinese popular culture, 108
Chinese primers, 86, 88, 90, 91, 108
Chinese reading, x, 185, 201, 203–207
Chinese spoken language, viii, ix, x, 64, 143
Chinese teacher, 61, 123, 137, 138, 142, 178, 195
Chinese textbooks, 36–40, 44, 45
Chinese writing, viii, 1, 3, 19, 23, 24, 144, 187, 200
Chinese written language, vii, viii, ix, 1–15, 19–22, 25–32, 102, 204, 205, 207, 208
Chinese youth literature, 107–124, 157, 172, 176
Chinese Yuwen instruction, 59
Civil service examination system (Imperial exams), 10, 11, 14, 29, 64
Civil war, 62, 89, 112, 143, 164, 168
Classical Chinese, 38, 39, 108, 133, 172
Classical texts, 66, 112, 137
Classroom-based research, 196
Collaboration tools, 186, 188–189

Index 213

Collaborative learning, 133, 188, 189, 195, 196
Collaborative writing, 188, 189
College entrance exam, 115, 124, 154, 155
Comic books, 120, 121, 158, 175–178
Common core courses, 150
Communication tools, 146, 187–189
Community literacy activities, 200
Competition from foreign imports, 120
Compound ideographic characters, 3
Compulsory education, 35, 118, 123, 129, 131, 133, 141, 146, 150, 184, 200
Compulsory Education Law of the People's Republic of China, 118, 131
Compulsory education standards, 123
Computer programs for word recognition, 184
Confucian classics, 51, 82, 84, 102
Confucianism, viii, 61, 62, 82, 102, 142
Confucian texts, 9, 10, 12, 86
Confucius, 2, 8, 12, 14, 21, 26, 27, 51, 61, 62, 74, 82, 83, 136, 142
The Count of Monte Cristo, 40
Criticize Confucius Campaign, 74
Cross-age reading, 108, 178
Cultural heritage, 27, 30, 64
Cultural Revolution (Great Proletarian Cultural Revolution), x, 49–59, 61–78, 94, 97, 110, 114–119, 130, 131, 145, 153, 160, 168, 170–172, 178
Cultural taboos, 27
Curriculum guides, 135, 141, 184
Curriculum reform, 97, 129–139, 141–155, 184, 195
Curriculum standards, 37, 91, 129, 136, 138, 139, 141–150, 153, 184, 200
Curriculum syllabus, 142

D
Dalton System, 37
Daudet, A., 36, 41
"The dawn of civilization," 42, 44
De Amicis, E., 38, 41, 43
Debate, ix, 50, 53, 64–66, 94, 136, 148, 153
Decline of Chinese LHH, 173
de Maupassant, G., 41–43
Dewey, J., 65, 89, 90, 109, 143
Dialects, viii, ix, x, 2–3, 13, 14, 20–22, 24, 25, 29–31, 108–109
Dialogic reading, 200–203, 207
Dictionaries, ix, 9, 21, 84, 116, 204
Die Passion eines Menschen, 163
Discussion-based learning, 134

Dispositions, 41, 133–135
Divination, 1, 8, 12
Docin Network, 191
The Doctrine of the Mean, 83, 142
Down to the Countryside Movement, 57
Dragon Seed, 168
Dumas, A., 40

E
Early childhood curriculum reform, 97
Early childhood education standards, 91
Early literacy, 81–103, 201
  curriculum, 83–86
  education in China, 81–103
Eastern Jin Dynasty, 23
Editors, 69, 71, 72, 74, 77, 111, 118, 120, 170–173, 176
Educated peasants, 57
Educational barriers broken, 57
Educational policies, 59
Educational standards, 59
Educational tool, 109, 110, 169
Educational value of children's books, 121
Educational value of LHH, 177
Education policies, 94
Education reform, 101, 121, 129, 132, 133, 141, 147, 184, 196
Elective series, 150, 151
Email, 152, 187–189
Embodiment, 63, 78
Emperor Qin Shihuang, 26
Emperor Wu Di, 82
Emperor Yong Zheng, 29
"Enemies," 42, 44, 53, 56, 112, 114, 117, 167, 168, 174
Engagement in reading, 206
Engles, M., 55, 56
Exemplar lessons, 61
Experimental research, 102

F
Fables, 108, 109, 123, 170
Factory training schools, 58
Fairy tales, 92, 109, 110, 118, 119, 123
Family literacy, 199–208, vii
Family literacy in China, 199–208
Family school, 83
Fanqie, 22
Fantasy and science fiction, 176
Finger-play rhymes, 91
Five Classics, 82, 142

Five Heroes at the Langya Mountain, 167
Five-step model, 65
Folktales, 108, 117, 170
Foreign literature education, 35–48
Formative assessments, 134
Founding of People's Republic of China (PRC), viii, 36, 49, 81, 93, 102, 112, 129, 141
Four Books, 82, 142
Four Olds, 51
Friends and Foes in the Battlefield, 164
Functions of literacy, 9, 14, 15, 49

G
Gang of Four, 67
Gender issues, 178
Geng, J., 36, 41
Geographical regions of China, 205
Globalization, 138, 147
Golden Age (of Chinese children's literature), 112, 114, 117
Google Pinyin, 188
Gorky, M., 42, 44, 166, 170
Graphic novels, 158
Great Leap Forward, 51, 57, 59, 115, 130, 145, 153
The Great Learning, 83, 142
Guo, J., 122

H
Half-study and half-work or half-farming schools, 59
Han Dynasty, 3, 9, 12, 22, 82
Han, H., 122
Han Li character style, 21
Harry Potter series, 121
Herbart, J.F., 142
Hero stories, 160, 165
He, Y., 173, 176
Higher education in China, 35, 123
High school Chinese textbooks, 36, 40, 46, 47
High school curriculum standards, 142–147
High school Yuwen, 141, 143, 144, 146–155
Home literacy, 107, 199, 200, 203–208
  environment, 200, 203–206
  practices, 199, 205, 208
Home schools, 199
Homophones, 5, 25, 27–31, 188
Homophone taboos, 27–30
Homophonic differentiation, 5
Homophonic family names, 25
Hong, B., 36

Hong Kong, 202, 205
"How the foolish old man removed the mountain," 58
How the Steel Was Tempered, 170
Huang, S., 164, 165
Hubei province, 90
Hu, S., 36, 39, 41, 43, 46
Hybrid input system, 188

I
Ibsen, H., 39
ICT integration in literacy education, 185, 186, 194–196
ICT supported pedagogy, 185
Ideological rectification, 58
Illustrated books, 88, 158
Imperial examinations, 82, 83, 91, 102
Imperial scholars, 82
Implementation of curriculum reform, 137, 148, 155
Inactivity (in Children's book publishing in 1990s), 120, 176
Independent learning, 131, 133–135
Information and communication technologies (ICTs), vii, x, 183–196
"In memory of Norman Bethune," 58
Inquiry, 131, 133–136, 138, 139, 149, 150, 152, 154, 157, 184, 194, 196
Inquiry-based learning (inquiry learning), 134, 135, 139, 150, 184
Inservice education, 153
Instant messaging, 188
Instructional methods, 65, 187
Instructional supersystems, 196
Integrated learning, 133, 136
Interest, vii, 11, 14 36, 39, 40, 45, 65, 87, 92, 93, 98, 103, 110, 114, 115, 120, 134, 144, 151–154, 160, 164, 172, 173, 176, 177, 185–189, 191–192, 195, 203
The Internationale, 55 172
Internet, 147, 184, 188, 189
Iron Buddha Temple, 167

J
Japan, 20, 22, 41, 43, 111–113, 116, 120, 121, 158, 164, 165, 169, 170, 177, 178
Japanese manga, 173, 175–178
Jiang Qing, F., 122
Jianpin, 187
Journey to the West, 92, 108
Junior high Chinese textbooks, 39–43, 46–47, 133

K

Kai character style, 21
Kairov's pedagogy, 65, 130
Kästner, E., 120
Kindergarten, 69, 89–92, 95–98, 100, 109, 202, 203
Knowledge and skills, 66, 68, 92, 96, 130–136, 138, 144–147, 150–152, 154, 184, 193, 195
Korea, 20, 22, 72
Kung fu stories, 121, 158, 160, 163

L

Laborers, 51, 57–59, 70, 73, 113, 115, 162, 170
Lao Zi, 8
The Last Class, 36, 41, 43, 45Latin of the Far East, 20
Learner corpora, 190
Learning management systems, 189
Lenin, V., 55, 56, 170
Lian huan hua (LHH), 108, 157–178
Librarians, 123, 124, 177
Libraries, 53, 111, 123, 124, 162, 164, 178, 184, 203, 204, 207, 208
The Life of Li Chao, 39
Lifelong learning, 149, 152, 153
"The life of a useless man," 42, 44
Li or Cleric style characters, 9
Lisa and Lottie, 120
Literacy (illiteracy), vii, viii, ix, x, xi, 1–15, 19–32, 35, 39, 49–59, 81–103, 107–109, 112, 116, 118, 122, 129–139, 141–155, 157–178, 183–196, 199–208
  criticism, 157, 178
  development, vii, x, xi, 102, 103, 162, 172, 199–201, 203–208
  learning in ancient China, 1, 11, 12, 19–32
  rate in China, ix, 49, 53, 160, 169, 173
  rich environment, 199, 207
The Little Elf, 176
Little Friends, 111
"The little patriot of Padua," 41, 43
The Little Red Book, 54, 55
Little Red Guard, 116
Little Soldier Chang Ka-tse, 114, 159
Little Sparrow, 92
"The little vidette of Lomdardy," 41
Liu, B., 36
Logographic/ideographic nature of characters, 1–4, 21, 22, 24, 25, 55
Lowell, J.R., 38
Low-risk learning environment, 136
Lu, X. (鲁迅), 36, 41, 43, 92, 163, 166, 168

M

Mandarin, viii, 2, 5, 108, 133, 169
Mao Zedong., 49, 52, 54, 55, 58, 102, 115, 167, 170, 171
Maple Leaves, 171
Marriage Law of 1950, 169
Marx, 55, 56
Marxism-Leninism, 52
Marxist, 53, 145, 147, 163
Masereel, F., 163
Mass communication, 160
Master teacher, 63
May Fourth Movement, 35, 64, 65, 81, 89, 109, 110
Memorization, 55, 66, 83–85, 135, 145, 146
Mencius, 8, 26, 82, 142
Metacognition, 186, 195
Microsoft pinyin, 188
Middle school, 38, 47, 48, 53, 56–58, 109, 114, 115, 119, 123, 138, 143–147, 185, 189, 190, 206
Ming dynasty, 10–11, 28, 88
Minority groups, 149, 169, 208
Missionaries, 89, 90, 108
Mobile libraries, 162
Mobile technology, 186, 189–190
Modern Chinese writing system, 1, 3
Montessori, 97, 101
Motivation, 12, 102, 135, 152, 164, 186, 191–192, 195, 200, 206–208
Movie adaptations, 116, 177
Multimedia instruction (courseware and programs), 186–187

N

Nala, 39
Names of a hundred families, 86, 87
Nanjing, 90, 92, 96, 97, 164, 165, 168, 201
Narrative publications, 158
National Conference on Education (1978), 67
National Forum on Publishing for Youth (1978), 118
National identity, 20–21, 30
Nationalist government, 116, 117, 161, 163–165, 167, 170
Nationalists, 62, 89, 111, 116, 117, 143, 161, 163–170
"Navigation" by Ivan Sergeevich Turgenev, 36, 41
Nebiolo, G., 160
New China, 49, 58, 110, 130
New Culture Movement, 35, 36, 38, 43, 46, 102, 109, 110, 142
New Literature Movement, 36, 42

O

One child policy, 101, 118, 147
Open door policy, 120
Open the Skylight, 122
Oracle bone characters, 1, 7, 21
Oral communication, 2, 21, 130, 133
Oral language, viii, 2, 3, 20–22, 94, 95, 98, 134, 201, 205, 207, 208
Oral language play, 94
Orthographic nature of Chinese characters, 15, 199
Ostrovsky, N., 170
Out-of-school reading, 134, 200, 203

P

Paper, 9, 12, 15, 22, 23, 50, 53, 108, 109, 115, 134, 147, 158, 165, 183
Paradigm shift, 93, 97, 103, 136, 137, 139, 155, 195
Parental education, 199, 203
Parent attitudes towards reading, 205–207
Parent beliefs, 100, 206
Parent–child relationships, 199
Parent educational level, 203, 204
Paris Commune, 55, 170
Part-time schools, 59
Patriotic beliefs, 78
Patriotic education, 111, 112
Peasants, 50, 55, 57–59, 62, 66, 113, 115–117, 160, 161, 167, 174, 175
Pedagogic models, 63, 75
Pedagogy, 61–78, 83–86, 91–95, 97–100, 102, 103, 130, 131, 185
People's Daily, 52, 53, 56, 66, 113, 116, 168
People's Education, 65
People's Education Press (PEP), 55, 112
People's Fine Arts Publishing House, 173, 174
People's Liberation Army, 52, 54, 58, 116, 168
People's Liberation Army Daily, 52, 54
People's Republic of China (PRC), vii, viii, 2, 36, 49, 51, 54, 55, 61, 62, 65, 81, 93, 102, 112, 114, 118, 129, 131, 141, 143, 169, 170
PEP. *See* People's Education Press (PEP)
Perceptions of reading, 206, 207
Phonemes, viii, 3, 5, 7, 20
Phonetic-based input system, 187, 188
Phonetics, 3–6, 9, 10, 14, 31, 32, 116, 187, 188
Piaget, 97
Pictographic characters, 3, 14

Picture book reading, 93, 98, 100, 101, 201
Piloting (stage of standards implementation), 149
Pinyin, viii, ix, 94, 95, 98, 116, 132, 187, 188, 192, 193
Pippi Longstocking, 120
Pleasant Goat and Big Big Wolf, 177
11th Plenum of the 8th Chinese Communist Party Central Committee, 50
Politburo, 50
Political ideology, 78, 109, 130, 131, 147
Political implications of Chinese written language, 20
Political infrastructures, 20
Political record, 69, 70
Political satire, 163
Political socialization, 116, 163, 168, 169, 172, 177
Pottier, E.E., 55
PRC. *See* People's Republic of China (PRC)
Preschool, 81, 83, 89–98, 100–103, 201–203, 205
 curriculum, 83, 91, 94, 96, 97, 103
 education, 89–91, 96, 102, 103
 guidelines, 96–98, 100, 103
Preservice teacher preparation, 138
Primary school, 41, 47, 58, 62, 69, 72–74, 83, 101, 109, 110, 112, 116, 117, 119, 129–139, 143, 162, 184, 185, 190
Primary teachers, 69, 138, 185
Primary Yuwen, 129–138
Primary Yuwen standards, 148
Primers, 86, 88, 90, 91, 108
Problem solving, 134, 152, 194, 196
5155 Project, 176
Proletarian ideology, 51
Proliferation of Chinese youth literature, 118
Pronunciation units, 5
Propaganda, 50, 52, 59, 66, 70, 113, 163–167, 170, 171, 176
Protecting the Children, 168
Public and school libraries, 123
Publishing, 40, 46, 54, 55, 111, 112, 118, 120, 121, 145, 160, 164, 165, 170–174
Putonghua, viii, 2, 133

Q

Qian, X., 160
Qin character style, 21
Qin dynasty, 8–9, 12, 21
Qing dynasty, 11, 29, 84, 85, 88–91, 108, 158

Qinghua University, 53
Qing, J., 50, 56, 171
QQ, 189
QQ Pinyin, 188
Quality education, 132, 133, 145, 147
Quanpin, 187
Qzone, 189

R
Race between the Tortoise and the Rabbit, 92
Radicals, 3–7, 13, 15, 20, 24, 25, 70, 89, 102, 115, 163
Radio serials, 116
Read-aloud activities, 207
Read-aloud stories, 118
Reading aloud, 10, 12–13, 98, 201
Reading Chinese, 203, 204, 206
Reading comprehension, 75, 112, 177, 187, 192, 194, 204
Reading motivation, 206–208
Recitation, 11–14, 55, 83–85, 90, 135, 137
Red Flag Magazine, 52
Red Guards, 51, 53, 57, 70, 74, 75, 116
Redness, 78, 115
Red-Scarf Teaching Approach, 65, 75
Reluctant readers, 178
Renzhi Ma method (these three are structure-based input methods), 118
Revolutionary diaries, 56–57
Revolutionary plays, 56
Rhymes, 86, 91, 92, 94, 95, 118
Role of ICT (Information Communication Technology), 191oles of Chinese written language, vii, 30, 31
Rural education, 59, 96
Russian influence on Chinese preschool education
Russian pedagogy, 94

S
Sanmao series, 165, 166
Scar literature, 171, 173
Schreiner, O., 42, 44
Secondary Chinese education, 46
Secondary teachers, 68
Self-regulated learning, 194, 195
Semantic-phonetic compound characters, 3, 6
"Serve the people," 58
Shakespeare, W., 37, 42
Shang dynasty, 1, 7–8, 26

Shanghai, 27, 29, 40, 46–48, 53, 55, 56, 69, 71, 72, 92, 111, 113, 118, 119, 122, 152, 158–163, 165, 166, 168, 173, 205
Shen, M., 160
Shimin, E.L., 28
Shining (*Red Star*), 116, 117
Shuangpin, 187, 193
"The siege of Berlin," 41, 43
Sienkiewicz, H., 42
Simple ideographic characters, 3
Simplified Chinese characters, ix
Simulated environment, 187, 192, 193
Sino-Japanese War, 110, 111, 114, 161, 164, 167, 169, 174
Sixteen Points, 50, 54
Skill development, 191–193, 195, 203
Social commentary, 119, 163
Socialist Education Movement (1962), 56, 57
Sociocultural factors of literacy, 19
Sociocultural perspective, vii, 155
Socio-dramatic play, 101
Socioeconomic status (background), 199, 200
Soldiers, 43, 50, 55, 58, 62, 66, 112, 116, 117, 165, 167
Song dynasty, 10, 11, 13, 21, 23, 85–87
"Song of the shirt," 36
Song or Fan-Song fonts, 21
Songs for children, 95
Sougou Pinyin, 188
Soviet style preschools, 93, 96
Soviet Union influence, 81
Special Rank Teacher (SRT), 61–78
Splitting the Chinese Language Curriculum into Literature and Language Strands reform, 65, 66, 75
The Spring and Autumn Annals, 8, 26, 142
Spring and Autumn Period, 8, 26, 82, 142
Steel Meets Fire, 173–175
Storybook reading, 202
Story of Erxiao, 112
Storytelling, 101, 108, 117, 119, 173, 176, 178
The Strives of Three Kingdoms, 24
Strokes, 6–7, 9, 13, 15, 20, 29, 88, 188, 192, 202
Structure-based input system, 186, 187
Student-centered curriculum, 138, 152
Student ownership of learning, 134
Sub-dialects, viii, ix, 2
Sui Dynasty, 10, 12
Sukhomlynsky's aesthetic approach to learning, 131
Summative assessments, 134

T
Tagore, R., 38
Tang Dynasty, 21, 22
Teacher accountability, 138
Teacher biography, 150
Teacher-centered curriculum, 154
Teacher education, 138, 154
Teacher effectiveness, 154
Teacher expertise, 136
Teacher paradigm shift, 155
Teacher professional development, 154, 196
Teacher quality, x, 136, 154
Teachers as facilitators, 151, 152, 195
Teachers of Chinese classics, 51
Teaching aids (pictures), 95
Teaching award, 63, 67
Teaching Chinese characters, 191
Teaching excellence, 63, 67, 70, 78
Teaching resources, 190
Teaching syllabus, 130–132, 141, 144–146, 148–150
Teaching syllabus (primary), 131, 141, 145, 146, 148, 150
Television shows, 177
Test-driven Chinese society (testing culture), 138, 154, 155
Test preparation materials, 121
Textbooks, 11, 36–48, 50, 51, 54–56, 58, 65, 66, 72, 76, 85–88, 92, 93, 96, 97, 107, 109, 111, 112, 123, 132, 135, 137, 143, 145, 150, 154, 155, 167, 177
  development, 145
  editorial teams, 55
  guidelines, 55
  middle and high school, 57, 146
  preschool, 97
  primary, 62
The Third Way, 122
Thomas Hood, 36
Thousand-Character Text (千字文), 87
Three-Character Classic, 86, 88
"Three dreams in a desert," 42, 44
Three Great Treatises, 58
"Three questions," 36, 41
Tolstoy, L., 36, 41, 166
Tones, x, 3, 5, 10, 205
Tracing characters, 12, 13
Trade books for young readers, 107
Translated folk tales, 92
Translated foreign literature, vii, 35–40, 44
Translations of children's literature, 107, 109–111, 113, 115, 123, 162
Translators, 40–43, 45, 65

Turgenev, I.S., 36, 41
Tutors, 83–85
"Two Friends," 41, 43
Two Newspapers and One Magazine, 52–54

U
Urban education, 59, 96, 101, 103, 115, 118, 154, 163, 208
Urban families, 118
US–China rapprochement of 1972, 170

V
Vasil, E., 41
Verbal persecution, 29
Verbal taboo practices, 25
Verbal taboos, 28, 29, 31
Vernacular Chinese, 36, 38–40
Vernacular Chinese textbooks, 38, 40
Vernacular language, 109
Vietnam, 22
Vocabulary development, 201
Voice recognition systems, 188
Vygotsky, 97, 100

W
Wang, P., 159, 176
War propaganda, 164, 167
Warring States Period, 8, 82
"The waves striving for freedom," 42, 44
Website development, 184
Wei-Jin Southern and Northern Dynasties, 9, 21
Wen (文) versus dao debate (道), 64
Western ideas, 153
Western influences, 46, 81, 89–93, 97, 101, 102, 108, 109, 120, 121, 128, 131, 134, 136, 137, 142, 148, 152–154, 159, 175
Western Zhou Dynasty, 26
White, E.B., 120
Wikis, 188
Winter schools, 59
Woodcut stories, 163–165, 167
Workers, 50, 51, 54, 55, 57–59, 62, 66, 71–74, 117, 160, 170, 172, 192
World Trade Organization, 147
Writing Chinese, viii, 1, 3, 19, 23, 24, 144, 187, 200
Writing disabilities, 188

Index

Writing implements, 8
Writing strokes, 6–7, 192
Writing surfaces, 8, 12
Written script universalization, 8
Wubi method (五笔字型输入法), 188

X

Xia, M., 41–43
Xiaoping, D., 67, 96, 117, 118
Xing [行] style, 21, 23
Xu, G., 114, 159, 161

Y

Yan'an forum, 167
Ya Yan, 2, 21
Yosuke, T., 41, 43, 44
Yuan Dynasty, 10–11, 21
Yuanzi, N., 53

Yuwen curriculum, 54, 129–134, 136, 141, 142, 146, 148–153, 200
Yuwen curriculum reform, 129, 132–134, 136, 138, 141, 144, 147–153, 155
Yuwen education, 53, 129, 131–133, 137–138, 141, 145, 148, 151, 154

Z

Zankof, 94
Zhang, L., 165, 166, 176
Zhang, Y., 122, 171
Zhao, H., 160
Zheng method, 188
Zheng, Y. (China's King of Fairy Tales), 118–119
Zhou Dynasty, 8, 21, 26
Zhou Enlai, 50, 170
Zhou, Z., 11, 22, 36, 42, 43, 109, 115
Zola, E., 42

Printed by Printforce, the Netherlands